Langston Hughes & the Blues

LANGSTON HUGHES & THE BLUES

STEVEN C. TRACY

UNIVERSITY OF ILLINOIS PRESS
Urbana and Chicago

Publication of this work was supported in part by a grant from the Andrew W. Mellon Foundation.

Library of Congress Cataloging-in-Publication Data

Tracy, Steven C. (Steven Carl), 1954–
    Langston Hughes and the blues / Steven C. Tracy.
        p.   cm.
    Bibliography: p.
    Discography: p.
    Includes index.
    ISBN 0-252-01457-X (alk. paper)
    1. Hughes, Langston, 1902–1967—Knowledge—Folklore, mythology.
2. Blues (Songs, etc.)—United States—History and criticism.
3. Folk poetry, American—Afro-American authors—History and
criticism. 4. Literature and folklore—United States—History—20th
century. 5. Folklore in literature. 6. Afro-Americans in
literature. 7. Afro-Americans—Folklore. I. Title.
PS3515.U274Z8   1988
818'.5209—dc19   87-28753
                                                                CIP

To Cathy and Michelle

CONTENTS

ACKNOWLEDGMENTS

A book, and particularly a first book, is really the result of a collaboration of many people, no matter whose name ends up on the cover. I have been particularly fortunate in the collaborators I have had. The people who first read my manuscript, especially Dr. Amy Elder, taught me to be more careful and comprehensive in what I said, contributing a great deal to this book as it now reads. Dr. Elder's expertise in African and African-American literature, Dr. Edgar Slotkin's knowledge of folklore, and Dr. Wayne C. Miller's emphasis on the multicultural perspective in American literature contributed greatly to my development before the manuscript was begun as well as during its composition. I could not have been more fortunate in my choice of teachers, advisers, and friends. Their professional demeanors and accomplishments serve as models for what I hope to achieve in the future. My thanks go in addition to Dr. Arnold Rampersad, who read the manuscript and made many insightful comments and suggestions that have greatly improved the work. Very special thanks in a more general sense go to Wayne Miller for his patience, outstanding support and encouragement, and friendship that has benefitted me in many ways.

I must also express my gratitude to blues enthusiast and musician Dudley Radcliff for reading the sections of the manuscript dealing with the blues and for checking on my presentation of information about the blues. Radcliff also referred me to William L. Schurk, Sound Recordings Archivist at Bowling Green State University, who provided me with a number of Langston Hughes's recordings not previously in my collection. Jim Cummins of the

Elliston Room at the University of Cincinnati also provided assistance, and the Elliston Room itself proved an important source of poetry and recordings. Those books I was not able to locate at the University of Cincinnati were found in a swift and professional manner by the personnel in the university's Interlibrary Loan Department, who also deserve my deepest gratitude. All of these contributions strengthened my manuscript. The remaining weaknesses are my own.

A number of other teachers not directly involved with this work have assisted in sharpening my analytical skills and broadening my knowledge of American literature, especially Dr. Robert D. Arner, whose teaching, scholarly commentary, and breadth of knowledge have been an inspiration, and Dr. Angelene Jamison-Hall, whose discussions of African-American literature first allowed me to link my interest in blues music with literary criticism. Their teachings are part of whatever I write or teach.

The countless blues performers whose artistry has been consistently underrated by most scholars are, in a sense, the soul of my work as they are the soul of Langston Hughes's work. They helped me enjoy writing this book and I hope that I have faithfully represented them and motivate readers to search out their recordings, as I think Hughes wished to do in his works. If the academic discussion of their work has digressed from their spirit, I hope the material in the footnotes and discography will help bring that spirit back. There are few experiences that equal listening to the recordings of people like Charley Patton, Lonnie Johnson, Blind Lemon Jefferson, Memphis Minnie, Skip James, Bessie Smith, and other great blues singers.

I'd also like to thank Richard Wentworth and Carol Betts of the University of Illinois Press for their assistance with the manuscript.

On the personal side, I thank my mother and father, Jean and Edward Tracy, whose love, support, intellectual stimulation, and hard work can never be adequately repaid. I appreciate them more and more as the years go by, and my own daughter, Michelle, reminds me what an awesome task parents have before them. I also thank my in-laws, Teresa, William, and Angie Taylor, for babysitting, as my own parents did at times, during the final hectic days of preparing the manuscript.

Finally, I thank my wife, Cathy, the most important collaborator of all. Her advice, support, patience, encouragement, comments, assistance in research, and typing and proofreading of my manuscript were an essential part of making this book what it is. Her selflessness and diligence are an inspiration to me.

INTRODUCTION

Since at least the time that Washington Irving transplanted the German folktale "Peter Klaus" on American soil for his "Rip Van Winkle," American writers have realized the value of folklore for their literary productions. With the writings of the local colorists of the nineteenth century, the interest in Southern folklore generated by the contact between the North and South during the Civil War, the Port Royal experiment and the publication of *Slave Songs of the United States* in 1867, and the founding of the American Folk-Lore Society in 1888, writers and critics began to recognize more fully the importance of African-American traditions in particular. African-American intellectuals and a variety of folklorists since the turn of the century have collected and written about the importance of those traditions as reflections of African-American attitudes, aspirations, fears, and creativity. African-American writers in the 1920s—the "Harlem Renaissance" period—brought to full flower this interest in traditional African-American folklore as a resource for works of "legitimate" literature, as Robert Burns or W. B. Yeats drew on oral tradition, in their own very different ways, for strength and vitality. Langston Hughes has been considered the most important of the Harlem Renaissance writers, and he had a special relationship with the blues tradition, considering it beautiful folk poetry worthy of comparison with the best folk literature in the world.

Hughes was, of course, not alone in this opinion; among his contemporaries, James Weldon Johnson, Sterling Brown, Zora Neale Hurston, and many other writers and folklorists have supported his contentions, and critics such as Cleanth Brooks, R. W. B. Lewis, and Robert Penn Warren, writing about folk poetry in *American Literature: The Makers and the Making,* felt that "much of the poetry recognized as 'literature,' white or black, seems tepid beside it." In a very real sense, the blues, a form of folk poetry, is the soul of Langston Hughes's work, for it is the very essence of the souls of the black folk who were so important to Hughes's artistic expression. And it is the mining and the development of this important alternative American tradition that has given impetus to the works of subsequent black writers like Richard Wright, James Baldwin, Ralph Ellison, and Michael Harper, and white ones like William Carlos Williams, John Berryman, Allen Ginsberg, and Jack Kerouac.

Although the importance of Langston Hughes's work has long been recognized by both scholars and non-scholars alike, and the influence of African-American folklore on his work has been acknowledged, existing Hughes scholarship has dealt with general impressions about the influences of the oral tradition on Hughes. It is almost as if Hughes's working with the oral tradition precluded for many scholars any close textual study of his written work. In this book I will trace the influence of the oral blues tradition on Hughes's blues poems, demonstrating how Hughes merged the African-American oral and written traditions, exploiting conventions, techniques, and the goals of both to achieve a poetry that is intellectually stimulating, sociopolitically responsible, and aesthetically pleasing both as folk poetry and literature.

My work will begin with a discussion of Hughes's literary aims and practices in relation to the Harlem Renaissance of the 1920s. First, in chapter 1, I will explore the development of a body of attitudes toward the folk roots of African-American culture that rose to importance with this movement and its major leaders. After surveying the "Old Guard"—DuBois, James Weldon Johnson, Alain Locke, who manifested varying but distinct leanings toward the aesthetic of the younger writers, Locke so far as to be almost in the new camp—I will deal with the younger generation and their attitudes, with particular emphasis on Zora Neale Hurston and Sterling Brown. Once I have established this context of the increased interest in folk materials and the atmosphere of an intellectual movement that sought to mine that material for literary purposes, I will turn in chapter 2 to a discussion of the origin of the blues—in Africa, slave experiences, work songs, field hollers, and religious music—as a means of establishing racial and cultural parameters. I will also discuss Reconstruction, which is often associated with the emergence of an identifiable blues-song pattern, a pattern explored in the work of folklorists and arrangers like W. C. Handy, Guy B. Johnson, and Howard Odum. Finally, I will consider the emergence of the Harlem Renaissance movement and commercial blues recordings as a natural historical consequence of what had gone before.

The following section will survey the various definitions of blues as offered by blues artists, folklorists, literary artists, researchers, and aficionados. This is important for establishing a number of ideas about what the blues are and what function they serve in society. Discussions of blues stanzaic structures and the generations of song texts as well as the sociopolitical implications of the genre will be the concern here, as will the differentiation between folk and commercial blues, as far as that is possible.

After surveying the various attitudes toward the blues from these sources, I will discuss the place of the blues in Hughes's world view as mirrored in his nonfiction prose discussions of the blues, his fiction, and the work he did as editor of collections that contained blues, including phonograph records. Once I have placed Hughes's outlook within the context of the attitudes surveyed earlier, I will discuss in chapter 3 individual poems that demonstrate clearly the ways in which Hughes used blues structures, themes, imagery, patterns, and voices to link his literary work to the productions of "the folk," establishing the continuity of the African-American creative mind that he felt was so necessary to foster a racial self-awareness and pride. Specific recordings by blues performers named by Hughes in his writings will be used to exemplify various aspects of the blues tradition, while performers not named by Hughes will be cited to highlight some materials with which he was unfamiliar or which he avoided at various points during his career.

There is not really a steady development of direction in Hughes's blues poems from volume to volume regarding the use of stanzas or the sex of the speaker in the poems, but there are some differences among the blues that Hughes wrote at various times over the years. The blues poems of *The Weary Blues,* for example, present us with an observer of the blues singer or situation, and they place the blues stanzas within a poetic or descriptive frame, looking at "the Negro" perhaps in the spirit of questioning brought on by the New Negro movement and the sudden "vogue" of the African-American. Hughes felt that his next volume, *Fine Clothes to the Jew,* was a better book (though critics were divided), because "it was more impersonal, more about other people than myself, and because it made use of the negro folk-song forms and included poems about work and the problems of finding work, that are always so pressing with Negro people."[1] *Fine Clothes* was an advance over the blues poems of *The Weary Blues* because of its greater variety of stanzas, speakers, subjects, and literary effects. It should be remembered, however, that some of these poems were written before or at the same time as some of the poems in his first volume, so the order of publication in his volumes does not necessarily reflect a chronological change in attitude. Of course, Hughes was soundly criticized by middle-class blacks for his depictions of the "lowlife" element, figures which were not stripped of any exoticism and were presented from their own point of view rather than filtered through a poetic speaker. By letting the "low-down folks" speak for themselves, he was doing something similar to what George Washington Harris and Mark Twain had done for the humor of the old Southwest. He was rebelling against the middle-class outlook of the Negro movement, searching for an unpretentious "people" poetry, and moving almost imperceptibly toward an involvement with Communism.

Hughes's next major original volume of new poetry, *Shakespeare in Harlem,* presented, in Hughes's words, "a book of light verse. Afro-Americana in the blues mood. Poems syncopated and variegated in the colors of Harlem, Beale Street, West Dallas and Chicago's South Side. Blues, ballads, and reels to be read aloud, crooned, shouted, recited, and sung. Some with gestures, some not—as you like. None with a far-away voice."[2] Having presented a series of dramatic monologues in a variety of forms using blues stanzas and rhythms in *Fine Clothes,* Hughes went one step further by explicitly inviting performance and audience participation in this volume; the invitation had been only implicit in the oral base of the earlier poems. Donald Dickinson felt that "the subjects are lighter in mood than those in his early blues," citing a letter from

Hughes to Mrs. Knopf about these poems: "I selected a number [of poems] that it seems to me might suit the public mood of the movement, the trend toward lighter things during the war, and the current interest in blues music and swing, Negro bands and singers."[3] Indeed, though the poems are blues poems, a number of them, like "Six-Bits Blues," "Evenin' Air Blues," "Brief Encounter," and "Morning After," are more lighthearted blues than in previous volumes. However, the potential violence of "In a Troubled Key," the low-down moaning of "Death Chant," the protest of "Southern Mammy Sings," and the loneliness of "Reverie on Harlem River" prevent the volume from being too lighthearted. In fact, "Southern Mammy Sings" represents a more overt use of protest and an experimentation with the blues stanza form beyond what Hughes had done in the blues poems of earlier volumes.

That overt protest, probably fueled by Hughes's rejection of the middle-class orientation of the Harlem Renaissance and his connections with the Communists in the thirties, mirrored in "Red Clay Blues," is also discernible in the few blues-influenced poems of *Jim Crow's Last Stand* (1943), such as "Big Buddy" and "Note on Commercial Theatre." The latter complains of the commercial co-opting of the blues and suggests that if the blues are to be used honestly (and Hughes is still talking about using them), they will be used by people who have some crucial connections with them, not by white Broadway moguls out to make money. Some of these poems were repeated in *One Way Ticket* (1949), but in general the other blues poems are somewhat lighthearted or undistinguished, lacking the craftsmanship of the poems of *Fine Clothes* and *Shakespeare*, and there are fewer of them, too. Only "Juice Joint: Northern City," which had been published in slightly different form earlier as "Barrel House: Industrial City," has the poignancy or power of Hughes's earlier blues poems, but it does not use the blues stanza form.

If Hughes's abilities seemed to diminish in terms of his blues poems in these volumes, his power returned in *Montage of a Dream Deferred* (1951), where his experimentation and reliance on music revitalized his work and helped him come up with some of his best blues poems. The boogie poems, including the marvelous "Same in Blues" and the deceptively simple "Blues at Dawn," all tackle personal and social themes, and work with and alter blues stanzas to their best advantage. Furthermore, the poems gain from their placement in the volume, resounding off and segueing into poems whose rhythms are different but not incompatible. The result is a wonderful, coherent whole that makes use of the spirit and rhythms of the blues as they relate to the life of urban blacks of the time.

Hughes's next big poetic project was the preparation of his *Selected Poems* for publication. In her recent biography of Langston Hughes, Faith Berry wrote of this 1959 volume that Hughes "had selected not his best poems, but those he thought would go over best with the public. He aimed to please."[4] If we focus on the poems that Hughes chose to include in that volume, we can see that, as with many other poets preparing selected or collected poems late in their careers, Hughes made a number of revisions of poems that had appeared in his previously published volumes. However, these were not always the first revisions of the poems in print; in fact, in some cases the versions of the poems in his earlier volumes were actually revisions of those that first appeared in journals. The verses in *Selected Poems* were smoothed out and made more palatable to middle-class blacks, as will be discussed later.

Hughes's final volume, *The Panther and the Lash* (1967), was subtitled "Poems of Our Times" and dedicated to "Rosa Parks of Montgomery." On the whole this collection contains more poems of open protest than any of the other volumes. A little over one-third of the poems are drawn from his other books. Only one poem in this volume takes the blues form, "The Backlash Blues," and it, too, is one of Hughes's most overtly protesting blues lyrics. Perhaps the reason for the paucity of blues in this volume is Hughes's belief that the blues were not the best vehicle for this type of protest, or that they were no longer usable with as much frequency as earlier. Certainly after *Shakespeare in Harlem* they appear less often. Still, Hughes knew that he could not leave the blues out of these "Poems of Our Times," and "Backlash Blues" is one of the most complaining, defiant, and optimistic poems in the group.

Previous articles and sections of critical books dealing with Langston Hughes and the blues tradition have been written primarily by scholars whose main expertise is in African-American literature rather than in the blues tradition. Since the oral tradition is centrally important to the literary productions of African-Americans, a fuller exploration of the blues tradition and its contributions to African-American literature would be a major step toward establishing the total context for the poetry in a specific and detailed manner that would make discussions of Hughes far more accessible both to scholars and students. Studying Hughes without full knowledge of the oral tradition is a bit like studying Whitman without a full knowledge of Emerson: Hughes was simmering, simmering, simmering, and the oral tradition brought him to a boil. My extensive references to blues lyrics throughout this book are intended to give those unfamiliar with the blues actual blues texts to read and to provide them with ideas about where the original performances can be found. Ultimately my work should lead to a greater appreciation of the blues tradition, a clearer understanding of how Hughes used it to accomplish his aims, and a more serious consideration of both the blues and Hughes as important contributors to the literature of America. This, in turn, should make Hughes's blues poem more accessible to teachers, and, therefore, to their students. The extensive references to blues songs and the discography will help teachers bring more of the oral tradition into the classroom. I'm sure Hughes would approve.

Times and temperaments have changed since Nat Hentoff declared in 1958 that "Hughes is not a major poet as Auden or perhaps Roethke are."[5] The most Hentoff could say about Hughes was that he was "an honest, unpretentious versifier." Hentoff then cited Ezra Pound's recommendation of Hughes's poetry, quoting a comment that sounds rather ironic coming from Pound: "Thank God; at last I come across a poet I can understand."[6] In view of Pound's inability to use American vernacular speech effectively in his own poetry, Hughes's achievement seems all the more notable. In 1967 Dickinson was still backing off from considering the importance of Hughes's work in this area:

> Critics do not rank Hughes as a writer of the first class. He has done little with the deeper questions of life and often his work is confined to a certain predictable scope. In some cases he expresses the experimental at the expense of sound literary values while at other times he tends toward a journalistic facility. Considering the amount of work Hughes has done it is little wonder that some of his pieces are less polished than others. One might wish that he had spent more time

perfecting certain poems or stories rather than branching out into theatre work and editorial projects.[7]

The problem with Dickinson's evaluation is that it presents the theater work and editorial projects as expendable additions to Hughes's output rather than crucial elements of it. Hughes was a champion of the oral tradition, audience participation, and pride in African-American culture in his poetry, and his extension into other activities, similar in breadth to the efforts of Carl Sandburg, was a natural result of his aesthetic. When the Newport Jazz Festival was to be closed down due to riots in 1960, it was no surprise to find Hughes there, collaborating with Muddy Waters on a blues song to lament the occasion.[8] Today, poets like Etheridge Knight assert that "it's *all* oral,"[9] so Hughes, anticipating some of the Beat experiments with oral performance in the 1950s, was one of the forerunners of the present poetry-as-performance movements and the attempts to draw the oral vernacular tradition into "legitimate poetry."

It is Hughes's *seeming* facility, his experimentation, his reliance on the oral tradition, and his commitment to the "deeper questions of life"—questions about freedom, identity, existence, and man's relation to others and his environment—that make Hughes the great poet that he most definitely is. But these "deeper" questions have to do with day-to-day existence as well. When Hughes recognized that jazz musicians played for money, he was recognizing a fundamental truth: man does not live by art alone, especially an art that doesn't growl with the hungry bellies of the dispossessed or eagle rock to the tune of those weary blues. Hughes is a poet of the body, the soul, and the mind, relying on what Jemie calls the "confident humanity"[10] of the Black masses to offer an affirmative answer to the question, "don't you want to be free?"

Hughes's attitude toward the folk tradition was a natural extension of the attitudes of his forerunners DuBois, Locke, and Johnson, and a part of the Harlem Renaissance movement that at first took a romantic view of the "folk past" but quickly hardened into a truer realism. It was an attitude that prepared him for his many encounters with the blues. When he found them, in the country and in the city, in the field, the alley, and on the stage, he listened and he heard what they had to say to and for him. Forming his own ideas

about what the blues are and do, he sought to employ their structures, rhythms, themes, and words in his blues poems, though
obviously the blues poems of one person cannot cover all aspects of
the blues tradition. But he was working outside the oral tradition
as well, and the ways he attempted to capture and extend the
nuances of the oral blues tradition reveal an individual talent and
meticulous craftsman. The images of his poems are not as startling
as those of some of the most imaginative blues performers, like
Robert Johnson or Peetie Wheatstraw, nor as striking as some of
the traditional lyrics. His images are more in line with the expressions of the average, everyday, honest and unpretentious person
who expresses himself in a simple, heartfelt, and interesting manner. However, Hughes makes his special contribution in the area by
exploring the ways in which the oral and written traditions can be
applied and intertwined to great effect. Perhaps his stage directions
to act 2, scene 1, of *Simply Heavenly* indicate his feelings:

> The music of the blues
> on the guitar, slow
> haunting, syncopated,
> precedes the rise of
> the curtain . . .[11]

NOTES

1. Langston Hughes, *The Big Sea* (New York: Knopf, 1940), 263.
Reviewers like DuBose Heyward praised the poems of Hughes's first
volume, though the reviewer of the *Times Literary Supplement* found
them to be superficial (see DuBose Heyward, "Review of *The Weary
Blues*, by Langston Hughes," *New York Herald Tribune Books* [August 1,
1926], 4, and "Review of *The Weary Blues*, by Langston Hughes," *The
Times Literary Supplement* [July 29, 1926], 515). *Fine Clothes to the Jew*
sparked fiercer debates as to the value of that volume. Hughes himself
discussed the negative response in *The Big Sea* (264–68), repeating un-
favorable reviews from the *Pittsburgh Courier*, the *New York Amsterdam
News*, the *Chicago Whip*, Benjamin Brawley, and Eustace Gay, while
noting the positive reactions of James Weldon Johnson, Dewey Jones,
Alice Dunbar-Nelson, the literary magazines, and the white press. The
negative responses seemed to center around a feeling that Hughes was
parading disgusting lowlife figures before whites, who could use the
portraits to justify prejudice and stereotyping. Much of the objectionable

material was in Hughes's blues poems. The reviewer from the *Independent,* however, felt that "Mr. Hughes is best in his 'Blues'" (Review of *Fine Clothes to the Jew,* by Langston Hughes, *Independent* 68 [April 9, 1927], 396). Hughes, it seems, refused to be ashamed of the blues or blues people, finding them instead a compelling and natural source and subject for poetry. White critics, who could not feel threatened by the portraits, and black critics comfortable enough with themselves not to feel threatened, joined in praising Hughes.

2. Langston Hughes, *Shakespeare in Harlem* (New York: Knopf, 1942), 1.

3. Donald C. Dickinson, *A Bio-Bibliography of Langston Hughes* (Hamden, Conn.: Archon Books, 1967), 82–83.

4. Faith Berry, *Langston Hughes: Before and Beyond Harlem* (Westport, Conn.: Lawrence Hill, 1983), 321.

5. Nat Hentoff, "Langston Hughes: He Found Poetry in the Blues," *Mayfair* (August, 1958): 27.

6. Ibid. Jean Wagner referred to Hughes's occasional "excessive facility" in *Black Poets of the United States,* 386.

7. Dickinson, *Bio-Bibliography,* 115.

8. Langston Hughes and McKinley Morganfield, "Goodbye Newport Blues," *Muddy Waters at Newport,* Chess LP 1449, n.d. The song is actually sung by Muddy's half brother, pianist Otis Spann. Though Hughes was aware of the Mississippi/Chicago blues of Muddy Waters as early as 1960, he never mentioned Waters as one of the greatest blues singers. Since Waters is now recognized as one of the best, it seems odd that Hughes did not name Waters in either "I Remember the Blues" or *Black Magic,* where Waters's name might have been mentioned. However, Hughes never noted any blues figure associated with Mississippi Delta blues in any of his essays, nor did he name any of the other great post-World War II Chicago blues performers like Howlin' Wolf, Little Water, or Elmore James. Perhaps Waters's mixture of deep Delta blues with a rhythm and blues beat and amplification struck Hughes as an incongruous mix, much the way it initially grated on the sensibilities of some of Waters's British audiences during his first tour with his band. On the other hand, maybe the lionization of Waters by white British and American blues bands in the mid-to-late 1960s came too late for Hughes to see Waters's importance.

9. Steve Tracy, "Interview With Etheridge Knight," *MELUS* 12, no. 2 (1985): 7–23.

10. Onwuchekwa Jemie, *Langston Hughes: An Introduction to the Poetry* (New York: Columbia University Press, 1976), 77.

11. Langston Hughes, *The Langston Hughes Reader* (New York: Braziller, 1958), 282.

1

FOLKLORE AND THE HARLEM RENAISSANCE

1

It is no coincidence that the commercial recording of blues music by African-American performers and the cultural/artistic movement known as the Harlem Renaissance began at roughly the same time. Despite the existence of Edison's first phonographs in 1877 and the issuance in 1902 of six single-sided recordings by the Dinwiddie Colored Quartet, the recording of African-American blues artists was not considered in any serious way until 14 February 1920. On that occasion, Cincinnati native Mamie Smith recorded Perry Bradford's "That Thing Called Love" and "You Can't Keep a Good Man Down" in place of white singer Sophie Tucker. On 10 August, one month after the record was issued, Mamie was back in the studio, owing to the success of the release, to record two other tunes, "Crazy Blues," and "It's Right Here For You (If You Don't Get It . . . 'Tain't No Fault of Mine)." The latter title not only had sexual connotations, but was also peculiarly appropriate in terms of the appearance of blacks on phonograph records. Because the black press had been stumping for recordings by black artists and because of wide advertising in the black community, the record, Okeh 4169, in its "first month of issue . . . sold 75,000 copies at a dollar each, and continued to be highly successful for many months."[1] It was another chapter in the rebirth of the blues: the folk-blues that had been written down and arranged by W. C. Handy were beginning to make a big noise on the mass market, bringing on a blues craze that drew many other black singers into the spotlight.

These facts transcribe as easily and dispassionately as the fact of the publication of Claude McKay's *Harlem Shadows* in 1922; or Langston Hughes's acceptance of first prize in the first poetry competition sponsored by the National Urban League's *Opportunity Magazine* on 1 May 1925; or Hughes's placing three of his poems next to the plate of white poet Vachel Lindsay at the Wardman Park Hotel in December 1925, which subsequently led to Lindsay's public reading of the busboy's poems and a flurry of attention. What the facts do not convey is the drama that led to these events, to the popularity of the blues, and to the Harlem Renaissance. Neither do they indicate the complex, varied relationship between the recording movement and the Harlem Renaissance. In fact, both were renaissances—rebirths and reformations—that reworked themes and genres that had gone before, transforming them into something new. They drew upon individual creativity, organized black support, and white patronage, cooperation, and, in some cases, exploitation to achieve success.

Both the writers of the Harlem Renaissance and blues recording artists of the 1920s were working with African-American folklore; indeed, they owed much of their success to it. The task of defining what folklore is and recognizing what is "authentic" is central to understanding both the blues and the Harlem Renaissance completely, and it has been one of the most difficult ideas for folklorists to agree upon. Barre Toelken provided one of the best contemporary definitions in *The Dynamics of Folklore,* describing the materials of folklore as "tradition-based communicative units informally exchanged in dynamic variation through space and time."[2] *Tradition* refers to "culture-specific materials and options" available to the performer; *dynamic* to the performer's ability to exercise his inventiveness within the tradition. Although in the broadest sense of the term we are all "folk," generating folklore related to our background and region, the focus of many folklorists has often been on the productions of a regional or ethnic group that has fostered its ways and maintained its traditions in relative isolation—either imposed or voluntary—from other regional or ethnic groups and from a society dominated by a written heritage (though, inevitably, some influences from other groups or society may creep in). The folklore is generated by a group with a particular ethos related to time, place, and socioeconomic condition as well, and because it comes into being in this type of "exclusive" environment, it reflects all aspects of this environment: speech, sayings, tales, songs, religion, superstitions, signs, symbols, crafts, clothes, gravemarkers—all these and more are part of the folklore of a particular group. In fact, if Stephen Henderson was correct in identifying folk material as offering an "interior dynamism" that underlies the best contemporary black poetry, then perhaps some contemporary poetry by black writers can be considered folklore.[3] This is especially true of poets like Etheridge Knight, whose "Shine and the Titanic" seeks to work within and extend the tradition, and who felt that poetry is meant to be oral anyway, that performance is an essential part of the poem.[4] Thus collections of his poetry are merely conveniences, written transcriptions of what are naturally oral productions derived from and speaking to his people. Poetry needs the poet, the performance, and the audience to be complete.

Ideas and attitudes toward folklore have, of course, changed over the years. Alan Dundes suggested that there is a devolutionary premise in folklore theory that folklore "decays through time" or runs down "by moving from 'higher' to 'lower' strata of society";[5] he believed that this premise "is a culture bound product of a larger nineteenth century European worldview, a worldview which favored romanticism and primitivism, and which encouraged scholars in many disciplines to look and work backwards, that is, toward the presumed perfect past."[6] Elliott Oring challenged Dundes's claim that there is a devolutionary *premise* among folklorists, suggesting instead that there have been and are some devolutionary *tendencies* among some folklorists. These tendencies are often related to restrictive definitions of folklore that include, for example, only oral or unwritten lore, allied with multiplicity of criteria for judging progress. For example, Oring defended Edward Burnett Tylor against Dundes's claims, asserting that the identification of folklore as "survivals" from the past (or "popular antiquities," as folklore had been called) does not necessarily suggest that these "survivals" cannot *evolve* into what Tylor called "revivals."[7] William A. Wilson, too, recognized devolutionary tendencies, but he felt that "evolution and progress have had far more influence on the development of folklore study than Dundes is willing to admit."[8] However, it seems logical that by primarily associating folklore with the past, by seeking the oldest versions of particular works of folklore as if they would be the most complete and "authentic," and by collecting folklore with the attitude that it must be preserved before it is gone, some folklorists have implied that folklore is at least static, if not devolutionary. By approaching and defining folklore as static they are leaning toward a devolutionary approach by suggesting that folklore is at least unchanging in a changing world, increasingly anachronistic and irrelevant to contemporary concerns.

This romantic view of folklore, which sees it as primitive and fragmented, because it was current at the time of the education, apprenticeship, and literary emergence of the writers of the Harlem Renaissance, influenced those writers to look at African-American folklore, even that which was current, in a romantic and primitive light. These Harlem Renaissance writers seemed to feel that they were separate from the "peasant folk," despite the fact that very often they knew that the folklore that the (primarily white) critics labeled a survival of the primitive past was in fact being used and modified every day. For example, Bernard Bell called attention to the theory of Johann Herder, which influenced the Harlem Renaissance writers. Herder defined folk song as "a spontaneous, indigenous expression of the collective soul of a people."[9] The definition smacks of the pastoral, of an unselfconscious simplicity and almost magical communicative power that calls up a part of the past, a heritage of almost dreamlike dimensions from which people like Herder (or DuBois and others) were separated by education and sophistication. In this attitude we can see implicit the idea that folklore is a resource upon which one can draw if one wishes to get in touch with one's past and memory (self) while still maintaining a social and aesthetic distance.

Thus, on the theoretical side folklore was, in a sense, something primitive and mysterious for the Harlem Renaissance writers; but on the personal side it was contemporary and magical, something that drew African-Americans together. John Work believed that folk song was the folk's "natural means of communication, which they understand among themselves," and that slaves deliberately encoded their music—creating "a kind of secret password"[10] into the lives of the slaves—in order to prevent whites from understanding what the slaves understood among themselves. This was certainly true in regard to the slaves' intentions: they did deliberately encode their music and express themselves metaphorically to disguise their attitudes about their lives. However, Work's assertion that song was their natural means of expression, when, of course, we know that they talked with each other, creates a romantic picture of the naturally artistic singing slaves—an idyllic scene in a non-idyllic environment. It also creates the sense of a more primitive time when man was more in touch with himself, more naturally artistic, and highlights the disparity between those times and the times of the people who are writing about them.

Work's suggestion that the lore itself belonged to the individual group that created it and fostered it is a valid one. Carl Sandburg may have recorded folk songs; he may have been passionately interested in the folk; but he was not an "authentic" folksinger. Rather, he was a trained literary artist looking at the lore of a group from a perspective foreign to the group. There is a problem, though, in defining what the perspective of the group is. For example, does the performer have to remain in the same location as the entire group in order to maintain authenticity and perspective? That would limit African-American folklore to rural areas and confine the performers to particular geographical locations. Certainly professional folklorists and amateur collectors are today penetrating isolated communities all over America, "discovering" folk performers who fit these criteria. But are those performers the only ones who are "a medium for community concern, decorum, and traditional standards?"[11] An urban environment does often cause rural folklore to undergo changes that are more relevant to the urban environment, but those changes do not invalidate the material as folklore. A Northern urban community made up of formerly Southern rural inhabitants is still a community, and what they make of their lore is still lore.

The study of folk material, as with any study, is certainly affected by both personal and group preconceptions and prejudices. The collection, presentation, and interpretation of this material may be distorted by these preconceptions and prejudices; therefore, because the intrusion of anything foreign to the environment of the folk may distort it, it can be advantageous to have a collector who is connected in some crucial way to the group from which he is collecting. Both the folklore and the folklorist must be subjected to intense scrutiny in order to verify the honesty of the material. At that point, then, other outsiders can begin to subject the material to their own distortions, and *their* conclusions must be scrutinized.[12] Interpretations of the folk have been wide, and wild, but they have remained central to our understanding of not only what folklore is, but who the people are who are doing the interpreting.

In the years before the Harlem Renaissance, folk materials were not used extensively as a positive force in African-American writing. The ministers, educators, and activists of the Civil War and Reconstruction concentrated largely on asserting the capability of the African-American to achieve within the boundaries of the dominant white culture, exploring antislavery themes and the popular image of the tragic mulatto who was caught between the culture and values of the black world and the white world. They did this in order to make their calls for integration seem more legitimate. That is not to say that sketches of African-American folk life—customs, speech, tales, music, and art—by African-Americans were unheard of. William Wells Brown's *My Southern Home,* Charles Chesnutt's *The Conjure Woman,* and dialect poetry by Paul Laurence Dunbar, Daniel Webster Davis, James Edwin Campbell, and James D. Corrothers, among other works, all employed some aspect of African-American folk life to some degree; however, except for Chesnutt, the portraits were in most cases limited in scope and subordinated to the themes mentioned above or to romanticized reveries on the Southern past that were based on acceptance of popular white literary standards and social mores of the genteel tradition. Chesnutt and Sutton Griggs seem to have been the most successful in fiction; and Dunbar seems to have been the most successful poet, though he did not expose the dire poverty that was known to be prevalent, nor did he solve the considerable problems presented by dialect usage. However, he was, as Sterling Brown wrote, "the first American poet to handle Negro folk life with any degree of fullness,"[13] and in his poetry he generally transformed the clownish Negro of white popular verse into a more psychologically complete and attractive character. Still, these were very tentative, very self-conscious forays that prepared the way for the more assertive employment of folk materials by the writers of the Harlem Renaissance.

The essential problem of the Harlem Renaissance was that of establishing African-American identity, considering both the African and African-American heritage. That identity had to be established within the context of the growth of self-awareness within the black community and the various responsibilities—to self, to the community, and to art—that those who took part in the Harlem Renaisssance felt so acutely. The mass black migration from South to North, which peaked at the turn of the twentieth century, the over-speculation by real estate investors that glutted the Harlem market and drove down the rent prices, and New York's position as a booming metropolis combined to make Harlem the gathering place for a diverse group of African peoples on whom the writers among them could draw for folk materials. As George Kent stressed, the most important quest of the artists of the Harlem Renaissance was "to gain authority in [their] portrayal of black life by the attempt to assert, with varying degrees of radicality, a dissociation of sensibility from that enforced by American culture and its institution."14 Those varying degrees of radicality, both in politics and art, were what prevented a monotony of theme and approach in the productions of the movement; additionally, there were numerous attitudes toward folk materials, both in terms of whether they should be used at all and, if so, how they would be employed most successfully.

Those espousing the different approaches have often been divided into two major groups, the Old Guard and the New, based largely on the degree to which they accepted white, middle-class, European standards. Although the leaders of the Old Guard tended, in fact, to be chronologically older, the classifications are based on their philosophical stance. The Old Guard tended to be more ambivalent in their attitudes toward folk materials, attempting to balance their own racial pride with their middle-class values. For them, the New Guard relied far too much on black underworld characters and "lowlife" types in their depictions of African-American experience, rather than setting up examples of respectable Negroes for others of their race to follow; and they drew too much on and identified too fully with folk forms for their experimentation, particularly the "vulgar" blues and jazz. Of course, attitudes varied, but generally writers like W. E. B. DuBois, James Weldon Johnson, and Alain Locke—the Old Guard—differed from writers like Sterling Brown, Zora Neale Hurston, and Langston Hughes in their appreciation of folk materials.

As a philosopher, historian, social scientist, and political activist, W. E. B. DuBois towers as a prime motivator of the younger artists of the Harlem Renaissance. His *Souls of Black Folk* (1903), which was hailed as centrally important to the African-American cause, fixed "that moment in history when the American Negro began to reject the idea of the world's belonging to white people only, and to think of himself, in concert, as a potential force in the organization of society."[15] Still, though DuBois was an active Pan-Africanist, involved with the Niagara Movement in objecting to the conciliatory policies of Booker T. Washington, and a founding member of the NAACP, his position regarding the Harlem Renaissance was distinctly of the Old Guard because of his intensely middle-class outlook as a "devotee of white cultural expression."[16] DuBois's tutelage by Harvard English professor Barrett Wendell was at least partially responsible, and Wendell's elitism and Anglophilia affected not only his own aesthetic theories, but those of DuBois as well:

> Wendell's theory of literature was deeply influenced by his racial and national preferences. Literature in English was best written by those who were most English. . . . With little formal reading in literature himself, DuBois was being trained in the appreciation of letters by a charismatic figure disdainful of the problems of a struggling national literature, of the vitality of folk expression, or of the experimentation in forms and themes by which literature revitalizes itself.[17]

But DuBois was not Barrett Wendell; therefore, it would be a mistake to type DuBois as disdainful of folk expression. Rather, DuBois held a complicated position on folk materials, bounded on one side by his racial pride and on the other by his attempts to bring middle-class respectability to his people.

For example, DuBois was proud of African-American folk music, as Paul Robeson recounted:

> Dr. DuBois was a distinguished historian as well as a social scientist. We often talked about the wealth and beauty of our folk heritage, particularly about Negro music which he loved and found deeply moving. He often stressed the importance of this special contribution to American culture. We had interesting discussions about the

likeness of our Negro folk music to many other folk musics throughout the world.[18]

This "special contribution," described in *The Negro* (1913), was made not only in the African influence on the invention of musical instruments, but also in the mingled African and American contribution of "a new and original music to the western world, not only in the spirituals, but in the 'blues' and 'ragtime,'" which he felt launched modern dance music and represented "the only kinds of music brought forth in America by immigrants."[19] DuBois's love of African-American folklore extended most strongly to spirituals, which he treasured alongside his Brahms, Schumann, and Handel. His earlier essay, "Of The Sorrow Songs," included in *The Souls of Black Folk,* discussed "the rhythmic cry of the slave . . . as the most beautiful expression of human experience born this side of the seas . . . and the greatest gift of the Negro people."[20] He went on:

> These songs are the articulate message of the slave to the world. They tell us in these eager days that life was joyous to the black slave, careless and happy. I can easily believe this of some, of many. But not all the past South, though it rose from the dead, can gainsay the heart-touching witness of these songs. They are the music of an unhappy people, of the children of disappointment; they tell of death and suffering and unvoiced longing toward a truer world, of misty wanderings and hidden ways.[21]

Later in the essay, DuBois referred to the breaking down of the original African and African-American songs into pieces with a less distinct and integrated African-American purpose, where the words and music do not seem to work in concert, except for whites on the concert stage. The message of the songs that still remained among the folk became "naturally veiled and half articulate,"[22] since the songs were removed, as devolutionist folklorists would claim, from the spirit and meaning of the original sorrow songs. DuBois bemoaned the imitation and caricaturing of the "primitive" folk music that he felt expressed the soul-yearnings of the black slave and lived "in the hearts of the Negro people."[23] Characteristically, it was their usefulness to whites in their religious practice, as well as to blacks and their connection to both the African *and* Judeo-Christian traditions, that attracted DuBois most especially to these sorrow songs. The attention afforded them by the white organizers of the Port Royal experiment, which culminated in the publication of *Slave Songs of the United States* in 1867, also most likely contributed to DuBois's enthusiasm.[24]

It was apparently the distance of ragtime, blues, and jazz from that purity of expression that caused DuBois to reject them as "serious" music, though he bragged about them as sources of popular culture. They simply did not project the type of "cultured" image or adhere to the (largely European) standards that DuBois desired. DuBois found it difficult to accept African-American folk music like blues, jazz, and popular gospel. *The Crisis*, the journal he edited for the NAACP, scarcely hid its disdain for these kinds of music. In fact, the material published in *The Crisis* provides a fairly good index to DuBois's prejudices. Arnold Rampersad wrote of it:

> While it now and then praised black popular entertainers, especially the celebrated comedian Bert Williams, it seldom questioned the artistic criteria of the white world except on matters such as patronage and publishing. DuBois' idea of a notable musical event, of which he recorded hundreds in the *Crisis*, was a black performer interpreting serious Western music, or a white composer or musician introducing African or Afro-American themes into his work.[25]

Thus, in enumerating the achievements of Africans and African-Americans in art and music, DuBois called attention to "Bridgeworth, the friend of Beethoven, and the unexplained complexion of Beethoven's own father; Coleridge-Taylor in England, Tanner in America, Gomez in Spain," and referred to Henry Thacker Burleigh, who introduced African-American spirituals on the concert stage, Will Marion Cook, leader of Will Marion Cook's Southern Syncopated Orchestra, and choral conductor Hall Johnson as the men who were "making the new American syncopated music."[26] Artist Henry Ossawa Tanner was an appropriate choice for DuBois, since he turned from his compelling early work dealing with African-American themes, such as "The Banjo Lesson," to paintings based on religious themes, relocating himself in Paris in 1891. Tanner's subsequent prize-winning career, during which he received the Medal of Honor at the Paris Exposition and the Lippincott Prize, featured just the type of garnering of white recognition and achievement within European channels that DuBois sought. In DuBois's list there is no mention of the itinerant blues singer, or tent show singers like Ma Rainey, who began her singing career in a traveling show in 1902,[27] thirteen years before DuBois put his list together. In fact, when DuBois later expanded *The Negro* into *Black Folk: Then and Now* (1929), he increased his list to include composer-arranger W. C. Handy (but not his acknowledged sources) and concert artists Sissieretta Jones (called "The Black Patti," after Italian soprano Adelina Patti), Roland Hayes, and Marian Anderson. DuBois preferred the spirituals, which for him wed despair and hope, and drew on an ancient spirit and power connected partly to the struggles of the African and African-American tradition, partly to the Judeo-Christian. He also preferred black artists who embraced white Western traditions and the professionally trained arrangers of folk music, who could make the music more "respectable," rather than the untutored people who created the music. Writing in *Dusk of Dawn* (1940), DuBois presented an attitude about blues and jazz that was closely related to his championing of economic power and a black-controlled segregation in the 1930s as opposed to his earlier pressing for political rights and integration: "Most whites want Negroes to amuse them; they demand caricature; they demand jazz; and torn between these allegiances: between the extraordinary reward for entertainers of the white world and meager encouragement to honest self-expression, the artistic movement among American negroes has accomplished something, but it has never flourished and never will until it is deliberately planned."[28] DuBois's laudable call for self-definition and self-determinism unfortunately impugns the integrity of jazz performers; and his call for further education and culture among the segregated black group might have meant, as E. Franklin Frazier claimed, a genteel, middle-class program remote from an understanding and aesthetic of the black proletariat.[29] Still, DuBois could scarcely keep from bragging about African-American musics, despite the fact that he seemed to have disdain for them. That very fact is expressive of the dichotomy between his assertion of black pride and his partial capitulation to white European standards.

Like DuBois, James Weldon Johnson provided an example for the New Guard writers of the Harlem Renaissance, but his position differed from that of DuBois. Although Johnson was aware of the contributions of people of African descent around the world and felt "some cultural unity with the African people," that interest did not extend to "plans that included Negroes of the world, such as DuBois's Pan-African Congress."[30] Like DuBois, however, he rejected Booker T. Washington's admonitions for vocational training in light of what he considered to be his own excellent "classical liberal education" at Atlanta and Columbia universities, where he probably picked up his habit of naively underestimating "the many barriers impeding Negroes from gaining an education."[31]

In underestimating those problems, Johnson demonstrated a remoteness from the everyday problems of the laborer. It has been said that "Johnson rarely took any action particularly aimed at helping the Negro laborer. Probably there was little he could have done; but it was also true that he was hard pressed to personally involve himself in the laborer's struggle. He had little in common with the laborer. DuBois pointed out that Johnson, except for isolated incidents, never had any personal contact with the urban laborer."[32] This lack of personal contact with urban laborers made it hard for Johnson to understand their problems or identify with their views or aesthetics; indeed it was they who needed to adopt his values. Thus, Johnson's position was less international and economically determined than DuBois's, though it was still based on the belief in the power of a liberal education to uplift African-Americans. And, like DuBois, Johnson believed that this uplifting involved partially embracing white, middle-class values.

Johnson, too, was greatly concerned with the *image* of the African-American. The African-American must be the soul of propriety; he must look good, not only to other African-Americans, but to whites as well. Johnson emphasized this orientation in *The Daily American,* the newspaper he started in 1895, with its "prosaic style, its puritanical emphasis on clean living and clean government, its explicit attempts at objectivity,"[33] all aimed at emphasizing the African-American's responsibility and literacy. Johnson stated his concern about having two audiences with conflicting expectations in his essay "The Dilemma of the Negro Author" (1928), which outlined the special problems of the African-American author faced with audiences "with differing and often opposite and antagonistic points of view."[34] The white audience mainly expected stereotypes: portraits of blacks as poor, lazy, passionate,

savage, non-heroic. But the black audiences demanded more refined, educated characters governed by white, middle-class values:
they were in fact trying to adopt these values in order to change the
attitudes of the white middle class toward them. Though Johnson's
essay was perceptive in its analysis of the problem, it provided little
concrete advice on solving the dilemma; rather, it concentrated on
berating both black and white audiences for placing such con-
straints on the African-American artist. His response to those who
would simply ignore the white audience was to point out that
pleasing black audiences was difficult as well; in fact, it was no
answer at all. Johnson probably responded this way because solving *that* problem would be akin to solving the race problem itself.
Johnson could only conjecture that time might change things. His
general prescription made some attempt to reconcile his desire for
both audiences: "The equipped Negro author working at his best
in his best known material can achieve this end; but, standing on
his racial foundation, he must fashion something that rises above
race, and reaches out to the universal in truth and beauty."[35]

That desire to "rise above" race implied a desire to transcend the
local or national through the use of the local or national; yet as
Johnson had already said, one of the problems caused by his
double audience was that their contradictory points of view presented a great obstacle to success. Thus, Johnson was left resorting
to his African-American heritage on the one hand, while, on the
other hand, relying on white values. In fact, DuBois criticized him
"for too often asking advice from whites."[36] In the Preface to his
Book of American Negro Poetry (1922), Johnson expressed his
wish that the African-American writer would attempt to accomplish something akin to what Synge had done for the Irish:

> . . . he needs to find a form that will express the racial spirit by
> symbols from within rather than by symbols from without, such as
> the mere mutilation of English spelling and pronunciation. He needs
> a form that is freer and larger than dialect, but which will still hold
> the racial flavor; a form expressing the imagery, the idioms, the
> peculiar turns of thought, and the distinctive humor and pathos, too,
> of the Negro, but which will also be capable of voicing the deepest
> and highest emotions and aspirations, and allow the widest range of
> subjects and the widest scope of treatment.[37]

The "racial flavor" of which Johnson spoke was for him provided by the folk materials of the African-American. He exulted in the "power of the Negro to suck up the national spirit from the soil and create something artistic and original," which simultaneously possessed "the note of universal appeal."[38] Johnson seemed to admire a broader range of African-American folklore than DuBois, expressing his admiration for Uncle Remus stories, spirituals, ragtime, blues, and jazz. However, like DuBois, he considered the spirituals "the greatest body of folk song" that America had produced, in which the Negro had "sounded the depths, if he did not scale the heights, of music."[39] Johnson knew the spirituals firsthand and as a scholar—he collected and edited two volumes of spirituals himself during the Renaissance years. Johnson's inability to assert that spirituals could "scale the heights" betrayed his reticence to claim for the songs any serious intellectual value, or to categorize them with more "serious" Western music such as the kind he and his brother, J. Rosamond Johnson, were producing for shows on and off Broadway; rather, the spirituals plumbed the emotional depths. Also, like DuBois, he was aware of the imitation and adulteration of African-American folklore on Broadway and Tin Pan Alley, and he cared very much to preserve in some way the folklore he knew from his childhood in the Deep South and his time as a teacher in Georgia. Therefore, when he undertook to use folk materials in his greatest literary achievement, *God's Trombones* (1927), it was no surprise that he chose folk religion—the oral sermon—as his vehicle, or that he employed it so lovingly and diligently.

In this volume, Johnson had done what DuBois would never do: he employed the cadences and form of oral folk materials extensively as part of his written style. For Johnson this work was an attempt, poetically rendered, to capture the spirit of the sermon beyond transcribing the superficialities of dialect misspellings. By getting at the speech and the structure of the sermons, Johnson sought to portray the rhetorical genius of preachers whom he considered to be the earliest galvanizing and rallying forces of his people. It was Johnson's willingness to creatively experiment stylistically with folk forms that characterized his further admiration of and commitment to African-American folklore and pushed *God's Trombones* into an area where DuBois feared to tread.

To be fair, much of Johnson's other poetic work was either dialect poetry, which he quickly repudiated,[40] or verse bounded by conventional European forms unrelated to African-American folklore; and he spent some time writing minstrel and coon songs with his brother for popular consumption, though not all of their material was of this sort.[41] Much of this material was written early in his career under the influence of Dunbar. His rejection of dialect poetry's misspellings was likely related to the company he kept as a writer for *The New York Age* (1914–24), as secretary general of the NAACP (1916–30), and as a member of "society" in New York and Washington, all of which pushed him to a more middle-class outlook concerning dialect poetry and that part of his past. But *God's Trombones* was his shining poetic achievement, where he began to reject the "Rastus and Lishy Davis of the old Dunbar tradition," utilizing "the idiomatic folk patterns as an effective artistic instrument."[42] His attempts at capturing the tempo, dramatic pauses, syncopation, and rhythmic stress through line arrangement and other typographical accommodations served to move his written poetry back toward speech itself, speaking powerfully to the other New Negroes of the Harlem Renaissance because of their interest in the folklore of their people.

One of those who most directly encouraged the New Guard writers of the Harlem Renaissance was Alain Locke, Phi Beta Kappa Harvard graduate and the first black Rhodes scholar, who "was thoroughly convinced that there were enough black writers, artists, and thinkers to generate a new and distinctive cultural movement."[43] Like DuBois and Johnson, Locke was well acquainted with European culture, having lived and studied in England, Germany, and France, and he gave Langston Hughes "his first serious acquaintance with European culture."[44] It was no accident that the majority of the young writers whom Locke recruited for his ground-breaking anthology *The New Negro* (1925) were "anti-Garveyites, allied with the NAACP and the Urban League, college-educated, with many of the materialistic goals of American society within their grasp."[45] It must be noted, however, that those goals would have been far harder for them to achieve, and achievable on a more limited scale, than for their white counterparts. Locke's choice of writers reflected once again his racial pride balanced by his middle-class values.

Despite his middle-class leanings, Locke heartily encouraged the use of folk roots in the art of African-Americans, though, like DuBois, he expected artists to create "with the future of the race in mind."[46] Just as he sought sound criticism of African-American music by formally trained musicians who were not "divorced from the people and their vital inspiration by the cloister-walls and the taboos of musical respectability,"[47] he saw the need for a more complete exposition of the ideas of the folk Negro by the talented few of the intellectual artistic community. Moreover, he saw his desires coming to fruition: "What stirs inarticulately in the masses is already upon the lips of the talented few, and the future listens, however the present may shut its ears."[48] This folk experience was so important because, Locke felt, "in the very heart of the folk-spirit are the essential forces."[49] That spirit needed interpretation by the African-American intelligentsia because, as Locke said of African-American folk music, it was "produced without formal musical training or intention by the greatest and most fundamental of all musical forces,—emotional creation."[50] Thus, for Locke, there was a case of mutual interdependence. Just as African-American genius had to rely on "the race gift as a vast, spiritual endowment"[51] from which could be formed expressions of "high" art, so that endowment, forged from the emotions of the inarticulate masses, needed the New Negro to express it fully.

Locke, too, was familiar with a wide range of African-American folklore. Not only was he the founder of the Associates in Negro Folk Education, editing the series of eight *Bronze Booklets* that they published, but he also contributed two of the booklets, *The Negro and His Music* and *Negro Art: Past and Present,* in 1936. The volume on African-American music provided a good background discussion of the subject for its time and included readings and recorded references that indicate a fairly good knowledge of the various relevant historical, musical, and folkloric studies and contemporary commercial recordings. Locke's particularly broad list of blues recordings was the result of suggestions by the young Sterling Brown, as Locke acknowledged, but that willingness to listen to younger contemporaries like Brown was one of Locke's important traits. Locke was also a continuing observer of and commentator on African-American folklore until his death in 1954, and a sympathetic student of international African-American work. However, as with Johnson, Locke followed DuBois in seeing the spirituals as the "most characteristic product of Negro genius to date" and the race's "great folk gift,"[52] indicating once again the preference for material connected with white, middle-class religious values. Nonetheless, his broad knowledge, sympathy, and sense of purpose made Locke an important advocate of African-American folklore.

Locke was better able than DuBois to countenance the uses to which the New Guard put folk arts, primarily because DuBois's main artistic thrust was propaganda, while Locke called for "pure art"; however, Locke did feel that pure art must be undertaken with the full knowledge of the responsibility of the African-American artist to his people.

Surely their disagreement represents a fine distinction, but a distinction nonetheless. DuBois's note, affixed to his novel *The Quest of the Silver Fleece*, emphasized his idea, while still acknowledging the importance of the art as well:

> Who would tell a tale must look toward three ideals: to tell it well, to tell it beautifully, and to tell the truth. The first is the Gift of God, the second is the vision of Genius, but the third is the reward of honesty.
>
> In *The Quest of the Silver Fleece* there is little I ween, divine or ingenious, but at least I have been honest. In no fact or picture have I consciously set down aught the counterpart of which I have not seen or known; and whatever the finished picture may lack of completeness, this lack is due now to the storyteller, now to the artist, but never to the herald of the Truth.[53]

Locke countered, in "Negro Youth Speaks," with a call for art that did not self-consciously pose as Truth:

> Racial expression as a conscious motive, it is true, is fading out of our latest art, but just as surely the age of truer, finer group expression is coming in—for race expression does not need to be deliberate to be vital. Indeed at its best it never is. This was the case with our instinctive and quite matchless folk-art, and begins to be the phase of art that promises to be fully representative. . . . Our poets have now stopped speaking for the Negro—they speak as Negroes. Where formerly they spoke to others and tried to interpret, they now speak to their own and try to express. They have stopped posing, being nearer the attainment of pose.[54]

The fact that Locke likened this pure art to folk art in its lack of self-conscious mission further highlighted his admiration for folk art and what he saw as its motivation. Therefore, though the main objective of *The New Negro* was, as Robert Hayden has pointed out, "integrationist, not separatist,"[55] Locke was taking another step toward the direction of the New Guard artists, holding out against such cynics as George Schuyler. In "The Negro-Art Hokum" (1926), Schuyler found sectional, national, or economic characteristics rather than racial ones to be the main shapers of spirituals, work songs, ragtime, jazz, and blues, and he believed that African-American art was "identical in kind with the literature, painting and sculpture of white Americans."[56] Langston Hughes himself contradicted Schuyler, responding with his famous essay "The Negro Artist and the Racial Mountain" (1926), which was solicited by *The Nation*.

There were, of course, other African-American cultural leaders who valued black music: sociologist and *Opportunity* editor Charles S. Johnson, whom Langston Hughes considered first among "the three people who midwifed the so-called New Negro literature into being,"[57] wrote with bitter delight about the popularity of jazz and the critical debate over whether it was simply primitive, decadent jungle rhythm or expressive of the pace of modern American life. He came down on the side of Carl Van Vechten, Gilbert Seldes, and Leopold Stokowski, with an indignant sense of irony: "What an immense, even unconscious irony the Negroes have devised! They, who of all Americans are most limited in self-expression, least considered and most denied, have forged the key to the interpretation of the American spirit."[58] But it was the interpretation of the *African-American* spirit that was on the minds of the New Negroes, despite the fact that, like the Old Guard before them, they still had to come to terms with white America. And they attempted to express that interpretation in what they saw as the attitudes and language of the "folk."

Of all the New Negroes, Sterling Brown was the closest to the rural folk Negro in spirit and content. Brown cannot strictly be considered a member of the Harlem Renaissance for several reasons. For one thing, he didn't live in Harlem; rather he was born in Washington D.C., the son of a Howard University professor of theology, and following his education at Williams College and

Howard, and stints at several Southern colleges, he returned to Howard in 1929 to teach. Therefore, any geographical connection with Harlem is tenuous. Brown, in fact, rejected the notion that a Harlem Renaissance took place: "The New Negro is not to me a group of writers centered in Harlem during the second half of the twenties. Most of the writers were not Harlemites; much of the best writing was not about Harlem, which was the show-window, the cashier's till, but no more Negro America than New York is America."[59] What Brown said was, of course, partially true. The environment in Harlem was in many ways artificial, the gaudy creation of white philanthropic slummers and exploitative capitalist "gangsters" on their latest intense fling.

However, despite these orchestrated cultural dramatics, this extreme extravagance and artificiality, there was undoubtedly a spirit created by the gathering of African peoples and their artists and an attention attracted by the pageant atmosphere that made Harlem more than a nominal center of intellectual and cultural activity and provided opportunities both to improve and to corrupt art. Also, it's likely that Brown was at least partially speaking out of the years of relative neglect he suffered while other Harlem artists like Langston Hughes garnered more attention. Critics have also pointed out that Brown's first volume, *Southern Road* (1932), came out after "the first great upsurge of the Negro Renaissance had subsided,"[60] which would place him outside the movement that was bounded by the end of World War I and the stock market crash. If one is bothered by the book's publication after the unofficial end of the Harlem Renaissance, it could be pointed out that Brown had published five poems in Countee Cullen's anthology *Carolina Dusk* (1927), five poems in *Opportunity,* as well as one each in *Carolina Magazine* and *Anthology of Negro American Literature* before the decade was spent. For those less mindful of superficial boundaries, the spirit of Brown's work fits perfectly into the New Negro Renaissance movement, especially in terms of his use of folk roots. In fact, his employment of the rural folk roots of the African-American represented his generation's best use of that material in its range of expression and its reflection of the often heroic stature of the common man and his creations.

Brown addressed a conference on the character and state of studies in folklore in 1946 about "The Approach of the Creative

Artist," at which time he outlined succinctly his involvement with folklore. Discussing his experiences on the Federal Writer's Project, collecting the narratives of ex-slaves with John Lomax and B. A. Botkin, he classified himself "as an amateur and certainly not a scientist," though he found the scientific approach more important in the arena of reporting folklore.[61] His interest, as an amateur, was that of the creative writer: "I became interested in folklore because of my desire to write poetry and prose fiction. I was first attracted by certain qualities that I thought the speech of the people had, and I wanted to get for my own writing a flavor, a color, a pungency of speech. Then later I came to something more important—I wanted to get an understanding of people, to acquire an accuracy in the portrayal of their lives."[62] Brown classified his interest as a "social-historical approach," and that interest led him very easily to the desire to collect "living-people-lore, of groups that couldn't be considered folk except by a very wide extension of the word."[63] His study, then, extended to rural people in general, who would become the subjects of his writing.

Brown was unduly modest in denigrating his stature as a student of folklore. Admitting that he had "made a fairly close study of folk-ways and folk songs,"[64] Brown wrote extensively on African-American folklore, demonstrating a broad knowledge of the variety of historical, sociological, folkloristic, and literary studies of the blues, and distinguishing among the various types of sources of folklore.[65] His essays are characterized by references to relevant personal experience along with material from other scholars and regular specific references to examples of the folklore about which he was writing. This experience and knowledge, coupled with his studies of African-Americans as writers and subjects, made him "excellently situated to defend whatever had an authentic folk origin, and to utilize it without incurring the blame directed against the dialect writers who had preceded him."[66] If Brown was an amateur, he was an extremely thoughtful and learned one.

The authentic folk origin was so important to Brown because of his desire for authenticity in his own writing. As Sterling Stuckey has pointed out:

> Fortunately Sterling A. Brown, exposed to the critical realist approach to literature of George Dutton of Williams and the realism that characterized some of the best American poetry of the twenties,

especially the work of Edward [*sic*] Arlington Robinson, Robert Frost, and Carl Sandburg, was all the more prepared to take an uncondescending, that is to say genuinely respectful, attitude toward the folk whom he encountered in the South. . . . Brown realized the need to explore the life of the Southern Negro below the surface in order to reveal unseen aspects of his being, his strength and fortitude, his healing humor, and his way of confronting tragedy.[67]

For Brown, folk songs provided "a very adept self-portraiture" that "put to shame much of the interpretation of the Negro from without,"[68] and his use of African-American folklore represented his attempt to interpret the African-American as the African-American would interpret himself. Brown's viewpoint was an important advance over the position of the Old Guard writers, since it no longer implied the superiority of values external to the creators of the folklore; rather, it involved the creative infusing of his work with the folklore's "spirit, its practical philosophy, its humor, and its speech."[69] Brown was not one to identify with the pretensions of the middle class, as evidenced in his defense of the blues: "The blues tell a great deal about folk-life. The genteel turn away from them in distaste, but blues persist with their terse and tonic shrewdness about human nature. At times they belong with the best of folk-poetry, and the people who create them at their best cannot be dismissed as clowns."[70]

Indeed, not only did Brown refuse to see the folk artists as clowns, but he also began to drop the pretentious distinctions between literary and folk creations: "These blues belong, with all their distinctive differences, to the best of folk literature. And to some lovers of poetry that is not at all a negligible best."[71] If this claim, made in 1930, seems something of a backdoor compliment, his statement twenty years later was more assertively "front door," though he was referring to religious folk material:

The Negro slave's picture of Calvary in such lines as
> Dey whupped him up de hill . . .
> Dey crowned his head with thorns . . .
> Dey pierced him in de side,
> An' de blood come a-twinklin' down;
> But he never said a mumbalin' word;
> Not a word; not a word.

belongs with the greatest Christian poetry.[72]

Brown's claim was of course not uncritical; he realized that there were various levels of quality both in the folk and commercial fields: "Crudities, incongruities, of course, there are in abundance—annoying changes of mood from tragedy to cheap farce. There seems to be entering more recently, a sophisticated smut, not the earlier breadth of Rabelais, but the snickering of the brothel. Blues are becoming cabaret appetizers."[73] For Brown, though the folk roots were resilient and strong, in the city, where the folk become "a submerged proletariat,"[74] folk culture was being choked off by commercial interests whose "belt line productions" were "prurient and pornographic."[75] The answer clearly lay in restoring to folklore its original spirit in order to provide *spiritual* continuity and harmony.

In a sense, though, Brown had begun to sound a bit middle class in his distaste for the sexual element in the blues. Since the blues were well known to the brothels, why should Brown object to the use of brothel humor in the blues? The answer seems to lie partly in where this sexual element was being introduced. First, Brown's objections were directed against commercial recordings, which were, of course, not close to the folk roots in their origin, performance location, or intention. He was describing most often the compositions of professional writers which were being recorded in a studio for as broad a buying public as possible. The intention was not community oriented, but profit motivated, and the profit motive sent blues composers straining "to get double, even triple meanings, as close to obscenity as the law allows."[76] Therefore, Brown's concern was for the overemphasis of an unnatural, smuttily clever sexual element at the expense of the wealth of rich themes, images, and language that would project a more complete picture of the blues.

Additionally, Brown's enumeration of the influence of African-American folk music on other kinds of music does not result from the straining pretensions of a middle-class mind. When, in "The Negro in the Lively Arts," Brown called attention to its influence on composers as various as Stephen Foster, George Gershwin, Duke Ellington, Antonin Dvorak, Igor Stravinsky, Will Marion Cook, and William Grant Still, he did not seem to be attempting to garner legitimacy for folk music by associating it with more "serious" forms of music.[77] Indeed, Brown considered folk art to be serious music—serious enough to take its importance from its own context and on its own terms. And serious enough to turn up in his own poetry, where Stravinsky's music did not.

That is not to say that "free verse and the traditional forms as well as folk-forms"[78] did not appear in his poetry; but commentators from Locke and Johnson on down have recognized the superiority of his poems that draw on folklore.[79] Brown himself placed his efforts in the context of the reaction of twentieth-century American poets against "sentimentality, didacticism, optimism, and romantic escape" and the desire to use "fresher, more original language and to humanize poetry."[80] But Brown, writing about himself in the third person, asserted that he was "not afraid of using folk-speech, refusing to believe dialect to be 'an instrument of only two stops—pathos and humor.'"[81] Instead, he saw folk speech, within the variety of African-American folk forms, as liberating. The folk were not the untutored; they were the teachers. As Locke said, Brown "dared to give the Negro peasant credit for thinking."[82] And it is a credit to Brown's intelligence that he attempted neither to think for them nor speak at them, but always with them.

Zora Neale Hurston sought to establish a close relationship with the common folk as well. In *Mules and Men* she wrote: "The devil is not the terror that he is in European folklore. He is a powerful trickster who often competes successfully with God. There is a strong suspicion that the devil is an extension of the story-makers while God is the supposedly impregnable white masters, who are nevertheless defeated by the Negroes."[83] In a very real sense, Hurston was just such a trickster, the "devil's advocate" battling with the white man and his sociocultural gods and attempting to show her people that the trick is to turn to their own culture rather than the white man's to achieve and express psychic wholeness. Folklorist Alan Lomax praised her as "probably the best informed person today on Western Negro Folklore,"[84] and he attributed no small amount of the success of their 1935 Florida field expedition to Hurston's ability to ingratiate herself with their subjects, gathering religious and secular music in an area that had been poorly documented previously. He wrote to his father, "They have thronged our house by day and night ever since we have been here. They have been perfectly natural and easy from the first on account of Zora who talks their language and can out-nigger any of them. She always jokes, slaps backs, honies up the men a little when necessary and manages them so well that they ask for no money, but on the other hand cooperate in the friendliest sort of spirit."[85] Sterling Brown, too, recognized Hurston's obvious expertise in folklore and her joy in collecting it, calling her "zestful towards her material, and completely unashamed of it."[86] Langston Hughes discussed how much fun he had traveling with Hurston through the South in 1927, where she introduced him to rural folk artists who fascinated Hughes.[87]

As Lomax stated, Hurston not only collected folklore, but performed it as well; indeed, she performed both American and Bahamian folklore for the Library of Congress in June 1935, December 1936, and on 18 June 1938,[88] and she was well known to her Harlem Renaissance contemporaries as a vivacious storyteller. From all accounts, Hurston's career as a folklorist was unique and remarkable. Her only significant African-American contemporaries as folklorists were Thomas Talley, Arthur Huff Fauset, and J. Mason Brewer. Her career was characterized by a sympathetic understanding that helped make the recordings she gathered as close to "authentic" renderings of folklore as recordings by folklorists ever get—she seemed like less of an interloper to her African-American subjects than many folklorists would have. She belonged.

Part of the reason for Hurston's great success as a folklorist and a literary artist was her obvious respect for the folk from whom she collected. More belligerent than Sterling Brown, she was willing to accept the production and values of the folk as comparable to the production of "high" art: "There never has been a poet who has been acceptable to his Majesty, the man in the gutter before, and laugh if you will, but that man in the gutter is the god-maker, the creator of everything that lasts."[89] Her writing sometimes seems to crackle with pride in her people, to bristle with excitement and strength, as in her perceptive "Characteristics of Negro Expression":

Who has not observed a robust young Negro chap posing upon a street corner, possessed of nothing but his clothing, his strengths and his youth? Does he bear himself like a pauper? No, Louis XIV could be no more insolent in his assurance. His eyes say plainly "Female, halt!" His posture exults "Ah, female, I am the eternal male, the giver of life. Behold in my hot flesh all the delights of this world. Salute me, I am strength." All this with a languid posture, there is no mistaking his meaning.[90]

Hurston saw African-American speech and action as pregnant with drama; therefore, in her folklore collecting and her creative work she sought to deliver not just the artifact but the drama as well, paying particular attention to the processes by which people define themselves. The key to autonomy was self-definition, but that self-definition could only be depicted through a presentation that tapped the essential drama that Hurston saw at the root of African-American expression. Though there was a practical and economic motive to this technique as Hurston employed it in *Mules and Men* (Bertram Lippincott wanted "a very readable book that the average reader can understand, at the same time one that will have value as a reference book"[91]), the presentation was certainly consistent with Hurston's ideas about folklore.

When Hurston opened her introduction to *Mules and Men* (1935) by echoing Psalms 122:1, she was referring to a book of the Bible very appropriate to her purpose. "Psalm" comes from a Greek word meaning "to pluck the strings of the harp," and Hurston meant not only to expose the artistic genius of her people in the oral folk setting, but to ply her own artistic talents as well. The resonances her lines take from the biblical passages are great: the Bible reads,

> I was glad when they said unto me,
> Let us go into the house of the Lord.

and Hurston's lines read:

> I was glad when somebody told me,
> "You may go and collect Negro folk-lore."[92]

As African religion and art are inextricable, so *Mules and Men* was to be her hymn book for her people, as Psalms was the hymn book of the Jews. Hurston had a religious devotion to the folkways of her people, and she could have found no better way of expressing her zeal than by echoing the words from the King James Bible, which her Baptist preacher father most likely thumped often during her early days in Eatonville, Florida. The remainder of Psalms 122 deals with a city of unity, devotion, judgment, peace, and prosperity, another parallel to the portrait that Robert Hemenway painted of the town where Hurston spent her early years: "a self-governing, all-black town, proud and independent, living refutation of white claims that black inability for self-government necessitated the racist institutions of a Jim Crow South."[93] Returning there was not only a return to her historical past, but to a folk past and an ideal past as well (or, rather, an idealized one). Her childhood experiences at Eatonville, especially at Joe Clarke's general store, where she heard the stories, lies, superstitions, songs, and, in general, the creative voices of her unpretentious friends and neighbors, laid down the folk rhythms to which Hurston would improvise for the rest of her life. The experience became part of her character and her studies; indeed, where one ended and the other began is often difficult to discern.

Those early experiences with the environment and ethos of African-American folklore remained with Hurston even after she went to Howard University and Barnard College. At Barnard, under the tutelage and encouragement of Franz Boas, she learned to look at herself and her folk experiences differently, adding the perspective of the scientist's social anthropology to her habitual perspective of the participant. Because of the teaching of Boas, it must have been somewhat easier for Hurston to reconcile the two: Boas followed Humboldt in the belief that each language had an inner form (*Sprachform*) that revealed implicitly a peculiar outlook, and he believed that it was his task to establish the distinctive descriptive categories for the language. Thus, as a student of Boas and as a scientist, Hurston was prepared to relate the language of her people to their characteristic world view, relating cultural creativity to a unified, nurturing ethos that was often presumed to be nonexistent.

Since she knew the ethos from personal experience, her task as a scientist was somewhat easier than otherwise, for when Hurston was collecting folklore, she plainly felt that she was gathering information for an autobiography:

> When I pitched head foremost into the world I landed in the crib of negroism. From the earliest rocking of my cradle, I had known about

the capers Brer Rabbit is apt to cut and what the squinch owl says from the house top. But it was fitting me like a tight chemise. I couldn't see it for weaving it. It was only when I was off in college, away from my native surroundings, that I could see myself like somebody else and stand off and look at my garment.[94]

Basically, her learning process moved from the state of self-concious beauty to the self-concious realization of beauty, from the state of self as self to the sense of self as other. What Hurston had to do was reconcile not only the folk part of herself with its scientific counterpart, but with the creative writer as well. That reconciliation would here establish the status of African and African-American art as participatory, not elitist, though, naturally, one had to be comfortable enough to allow oneself to participate. Even in this reconciliation, she found an answer in her folk roots, in the conventional wisdom of an oppressed minority: "The theory behind our tactics: 'The white man is always trying to know into somebody else's business. All right, I'll set something outside the door of my mind for him to play with and to handle. He can read my writing but he sho' can't read my mind. I'll put this play toy in his hand, and he will seize it and go away. Then I'll say my say and sing my song.' "[95] Her answer was to play a number of roles, giving each audience what it wanted within the context of its realities. She thus became the orchestrator of her world, adapting her language and demeanor to the exigencies of the moment. The opening of *Mules and Men* is instructive. The narrative prose of the opening paragraph is standard English—a bit relaxed and colloquial, but standard nonetheless. As she first hails the inhabitants of the town, she goes "into neutral."[96] She crosses the Maitland-Eatonville township line and enters a transitional period in which one feels the tension between her scientific purpose and demeanor and her sense of community with those she had come to study.

At the time the narrator crosses that line, her language is mildly colloquial, standard English; her language becomes increasingly colloquial as she falls into the role of member of the community— or is it the consciously scientific decision to employ the language most effective in accomplishing her purpose? Or is it both? She moves from the "yep" and "I reckon" of her initial dialogue to the more conscious attempt at imitating the speech of the townspeople when she reveals her purpose: "Nope, Ah come to collect some old stories and tales and Ah know y'all know a plenty of 'em and that's why Ah headed straight for home."[97] Significantly, her speech becomes identical with that of the townspeople as she discusses her geographical homecoming. The landscape, too, is related to the language, the context to the demeanor, and thus Hurston's reason for doing what she did becomes less important than the fact that, by doing it, she emphasized the *unity* in community. She reconciles both her personal and professional objectives through astute stylistic adjustment, and revealed the unity of purpose of the scientific, literary, and folk elements of her personality. That purpose was to express herself as truthfully as possible and to depict "a black communal perspective in order to emphasize the *independent* cultural creation of black people."[98]

Hurston's desire to paint the folk as positively creative rather than negatively reactionary and Lippincott's desire for a commercially viable book did create problems for some reviewers, notably Sterling Brown. In his review of *Mules and Men* in the *New Masses,* he lamented that Hurston uncovers little that white folklorists couldn't have uncovered and that her characters were incomplete because they lacked the bitterness he knew existed:

> Her characters are quaint, complaisant, bad enough to kill each other in jooks, but meek otherwise, socially unconscious. This, to the reviewer, makes *Mules and Men* singularly *incomplete*. These people live in a land shadowed by squalor, poverty, disease, violence enforced ignorance and exploitation. Even if brow beaten, they do know a smouldering resentment. Many folk-stories and songs from the South contain this resentment. . . . *Mules and Men* should be more bitter; it would be nearer to the total truth.[99]

And although Brown had great respect for Hurston's abilities, he found fault with the language of *Jonah's Gourd Vine* in his commentary in the *The Negro in American Literature:* "The folk speech is richly, almost too consistently, poetic."[100] All in all, Brown saw Hurston presenting a view that was too pastoral, a bit touched up, which is, of course, true. But it is honest nostalgia, not the nostalgia of the white, Southern, local colorists.

She was not one to suffer "the white damsels who try to sing Blues"[101] nor the formally trained voices of African-Americans. She preferred the singing of a "cathead man in Florida" to that of

Roland Hayes and Paul Robeson because, although he didn't have their training, he exceeded them in "effect."[102] And it was that effect that she wished to emphasize, the created drama of African-American folklore that invited, even necessitated, the involvement and interaction of both performer and listener. Hurston was both, and Alice Walker was right in placing her in the company of Bessie Smith and Billie Holiday—an "unholy trinity": "Zora belongs in the tradition of black women singers, rather than among the 'literati,' at least to me. Like Billie and Bessie, she followed her own road, believed in her own gods, pursued her own dreams, and refused to separate herself from 'common' people."[103] If she left out too much of the bitter in her portrayals, it was not only because she was too busy enjoying the exuberance, but also because she may have had something to gain from her benefactors in excising the bitter. She was, after all, realistic about what she needed in order to survive and thrive.

2

Langston Hughes had varying degrees of personal and professional contact with both these Old and New Guard writers, and their influence on his personal aesthetic and professional career was significant. From the Old Guard he inherited a legacy of higher education and scholarship, a sense of racial pride and mission, an interest in both journal and book publication as a means of galvanizing his audience, and a belief in the importance of the African and African-American past in establishing the identity that the New Negroes were trying so hard to find. For Hughes, "Dr. W. E. B. DuBois, Alain Locke, and James Weldon Johnson were the deans"[104] of the New Negro movement, making significant contributions to the movement as well as to Hughes. In his brief, written tribute to him, Hughes demonstrated the central importance of DuBois by equating the educator's greatness with the principle Christian religious *writings* and a major African-American social rebellious *action,* uniting in DuBois both a religious and social sense of mission and emphasizing tradition as a means of gaining autonomy: "My earliest memories of written words are those of DuBois and the Bible. My maternal grandmother in Kansas, the last surviving widow of John Brown's Raid, read to me as a child from both the Bible and *The Crisis*. And one of the first books I read on my own was *The Souls of Black Folk*."[105]

Hughes related his being read to with tradition—personal and historical—and as he broke his dependence on others and asserted his independence by reading for himself, gathering for himself the information that would help him come of age, DuBois provided the continuity in his move toward autonomy. DuBois was there, too, when Hughes, the writer, came of age: DuBois's *Brownie's Book* accepted for publication two articles and a play by Hughes, leading to Jessie Fauset's solicitation of what became the first publication of Hughes's poetry, in DuBois's *The Crisis*.[106] This assistance (as well as DuBois's numerous accomplishments) was enough to panic Hughes at the prospect of their first meeting.[107]

Although Hughes maintained respect for DuBois, he did imagine the sting of DuBois's middle-class leanings, as Hughes had earlier felt his encouragement, when he reported erroneously that DuBois "roasted" the *Fire* quarterly.[108] Later the "proletarian" Hughes wrote, sensing DuBois's remoteness from the "low-down folks," that DuBois belonged to the class of "upper class Negro intellectuals" who turned up at select highbrow parties.[109] Hughes was aware that DuBois was balancing his own rebelliousness (John Brown) with his middle-class acquiescence (the Bible), and that their peaceful coexistence was hardly tenable.

Johnson, Hughes wrote, lived "in the very middle of Harlem,"[110] during the Renaissance, and his presence was central to Hughes in that he was one of three judges who awarded Hughes his first poetry prize in 1925.[111] Johnson later anthologized some of Hughes's poems in *Black Manhattan* (1930) and *Book of American Negro Poetry* (1931). Beyond that influence, Johnson was important as an African-American intellectual who understood Hughes's use of the "low-down" aspects of life in his art, defending Hughes against the "dozens like Eustace Gay" who lambasted Hughes.[112]

This type of patronage and understanding was evident in the treatment Hughes received at the hands of Locke as well. Locke, whom Hughes called "the granddaddy of the New Negro,"[113] secured Hughes's first foreign publication. Later he solicited Hughes's contributions to his special 1925 issue of *Survey Graphic* dealing with Harlem and, most important, he included Hughes in the ground-breaking anthology, *The New Negro*. Locke had drawn Hughes to Washington and to Howard University, encouraging him to look into various scholarship opportunities,[114] and it was there that Hughes was inspired by the songs and spirit of the religious and the secular, churches and barrelhouses, to write some blues and jazz poetry. Later, when Hughes employed those experiences in his own work, Locke defended *Fine Clothes to the Jew;* others were dubbing Hughes the "poet low-rate of Harlem" for some of the jazz poems of the type that traditional poets like Countee Cullen had criticized in *The Weary Blues*.[115]

Despite the support and encouragement of Dubois, Johnson, and Locke, Hughes still had his differences with them, related largely to their middle-class values and social status. At Johnson's parties one would meet "solid people like Clarence and Mrs. Darrow,"[116] Hughes wrote, connecting Johnson's social values with the white world and reinforcing Jean Wagner's assertion that Johnson "was a public figure" who was "imbued with the reserve and moderation that official responsibilities call for, . . . excessively concerned with respectability and conformity."[117] Locke was "a little, brown man with spats and a cultured accent and a degree from Oxford" and was "a charming conversationalist."[118] Hughes obviously had a slightly bemused attitude about the two; he found the mixture of their understanding of his work and their middle-class European quality incongruous. Hughes was most like the Old Guard in his own way, as evidenced in the compliment he paid to Locke, who seemed to him "a gentleman of culture, happy to help others to enjoy the things he had learned to enjoy."[119] Hughes, too, was a gentleman, cultured most in the sense of being aware of African-American culture and in accepting the beauty of the "low-down" folks, a ceaseless stumper for those things that he had learned not only how to enjoy, but to employ.

Brown, Hurston, and Hughes all shared the influence of the three older writers, but each brought to his or her subject matter a particular discipline. In the 1920s and 1930s, Hughes had little opportunity to meet Brown, since Brown did not live in or work around Harlem. Hughes knew of Brown as a scholar, critic, folklorist, and creative artist. Indeed, Brown gave a favorable review to *Not Without Laughter* in 1930, echoing that sentiment in 1937 when he called the novel "one of the best by a Negro author," finding it written "with poetic realism."[120] When, in the same passage, he called Hughes's Kansas town "a transplanted bit of the South," we see one of the essential differences between the two. Hughes was a big-city, Harlem poet, Brown more of a poet of the South. Brown himself acknowledged this difference when he called his own *Southern Road* "an attempt at folk portraiture of southern characters,"[121] while he characterized Hughes's *The Weary Blues* as an attempt "to celebrate jazz-mad Harlem."[122] Despite their familiarity with each other's work, the two did not have a close, ongoing, personal relationship that would have contributed significantly to Hughes's writing, except that Hughes was familiar with Brown's excellent scholarship, which contributed to the depth of Hughes's understanding of folk materials as it had to Locke's.

Since Hurston spent some time in Harlem and shared a patron, Charlotte Mason, with Hughes, her relationship with Hughes was much closer than Brown's. Hurston, whom Hughes called "one of the most sparkling Negro writers,"[123] had, before their collaboration on the folk play *Mule Bone,* a strong personal and professional relationship with Hughes. Beyond traveling together for a time collecting folklore, the two corresponded during her collecting trips; Hurston "saw the two of them as secret sharers of racial lore and as conspirators for the dramatic vehicle that would make it public."[124] Additionally, Hurston buoyed Hughes (as she over-flattered others) by writing him that his poems were going over well with "the folk" who heard them in her Southern forays. However, after their abortive collaboration on *Mule Bone,* they parted company far less than amicably, and Hughes's descriptions of her became patronizingly critical:

Of this "niggerati," Zora Neale Hurston was certainly the most amusing. Only to reach a wider audience, need she ever write books—because she is a perfect book of entertainment in herself. In her youth she was always getting scholarships and things from wealthy white people, some of whom simply paid her just to sit around and represent the Negro race for them, she did it in such racy fashion. . . . To many of her white friends, no doubt, she was a perfect "darkie," in the nice meaning of the term—that is a naive, childlike, sweet, humorous, and highly colored Negro.[125]

And later, though he recognized her abilities in collecting folklore, he made fun of her naive and eccentric ways: "I ran into Zora Neale Hurston walking intently down the main street, looking just as if she was out to measure somebody's head for an anthropological treatise."[126] Their relationship, which apparently sometimes approached but never culminated in a love affair, was over by 1931. Still, Hughes brought away from it a better knowledge of Southern African-American folklore, both the methods of collecting and the material; a belief that an educated literary artist could effectively mix and communicate with "the folk"; and a greater confidence in the "authentic" nature of his folk poetry.

It is important to emphasize that, unlike the "amateur" folklorist Brown and the "professional" folklorist Hurston, Hughes was not really a folklorist at all, despite his involvement with such volumes as *The Book of Negro Folklore, The Book of Negro Humor,* and *First Book of Jazz.* Rather, his interest in folk material was as a literary artist and as a popular historian of African-American culture—an editor and compiler, not a collector, of such material. Though he traveled both with and without Hurston in the South and read his poetry on lecture tours there as well,[127] Hughes knew both that the South was not his strong suit and that it didn't need to be: "I'm not a Southerner. I never worked on a levee. I hardly ever saw a cotton field except from the highway. . . . life is as hard on Broadway as it is in Blues-originating land."[128] In fact, when Hughes broke with Charlotte Mason, it was because he insisted that he was not a primitive but a city person, or rather, like Noah Faitoute Paterson, he was the city itself: "I was Chicago and Kansas City and Broadway and Harlem."[129] This assertion is as important as Hurston's changing to dialect speech when she drove into Eatonville: the location is connected with the speech, the spirit, and the aesthetic. Therefore, Hughes's outlook on and use of the material was bound to be different from both the Old Guard writers and the New because of his greater acceptance of secular songs on the one hand and of city songs, even the "composed," folk-based material, on the other.

Like Brown and Hurston (and in harmony with the African sensibility of unity), Hughes would accept secular folk music as being as valuable as the religious: "The Blues and the Spirituals are two great Negro gifts to American music."[130] However, like the Old Guard, he seemed to look toward "professional" artists to help legitimize the folk material, calling on "famous concert singers like Marian Anderson and Paul Robeson" to "include a group of Blues on their programs as well as the spirituals."[131] In a sense, this diversification would help Hughes enlarge his audience, but it would also bring about changes in Hughes's material and in perceptions of the blues as well, since singers like Anderson and Robeson did not sing like Bessie Smith or Blind Lemon Jefferson. The folk were fine for Hughes as folk material. However, as he described when discussing his travels in Georgia in *The Big Sea,* he felt such material was like an old Negro's patchwork felt hat that he came across and had to possess. The hat was "quaint and folk-like,"[132] something that he tried to lock away like a valuable specimen, only to have it destroyed in its isolated environment by moths. He ended up "brushing off moth eggs for fear they would turn to eating up the manuscripts next."[133] The lesson was that Hughes should use it or lose not only "it" but his other works as well. However, Hughes does not indicate that he learned the lesson that folk materials flourish best in their own environment; rather, he seemed to worry more about what the other people in the bank—particularly those with the fur pieces—thought about his appearance.

Of course, Hughes tried to maintain an authenticity about his work: "Since much of my work is concerned with Negro life, I seek to employ colloquial Negro speech as used in some stratas of colored life, but not in the educated classes, as simply as I can without distorted spelling, relying rather upon the idiom and turn of phrase for the flavor. I feel, in a sense, that the function of the poet is to interpret not only his own people to the rest of the world, but to themselves."[134] But that sense of mission put Hughes in a position that was difficult for him to define. He spoke tentatively and uneasily about his attempts to get an authentic quality into his "created blues," asserting "I guess you can't call them real folk blues, unless you want to say that I'm a folk poet, myself a folk person, which maybe I am."[135] Certainly he attempted to connect himself with the "common laborer"; in writing about the creation of his folk poems in *Fine Clothes to the Jew,* he described how they were written when he "was dragging bags of wet wash laundry about or toting trays of dishes to the dumbwaiter of the Wardman Park Hotel in Washington."[136] In essence, Hughes faced a problem that any "professional" artist must face in employing folk material—how to establish his relationship to that material and to his audience. He wished to be "authentic," though he knew that he wanted his poems to do more than he felt his sources did. Obviously, he felt that *his* perspective was necessary to interpreting his people to themselves, and that perspective implied some separation from the rural, traditional folk. In other words, Hughes was feeling the disfranchisement of an African-American artist from a traditional audience because of the influence of Western aesthetics. On the other hand, Hughes did not want to be trained too far away from the folk. He criticized the great singer-pianist Gladys Bentley for growing away from her roots and her environment, losing an almost African sense of unity: "But when the place where she played became too well known, she began to sing with an accompanist, became a star, moved to a larger place, then downtown, and is now in Hollywood. The old magic of the woman and the piano and the night and the rhythm being one is gone."[137] Clearly, Hughes wished to capture and maintain the type of unity he thought that Gladys Bentley had lost. What Bentley had abandoned, Hughes felt, was her self-reliance, humility, and geographical rootedness, and in the process she lost the spirit of performance and her original audience as well.

In his response to Schuyler's "The Negro Art Hokum," Hughes defined well his attitude toward the transplanted folk of the city, setting them in opposition to middle-class values and adding a third perspective to the two recognized by James Weldon Johnson in "The Dilemma of the Negro Author" (1928):

> But then there are the low-down folks, the so-called common element, and they are the majority—may the Lord be praised! The people who have their hip of gin on Saturday nights and are not too important to themselves or the community, or too well fed, or too learned to watch the lazy world go round. They live on Seventh Street in Washington or State Street in Chicago and they do not care whether they are like white folks or anybody else. . . . These common people are not afraid of spirituals, as for a long time their more intellectual brethren were, and jazz is their child. They furnish a wealth of colorful, distinctive material for any artist because they

still hold their individuality in the face of American standardiza-
tions. And perhaps these common people will give to the world its
truly great Negro artist, the one who is not afraid to be himself.
Whereas the better-class Negro would tell the artist what to do, the
people at least let him alone when he does appear. And they are not
ashamed of him—if they know he exists at all. And they accept what
beauty is their own without question.[138]

As the last three sentences indicate, Hughes knew that he didn't
need to make the folk his primary audience, though he certainly
attempted to *express* aspects of the folk experience. He didn't need
to interpret their lives for them because they already recognized
their own beauty, and, because of their grounding in orality, they
were already artists themselves. They were the ideal source for the
poetry that Hughes wanted to create; he wanted to demonstrate
their beauty for a black middle-class target audience that needed a
"legitimate" literary artist to sanction the folk materials for them.
Of course, as noted earlier, when Hughes first used secular folk
materials he was soundly criticized by middle-class blacks, though
the situation began to change in later decades. He also had trouble
understanding why other black artists were avoiding using indigenous black culture: "There is so much richness in Negro humor, so
much beauty in black dreams, so much dignity in our stuggle, and
so much universality in our problems, in us—in each living human
being of color—that I do not understand the tendency today that
some Negro artists have of seeking to run away from themselves, of
running away from us, of being afraid to sing our songs, paint our
own pictures, write about ourselves."[139]

Hughes embodied this situation in the Simple stories, in which
Jesse B., Joyce, and Boyd (as he is named in *Simply Heavenly*) make
exchanges based upon their sociopolitical stances. Jesse B. Semple
is the unpretentious barfly who loves the blues and sees race in
everything.[140] He is bedeviled by his alter ego, the middle-class
minded Joyce, whose name, which is very close to "Jess," also
suggests an exhortation to "just be simple." However, Hughes
makes it clear that Jess is being himself (*Simple*)—the representative of those who "are the soul of the race and most deserve to be
expressed in black art"[141]—by characterizing him with practicality, mother-wit, lively language, and self-acceptance. Mean-
while, Joyce is being *Simple* by embracing white, middle-class

values in the ideas of people like the confidence man Dr. Conboy in "Jazz, Jive, and Jam."[142] The narrator, Boyd, is a rationalist intellectual, educated and perhaps even a bit literary. He stands as an observer of the "Simple" lives, attempting to sort out the conflicting values as he leans at times toward Joyce, at other times toward Jess. Hughes seems to be using the three to represent alternate impulses within his own mind: he is the artist-creator using his rational observer-commentator (Boyd) to describe the alternate impulses to retain ethnic identity (Jess) and adopt white values to achieve social and economic stability in the white world (Joyce).

Hughes's problem, then, was to try to reconcile the three in his art. In his blues poems, he attempted to speak like one audience (the folk) and interpret to another (the black middle class), but this technique created a problem. Because Hughes was bringing techniques and ideas to his folk poems from what was normally considered to be outside the folk tradition (the most important example being the act of writing down his work), he was not actually referring his audience back to the folk totally. Rather, he was creating a middle ground that presented his audience with an enlightened professional poet's version of the unpretentious folk. Hughes's was a world where the intellectual had difficulty recapturing his folk roots because his mind would have been trained away from the folk ethos—by the socioeconomic lures dangled in front of upwardly mobile blacks every day as lessons in behavior, and by educational institutions as well. Of course, one of the additional problems here is the definition of folklore as survivals from the past, when in fact folklore was still being performed and growing; such a definition created for many people the idea that folk roots were a part of past, not present, life. Moreover, the higher education received by blacks in the United States and Europe would have fed that misconception. Thus, while Hughes often used urban, contemporary folklore in his blues poetry, his use of the blues caused people to think of the remote and primitive past envisioned by some folklorists, a past that middle-class blacks were trying to leave behind. Beyond that, Hughes's desire to explain his people to the rest of the world would violate his own definition of what the folk are like. It was Hughes's wish that the beauty, unpretentiousness, and vivacity of the folk could be infused into the all-too-reserved middle-class African-American; but the complex social interaction between environment and ethos made a complete sympathy and understanding nearly impossible.

Therefore, Hughes's intention to unite the intellectuals and near-intellectuals with the folk, to create the unity he felt necessary to the identity and progress of his people, was a difficult prospect, as he himself recognized:

> Let the blare of Negro jazz bands and the bellowing voice of Bessie Smith singing Blues penetrate the closed ears of the colored near-intellectuals until they listen and perhaps understand. Let Paul Robeson singing "Water Boy," and Rudolph Fisher writing about the streets of Harlem, and Jean Toomer holding the heart of Georgia in his hands, and Aaron Douglass drawing strange black fantasies cause the smug Negro middle class to turn from their white, respectable, ordinary books and papers to catch a glimmer of their own beauty.[143]

And, finally, Hughes believed the folk art was to be used by professional artists to interpret African-American life; it was something which showed its full importance only when united with the conscious purpose of the intellectual. The intellectual was necessary because the near-intellectual rejected his folk roots; but he was not to be merely a surveyor of material, but a user of it. In his usage, he would turn it into written words, but as an enlightened person, he hoped he would not violate its spirit.

These varied approaches to African-American folklore indicate how strongly these artists felt that folklore was central to the identity they were trying to establish during the Harlem Renaissance. And because the folklore was coming to them in pieces, from collectors whose reliability was sometimes questionable because of racist social attitudes that colored the material they collected, or from subjects who may have held back from telling all to white collectors, artists like Hurston and Brown sought to collect the material themselves. Those people, committed to "authentic" folklore, rejected much of the music recorded by record companies because it was remote from the folk and their values. Langston Hughes, though, attempted to use the resources of authentic folk *and* folk-based material in his work because they were both part of the city and the people who were being altered by the city and its burgeoning commercialism. That commercialism brought on a blues craze in the United States in the 1920s, a craze particularly for the female vaudeville blues singers. But their popularity was simply a rebirth and reformation of much that had gone before. In order to understand fully how Hughes used the blues, one must understand the various opinions about where the blues came from and what the blues are (and there are many different types of blues) and then place Hughes's attitudes and works in that context.

NOTES

1. Derrick Stewart-Baxter, *Ma Rainey and the Classic Blues Singers* (New York: Stein and Day, 1970), 12.

2. Barre Toelken, *The Dynamics of Folklore* (Boston: Houghton Mifflin, 1979), 32.

3. Stephen Henderson, *Understanding the New Black Poetry* (New York: William Morrow, 1973), 5.

4. Steven Tracy, "Interview with Etheridge Knight," *MELUS* 12, no. 2 (1985).

5. Alan Dundes, "The Devolutionary Premise in Folklore Theory," *Journal of the Folklore Institute* 6, no. 1 (1969): 6.

6. Ibid., 18.

7. Elliott Oring, "The Devolutionary Premise: A Definitional Delusion?," *Western Folklore* 34, no. 1 (1975): 38–39.

8. William A. Wilson, "The Evolutionary Premise in Folklore Theory and the 'Finnish Method,'" *Western Folklore* 35 (1976): 242.

9. Bernard Bell, "Folk Art and the Harlem Renaissance," *Phylon* 36 (1975): 156.

10. John Work, *Folk Song of the American Negro* (Nashville, 1915; rpt., New York: Negro Universities Press, 1969), 123.

11. Toelken, *Dynamics of Folklore*, 193.

12. Discussions of Zora Neale Hurston's *Mules and Men* and Sterling Brown's criticism of that work will be taken up in the sections on Hurston and Brown. In a later section on folklorists and their attitudes toward blues and blues singers, see W. Prescott Webb's comments on the blues of Floyd Canada. Of course, it is not necessarily true that a folklorist without a crucial connection with the group would distort the material. Someone too close could distort the material as well.

13. Sterling Brown, *"Negro Poetry and Drama" and "The Negro in American Fiction"* (1937; rpt., New York: Atheneum, 1972), 32. Dunbar, of course, practiced other ethnic writing as well, as in "A Border Ballad," "The Place Where the Rainbow Ends," "Appreciation," and "The Discovery."

14. George E. Kent, "Patterns of the Harlem Renaissance," in *The Harlem Renaissance Remembered*, ed. Arna Bontemps (New York: Dodd, Mead, 1972), 27.

15. Saunders Redding, "*The Souls of Black Folk:* DuBois' Masterpiece Lives On," in *Black Titan: W. E. B. DuBois*, ed. John Henrik Clark et al. (Boston: Beacon Press, 1970), 46. DuBois had other enemies besides Booker T. Washington, of course. Tony Martin outlines the disagreements that Marcus Garvey, Carter G. Woodson, William Ferris, and Arthur A. Schomburg had with DuBois in *The Pan African Connection* (Dover, Mass.: Majority Press, 1984), 101–10.

16. Arnold Rampersad, *The Art and Imagination of W. E. B. DuBois* (Cambridge, Mass.: Harvard University Press, 1976), 47. The idea of DuBois as a devotee of white culture would seem to sit very uneasily beside DuBois's Pan-Africanism and his Socialist and later Communist leanings. However, a number of points suggest that DuBois was affected by middle-class values, especially in his aesthetic judgments. In his essay "The Talented Tenth," DuBois praises the million blacks who, "judged by any standard, have reached the full measure of the best type of European culture" (*The Negro Problem* [1903; rpt., New York: Arno, 1969], 44). DuBois used the achievements of European culture as a standard because of his university training at Harvard, and in Germany. Paul Laurence Dunbar, in his "Representative American Negroes" essay in *The Negro Problem*, described DuBois as approaching truth "as a hard-riding old English squire would take a difficult fence" (199). Finally, DuBois himself, in a 1961 letter to Gus Hall, admitted that he lacked knowledge about Marx and Socialism when he was a member of the Socialist party in 1911–12 and that he began a new effort to learn about Socialism and Communism in 1926. His application to join the Communist party in 1961 rather than earlier suggests that he still had misgivings. See *Black Titan*, 304–6.

17. Rampersad, *Art and Imagination*, 39.

18. Paul Robeson, "Tribute," in *Black Titan*, 34–35.

19. W. E. B. DuBois, *The Negro* (New York, 1913; rpt., Millwood, N.Y.: Kraus-Thomson, 1975), 116–17.

20. W. E. B. DuBois, "Of the Sorrow Songs," in *The Souls of Black Folk* (Chicago, 1903; rpt., Greenwich, Conn.: Fawcett, 1961), 182.

21. DuBois, "Of The Sorrow Songs," 183.

22. Ibid., 186.

23. Ibid., 183.

24. See Elizabeth Ware Pearson, ed., *Letters From Port Royal* (New York: Arno, 1969) and the discussion in Dena J. Epstein's *Sinful Tunes and Spirituals* (Urbana: University of Illinois Press, 1977) for more background on the Port Royal experiment.

25. Rampersad, *Art and Imagination,* 188.

26. DuBois, *The Negro,* 141.

27. John Work, *American Negro Songs and Spirituals* (New York: Crown, 1940), 32–33.

28. W. E. B. DuBois, *Dusk of Dawn* (New York: Harcourt, Brace, 1940), 202–3.

29. E. Franklin Frazier, "The DuBois Program in the Present Crisis," *Race 1* (Winter 1935–36): 11–12. Writing in 1960, DuBois declared that what he had been fighting for and was still fighting for was "the possibility of black folk and their cultural patterns existing in America without discrimination; and on terms of equality." See "Whither Now and Why" in *The Education of Black People,* ed. Herbert Aptheker (New York: Monthly Review Press, 1973), 150. DuBois moved toward this position increasingly during his career, though the seeds were always there.

30. Lynn Adelman, "A Study of James Weldon Johnson," *Journal of Negro History* 52 (1967): 143.

31. Ibid., 129–30.

32. Ibid., 142.

33. Ibid., 131.

34. James Weldon Johnson, "The Dilemma of the Negro Author," *The American Mercury* (December 1928): 477.

35. Ibid., 481.

36. Adelman, "Study of James Weldon Johnson," 143.

37. James Weldon Johnson, Preface, *The Book of American Negro Poetry,* in *Voices From the Harlem Renaissance,* ed. Nathan I. Huggins (New York: Oxford University Press, 1976), 300.

38. Ibid., 288.

39. Ibid., 281–82. In *Autobiography of an Ex-Coloured Man,* Johnson's narrator praises ragtime, becomes enamored of it, and, finally, garners recognition as the best ragtime player in New York. However, part of his attraction is that he "first made ragtime transcriptions of familiar classic selections" (115). In addition, the narrator calls the Uncle Remus stories, Jubilee songs, ragtime music, and the cake walk "lower forms of art" that "will someday be applied to higher forms." See James Weldon Johnson, *Autobiography of an Ex-Coloured Man* (New York, 1912; rpt., New York: Hill and Wang, 1960), 87. Johnson admitted in *Along This Way* (rpt., New York: Da Capo, 1973), 113, that he "lacked religiosity," so his attraction to the spirituals does not seem to be based on religious fervor.

40. Johnson, *Along This Way,* 158–59.

41. The Cole and Johnson Brothers were foremost in the trend at the

turn of the century to move "away from the abusively racist lyrics in favor of words expressing more tasteful sentiments," according to Edward A. Berlin ("Ragtime Songs," in *Ragtime: Its History, Composers, and Music* [New York: Schirmer Books, 1985], 74). However their popular song "Under the Bamboo Tree" still presents a primitive exoticism that panders to white tastes.

42. Eugenia W. Collier, "James Weldon Johnson: Mirror of Change," *Phylon,* 4th quarter (1960): 359.

43. Faith Berry, *Langston Hughes: Before and Beyond Harlem* (Westport, Conn.: Lawrence Hill, 1983), 34.

44. Ibid., 51.

45. Robert Hemenway, *Zora Neale Hurston: A Literary Biography* (Urbana: University of Illinois Press, 1980), 40.

46. Ibid., 39.

47. Alain Locke, "Toward a Critique of Negro Music," *Opportunity* 12, no. 11 (1934): 328.

48. Alain Locke, "Negro Youth Speaks," in *The New Negro* (New York, 1926; rpt., New York: Atheneum, 1970), 47.

49. Alain Locke, Introduction, *The New Negro,* xv.

50. Alain Locke, *"The Negro and His Music" and "Negro Art: Past and Present"* (Washington, D.C., 1936; rpt., New York: Arno Press, 1969), 8.

51. Locke, "Negro Youth Speaks," 47.

52. Locke, *The Negro and His Music,* 18.

53. W. E. B. DuBois, *The Quest of the Silver Fleece* (Chicago, 1911; rpt., Millwood, N.Y.: Kraus-Thomson, 1974), 11.

54. Locke, "Negro Youth Speaks," 47–48.

55. Robert Hayden, Preface, *The New Negro,* xiii.

56. George Schuyler, "The Negro Art Hokum," in *Voices From the Harlem Renaissance,* 310.

57. Berry, *Langston Hughes,* 62.

58. Charles S. Johnson, "Jazz," *Opportunity* 3, no. 29 (1925): 133. It would be remiss to omit the name of Carl Van Vechten from a discussion of influences on the writers of the Harlem Renaissance, though that discussion does not belong in the main text here. Van Vechten, patron of the arts, photographer, critic, friend of and literary executor for Gertrude Stein, and novelist whose "sophisticated" novels were praised by people like James Weldon Johnson, F. Scott Fitzgerald, and Henry Seidel Canby, was well known for his New York parties that brought together artists from various socioeconomic backgrounds and facilitated a better understanding among them. Johnson mentions meeting Theodore Dreiser at a Van Vechten party, and there also one might find such people as Adelaide

Hall, Salvador Dali, F. Scott Fitzgerald, Helena Rubenstein, Chief Long Lance, Claude McKay, Emma Goldman, and Bessie Smith on a given night. But Van Vechten had also been called "an outrageous name dropper" and "a connoisseur of parties" (see James R. Mellow, *Invented Lives* [Boston: Houghton Mifflin, 1984], 178–79) and a collector of artistic curiosities who was particularly interested in gathering primitive and exotic artifacts and people to support his ideas about the nature of African-Americans. Though his *Nigger Heaven* was defended by Wallace Thurman, James Weldon Johnson, George Schuyler, Charles S. Johnson, and Langston Hughes, there was also a chorus of outcries against it, including Sterling Brown's accusations that it was exploitative and "partial to exotic singularities" (Sterling Brown, *The Negro in American Fiction*, 132). Regardless of Van Vechten's motives or intentions, he was important for providing an atmosphere for social and intellectual intermingling, for facilitating publishing contacts, and for giving financial assistance to a number of worthy causes. Nella Larsen's *Passing* was dedicated to Van Vechten and his wife. Van Vechten took Langston Hughes's first book of poems to Knopf, placed him in touch with *Vanity Fair,* was unwittingly caught up in the ill-fated *Mule Bone* affair when he sent the play to a theatrical agent, and remained a faithful acquaintance. Van Vechten's influence on Harlem Renaissance writers was more social and financial than literary, and the benefits *he* derived were social, financial, *and* literary. They provided him not only with material for his popular *Nigger Heaven*, but also with the help of Langston Hughes when Van Venchten had to replace some blues songs he used in the book without copyright permission.

59. Sterling A. Brown, "The New Negro in Literature, 1925–1955," in *The New Negro Thirty Years Afterward,* ed. Rayford Logan et al. (Washington, D.C.: Harvard University Press, 1955), 57.

60. Jean Wagner, *Black Poets of the United States* (Urbana: University of Illinois Press, 1973), 475.

61. Sterling Brown, "The Approach of the Creative Artist," *Journal of American Folklore* 59 (1946): 506–7.

62. Ibid., 506.

63. Ibid.

64. Sterling Brown, *Negro Poetry and Drama*, 77. Brown, of course, saw the blues performed firsthand. Joanne Gabbin reports his discussions of singer Calvin "Big Boy" Davis at Virginia Seminary in the mid-1920s as recounted in an 18 May 1973 speech. This guitar-playing performer of blues and spirituals, the inspiration for "Odyssey of Big Boy" and "When de Saints Go Ma'ching Home," may well be the "Big Boy" whose untitled "Blues" was recorded by Roscoe Lewis, along with a

version of "John Henry" and a number of spirituals, c. 1941 at Hampton, Virginia. Since Brown recalled bringing "Big Boy" in to sing spirituals and blues, and recalled a particularly good version of "John Henry," it is conceivable that this is the same person. See Joanne V. Gabbin, *Sterling Brown: Building the Black Aesthetic Tradition* (Westport, Conn.: Greenwood Press, 1985), 34–35, and *Tidewater Blues*, BRI LP 006, 1982, for Brown's recollections and a recording of "Big Boy's" "Blues." There was some communication between Brown and Lewis during Brown's tenure in the Federal Writer's Project related to Lewis's collection of ex-slave narratives, presenting us with another possible association between the two "Big Boys."

65. Brown's "The Blues As Folk Poetry," (in *Folk Say I,* ed. B. A. Botkin [Norman: University of Oklahoma Press, 1930], 339) calls attention to the work of Carl Sandburg and folklorists Howard Odum and John Jacob Niles; "The Negro In the Lively Arts" (*Tricolor* 3 [April, 1945]: 62–70) cites Abbe Niles, Newbell Niles Puckett, Katherine Dunham, Louis Harap, Ernest Borneman, Lafcadio Hearn, George Washington Cable, and Melville Herskovits; and "Negro Folk Expression: Spirituals, Seculars, Ballads and Work Songs" (*Phylon* 14 [1953]: 45–61) refers to the work of Stephen Foster, Frederick Douglass, John Lomax, and Zora Neale Hurston. The list of reading references at the end of his chapter on Negro folk poetry in *Negro Poetry and Drama* is distinguished for its breadth, including important work like that of Lawrence Gellert, W. C. Handy, and Guy Johnson.

66. Wagner, *Black Poets*, 479.

67. Sterling Stuckey, Introduction, *The Collected Poems of Sterling A. Brown,* selected by Michael S. Harper (New York: Harper and Row, 1980), 9.

68. Brown, *Negro Poetry and Drama,* 29.

69. Wagner, *Black Poets,* 477.

70. Brown, *Negro Poetry and Drama,* 27. In an interview with Steven Jones and Stephen Henderson in 1973, Brown echoed these sentiments and discussed the superiority of authentic folk blues to the productions of Gershwin and Roark Bradford and the stereotypes in *Cosmopolitan* and *Redbook.* See Gabbin, 36, for a partial transcript of Brown's words.

71. Brown, "The Blues as Folk Poetry," 339.

72. Brown, "Negro Folk Expression, 45–61."

73. Brown, "The Blues as Folk Poetry," 339.

74. Brown, "Negro Folk Expression," 60.

75. Brown, "The Blues," *Phylon* 13 (1952), 292.

76. Brown, "The Blues," 292.

77. Brown, "The Negro in the Lively Arts," 62–70.

78. Brown, *Negro Poetry and Drama*, 77.

79. See, for example, Alain Locke's comments in "Sterling Brown: The New Negro Folk Poet," in *Voices from the Harlem Renaissance*, ed. Nathan Huggins (New York: Oxford University Press, 1976), 251–57; James Weldon Johnson's introduction to the first edition of *Southern Road*, included in the *The Collected Poems of Sterling Brown*, ed. Michael Harper (New York: Harper and Row, 1980), 17; Sterling Stuckey's Introduction to *The Collected Poems;* and Stephen Henderson's "A Strong Man Called Sterling Brown," *Black World* 19, no. 11 (Sept. 1970): 5–12.

80. Brown, *Negro Poetry and Drama*, 61.

81. Ibid., 77.

82. Alain Locke, "Sterling Brown: The New Negro Folk Poet," 254.

83. Zora Neale Hurston, *Mules and Men* (Philadelphia, 1935; rpt., Bloomington: Indiana University Press, 1978), 254. Actually, Hurston is wrong about the perception of the devil in European folklore, since he turns up as a trickster there as well. The devil as trickster seems to be a *class* perception, not a black one.

84. Alan Lomax to Oliver Strunk, 3 August 1935, in Hemenway, *Zora Neale Hurston*, 212.

85. Alan Lomax to John Lomax in Hemenway, *Zora Neale Hurston*, 212.

86. Brown, *The Negro in American Fiction*, 160.

87. Langston Hughes, *The Big Sea* (New York: Hill and Wang, 1973), 296–98.

88. R. M. W. Dixon and John Godrich, *Blues and Gospel Records, 1902–1943* (Chigwell, Essex: Storyville Publications, 1982), 352.

89. Zora Neale Hurston to Langston Hughes, 22 November 1925, in Hemenway, Introduction, *Mules and Men*, xxvii.

90. Zora Neale Hurston, "Characteristics of Negro Expression," in *Voices From the Harlem Renaissance*, ed. Nathan I. Huggins, 225.

91. Zora Neale Hurston to Franz Boas, 20 August 1934, in Hemenway, *Zora Neale Hurston*, 163.

92. Hurston, *Mules and Men*, 3.

93. Hemenway, *Zora Neale Hurston*, 12.

94. Hurston, *Mules and Men*, 3.

95. Ibid., 5.

96. Ibid., 9.

97. Ibid.

98. Hemenway, *Zora Neale Hurston*, xxvi.

99. Brown, "Old Time Tales," *New Masses* (25 February 1936): 25.

100. Brown, *The Negro in American Fiction*, 160.

101. Hurston, "Characteristics of Negro Expression," 235.

102. Hemenway, *Zora Neale Hurston*, 54.

103. Ibid., xvii–xviii.

104. Langston Hughes, "The Twenties: Harlem and Its Negritude," *African Forum* 1, no. 4 (1966): 11.

105. Langston Hughes, "Tribute," in *Black Titan: W. E. B. DuBois*, 8. DuBois was, of course, aware of Brown's importance. The first congress of the "Niagara movement," of which DuBois was an organizing member, was held in 1906 at Harper's Ferry, West Virginia, the scene of John Brown's raid. DuBois also wrote a biography: *John Brown* (Philadelphia: George W. Jacobs and Co., 1909).

106. Hughes, *The Big Sea*, 72. Jessie Redmon Fauset's contribution as literary editor of *The Crisis* should not be overlooked. Carolyn Wedin Sylvander, in *Jessie Redmon Fauset: Black American Writer* (Troy, N.Y.: Whitson, 1981), reports that Fauset handled much correspondence, contest judging details, and office management while DuBois was away (57); that she had a "near full responsibility for the *Brownie's Book*" (59); and that she "discovered" Hughes when he submitted a poem to her (61). Hughes named her, along with Charles Johnson and Alain Locke, as one of "the three people who midwived the so-called New Negro literature into being," in *The Big Sea*, 216. Hughes in fact had a great respect for Fauset but was not intimidated, as he was at the thought of meeting DuBois, because of her friendly and encouraging demeanor, her acute artistic judgment, and her organized professionalism.

107. Hughes, *The Big Sea*, 92.

108. Ibid., 237. DuBois actually praised the journal and urged readers to look at it.

109. Ibid., 249.

110. Hughes, "The Twenties: Harlem and Its Negritude," 11.

111. Hughes, *The Big Sea*, 215.

112. Ibid., 267.

113. Hughes, "The Twenties: Harlem and Its Negritude," 11.

114. Berry, *Langston Hughes*, 57.

115. Hughes, *The Big Sea*, 266. Cullen's traditionalism in form and language in an age of experimentation by avant-garde poets has made him seem anachronistic to us, but at that time he was admired by many middle-class African-Americans because of his refusal to employ the folklore of the "low-down folks" in his work, as Hughes, Brown, and Hurston were doing in theirs. Cullen was indeed scornful of the employment of folk material and jazz, preferring to take what he felt was the "high road" of Keatsianism and Victorianism. In his review of *The Weary Blues and Other Poems* in the February 1926 issue of *Opportunity*,

Cullen confessed a "coldness" toward Hughes's poems, seeing them as intrusions in the book. Hughes upbraided Cullen a short time later in "The Negro Artist and the Racial Mountain" for what he saw as Cullen's desire to be white, and Hurston wrote a letter to Hughes laughing at Cullen for going to Europe to learn his trade, though she felt it was typical of his middle-class leanings (Hurston to Hughes, 12 April 1928, reported in Hemenway, 51). Cullen responded, in his own way, with "To Certain Critics" and a continuing commitment to his aesthetic. Though an extensive discussion of his poetry is not relevant to this study, it should be emphasized that not all African-American literary artists employed folk material in their work.

116. Hughes, *The Big Sea*, 249.

117. Wagner, *Black Poets*, 351.

118. Hughes, *The Big Sea*, 184–85.

119. Ibid., 186.

120. Brown, *The Negro in American Fiction*, 155.

121. Brown, *Negro Poetry and Drama*, 76.

122. Ibid., 71.

123. Hughes, "The Twenties: Harlem and Its Negritude," 14.

124. Hemenway, *Zora Neale Hurston*, 115.

125. Hughes, *The Big Sea*, 238–39.

126. Ibid., 296.

127. Langston Hughes, *I Wonder As I Wander* (New York: Hill and Wang, 1964; rpt., New York: Octagon, 1974), 45. Indeed, sociologist Guy B. Johnson, who had written about the blues, invited Hughes to speak at the University of North Carolina.

128. Langston Hughes, "Jazz As Communication," in *The Langston Hughes Reader* (New York: Braziller, 1958), 492.

129. Hughes, *The Big Sea*, 325.

130. Langston Hughes, "Songs Called the Blues," *Phylon* 2, no. 2 (1941): 143.

131. Ibid., 145.

132. Hughes, *The Big Sea*, 299.

133. Ibid., 300.

134. Langston Hughes to Mary Owings Miller, in *Contemporary Poetry*, Autumn 1943: 4.

135. Langston Hughes, *Langston Hughes Reads and Talks About His Poetry*, Spoken Arts 7140, 1959.

136. Hughes, *The Big Sea*, 272.

137. Ibid., 226.

138. Langston Hughes, "The Negro Artist and the Racial Mountain," 306. In his review of *Shuffle Along* in 1921, Claude McKay anticipated a

number of points that Hughes makes in this essay, rejecting "respectable" white middle-class standards and embracing the unpretentiousness of the "common" Negro. See Wayne F. Cooper, ed., *The Passion of Claude McKay* (New York: Schocken, 1973), 62–65.

139. Langston Hughes, "Springarn Medal Acceptance Speech," NAACP Convention, St. Paul, Minnesota, 26 June 1960. Hughes Archives, Schomburg Collection. Reprinted in Onwuchekwa Jemie, *Langston Hughes: An Introduction to the Poetry* (New York: Columbia University Press, 1976), 27.

140. "Bop," in *The Best of Simple,* ed. Langston Hughes (New York: Hill and Wang, 1971), 117.

141. Jemie, *Langston Hughes,* 27.

142. See Langston Hughes, "Jazz, Jive, and Jam," in *Simple Stakes a Claim* (New York: Rinehart, 1957). A fuller discussion of this story appears in my article "Simple's Great African American Joke," *CLA Journal* 27, no. 3 (March 1984): 239–53, where I discuss the story in the context of what Louis D. Rubin calls "The Great American Joke."

143. Hughes, "The Negro Artist and the Racial Mountain," 309.

2

DEFINING THE BLUES

1

Defining "the blues" has proved to be a difficult task for the scholar and the aficionado. The term is complex because it refers to a number of separate entities—an emotion, a technique, a musical form, and a song lyric—that are somewhat foreign to Western ways of thinking and notating, and also because the blues are the production of a nonwhite, nonliterate, oral society that primarily white critics from a literate society are attempting to interpret. In its most generalized form, a fit of the "blue devils," from which the term "the blues" derives, refers to a mood of despondency and can be experienced by everyone. In the nineteenth century both of these terms found their way into the writings of people like Thomas Jefferson, Washington Irving, and Lord Byron.[1] Under this definition, "the blues" can refer to a range of separate physical and emotional hardships that precipitate such a mood, signifying often a temporary emotional low that can be displaced by a solution to the specific problem. However, for African-Americans, as Franklin Rosemont pointed out, the blues are "a way of life,"[2] differentiated from the generic emotion because of the peculiar circumstances of African-American existence in the United States. A particular misery and sadness, a particular blues, unites African-Americans whose common heritage—in Africa, slavery, and a theoretical freedom—often provides a bond which is difficult for middle-class blacks to break. That bond implies neither an African-American singlemindedness of attitude nor purpose in ways of dealing with the oppressive system; rather, it implies a shared need to deal with the tension created by America's theoretical democracy in conflict with a systematic network of racist attitudes that were (and are) often granted the authority of law. The problems of those blacks who have accepted the vision of the American dream as possible for African-Americans, and, consequently, have attempted in many ways to leave behind the aspects of their folk culture that clashed with white, middle-class ideals, have been dealt with frequently in both fact and fiction. The basic message is that upwardly mobile blacks should adopt white, middle-class values and forget their own culture in order to succeed; but that success is always blocked by the memories of the same white people who have counseled African-Americans to forget. Since the network affects every aspect of which the secular blues technique, music, and lyric were born. Since blues performances are both communal and individual ex-tural meeting ground of African and European art in America, out of which the secular blues technique, music, and lyric was born. Since blues performances are both communal and individual ex-pressions, dynamic and varied, based on factors such as time, location, dominant local performers and traditions, availability of phonograph recordings, and individual skills and creativity, the depth and breadth of the term can indeed overwhelm anyone trying to reduce it to a pithy phrase.

Despite the frequent commentary on Africanisms in African-American music found in letters, diaries, journals, articles, and books since the early days of slavery, research dealing with African-isms in blues music of the twentieth century was ignored in favor of the study of "spirituals, Louisiana Creole folk music, and jazz"[3] until very recently. The research of musicologists, anthropologists, and folklorists has been employed by critics and professionals like Ernest Borneman, Rudi Blesh, Marshall Stearns, Harold Cour-lander, Gunther Schuller, and A. M. Jones, among others, in their treatises on jazz and folk music. Those works have in turn laid the pioneering groundwork which provided subsequent scholars with opportunities to extend or refute those early assertions. Musicolo-gists such as H. E. Krehbiel and Erich M. von Hornbostel looked to Africa for the origins of African-American music: Krehbiel did so very generally and unsystematically, and with a bias for "refined" culture; von Hornbostel was more specific, though he was limited in seeing the leader-chorus response as the sole African feature in

African-American spirituals.[4] Anthropologists Melville J. Herskovits, Richard Alan Waterman, and Alan Merriam sought to charac-
terize African music more fully and to suggest a more specific
relationship with the music of the Americas. Merriam, lamenting
that many studies had been "affective rather than analytical,"[5]
challenged Winthrop Sargent, Rudi Blesh, and A. M. Jones in their
assertions about the prevalence of the "blue notes" in Africa, particularly their claims about its common occurrence in the Guinea
Coast and Congo regions. Merriam's refutations indicate the great
need for more research into African music by jazz critics who can
lay aside preconceptions.

A good place to start would be with an examination of pre-jazz
African-American music to determine what elements have carried
over from African music. The influence of African music on African-American music before the twentieth century has been surveyed and discussed by Dena J. Epstein, who found many survivals
of African instrumental, vocal, and music techniques in the religious and secular music of African-American slaves through
1867.[6] A more specific discussion of the influence of Africanisms on
African-American music has been provided by Alan Lomax with
his Cantometric analysis, which consists of thirty-seven rating
scales that record characteristics of a particular performance. He
also found that "the song styles of black communities in . . . the
United States . . . adhere closely to the core Black African model."[7]
Lomax further theorized that African music is so attractive to the
world today because "it is so practical, . . . it operates successfully
in more of life's activities than any other musical system,"[8] presenting a "musical performance structure and social structure [that]
mirror one another, reinforce one another, and establish that spiritual quality of both African music and African society—whether in
Africa or in African enclaves in the New World."[9] Though Can-
tometrics has been challenged by those who find the scale categories too vague or impressionistic—especially since Lomax claimed
that anyone could do the analyses—the system raises some important points about the subject and provides a number of ways of
looking at the relationship between African and African-American
music.

With such a critical background in musicology, anthropology,
and folklore, the danger facing a Western blues critic is an over-

reliance on this previous, sometimes contradictory, research, which may have drawn from false information about African music and traditions. Indeed, because blues and jazz are different, though related, musical forms, it is necessary to look at African music with the blues specifically in mind; and, in fact, many blues researchers have found it necessary to go to Africa to do their own collecting and research to supplement their specialization in the blues field. As a result, our understanding of Africanisms in blues music has become fuller and more complex, though not definitively established.

Some of the earliest comments on residual African elements in blues music came from Janheinz Jahn, an important African scholar who was early among those who asserted the existence of an African culture and philosophy that was independent of European and Middle Eastern influence. In fact, he argued that Africa had exported its own ideas to the rest of the world. In *Muntu,* Jahn claimed that the suppression of drumming in the United States eliminated "the polymeter which carries polytheism,"[10] leaving polyrhythm, which is based on a single meter. This suppression prepared the way for *Kuntu* (modality or way of singing) to alter the existing European musical traditions and produced jubilees, ballads, spirituals, and blues. Although the theory is attractive and seems logical at first glance, the suggestion that drums exclusively carry polytheism is too broad. In fact, as Jahn himself as well as many other African scholars have recognized, both religion and music permeate everyday African life, so that any number of instruments, and vocals, could help carry polytheism as well as drums could. Jahn also asserted that "without the drums it was impossible to call up the orishas, the ancestors were silent; and the proselytizers had a free hand,"[11] but, again, a number of other percussive instruments, or instruments played percussively, could substitute. As Jahn himself acknowledged, the African *manner* of performing survived. Even more important, as African theologian John S. Mbiti pointed out, "There are about one thousand African peoples (tribes), and each one has its own religious system."[12] Thus, when Jahn generalized from the four concepts (*Muntu, Kintu, Hantu, Kuntu*) set down by Alexis Kagame with reference to the Bantu of Ruanda, he made a general application that could be invalidated by any number of the varied religious systems set up to satisfy the immediate needs of individual tribes. Indeed, Alan Dundes recognized that there are those who would wish "to dispute some of Jahn's definitions of African philosophic concepts,"[13] and Mbiti found that Jahn's eagerness to prove that Africa has much of philosophical value to offer may have caused him to overstate his case.[14] Undoubtedly, aspects of the life that the enslaved Africans had led previous to their captivity must have carried over to some degree in the United States, despite efforts to suppress them, but sweeping generalizations about diverse groups are more romantic than valid.

That is not to say that Jahn's writings on the blues are without value. His Ernst Dauer–influenced discussions of the misapplication of the term "improvisation" to what is essentially an African-influenced singing style, his assertion that African antiphony is the foundation of the sequence of voices in the blues, and his discussion of the African origin of the blue notes are all important points. Additionally, some of his subtle differentiations between the conventional white critics' attitudes about blues and his ideas based on (overgeneralized) African philosophical concepts raise important questions about the relation of African to African-American life and the blues. In *A History of Neo-African Literature,* Jahn commented that the central theme of the blues is "an individual's right to life and to an intact 'perfect' life," defined by the term *magara,* which is "the life force which one possesses, which one wants to increase, and which can be diminished by the influence of others."[15] Jahn saw the blues as an expression not of sad or happy moods but of "the attitude caused by the loss of life-force or leading to the gaining of life-force."[16] Essentially, then, Jahn found the blues to be an assertion of autonomy and the desire to consolidate one's power in a world where one's power is in danger of being lost. However, this idea that one is entitled to an intact, perfect life could also stem from the African-American's encounter with notions derived from Rousseau and Locke about the right to life, liberty, and the pursuit of happiness as expressed in the Declaration of Independence. That document theoretically referred to all Americans but actually formed the basis of the fundamental irony about America as it treated African-Americans. In fact, invoking the basic document of an oppressive country is an effective strategy to use in calling attention to the hypocrisy of that country.

Therefore, we might say that while African philosophy predisposed African-American slaves to claim the right to *magara,* American life certainly emphasized both the absence of *magara* in fact while positing the right to *magara* in law. Finally, Jahn's idea that the blues represent more than a happy or sad mood but may in fact be a political statement asserting a desire for personal and communal liberation is an astute observation that does not need African philosophical concepts to justify it. Further aspects of Jahn's theories about the blues will be discussed later, as various critical attitudes about the blues are surveyed.

Jahn's nationalistic pride in Africa was matched by the African-American pride of the members of the Black Arts movement in America in the 1960s, and some of those writers, especially Leroi Jones, wrote insightfully about the blues. Jones approached African-American music from a "socio-anthropological as well as musical"[17] standpoint, asserting that "blues could not exist if the African captives had not become American captives."[18] Jones felt that Protestant America's lack of something like the Catholic saints to replace the West African deities helped bring into being the link between pure West African songs and the postslavery music of the African-Americans. This link was the work song, which had its parallels in West Africa; however, those parallel songs had referred to West African religion and drums, which were forbidden in America, so a substitution of non-forbidden elements altered the African songs and made them African-American. Jones also contradicted H. E. Krehbiel, asserting that African-Americans may not have been using a diatonic scale, but an African scale instead, which accounts for blue notes. He also found Western rhythmic vapidity to be the reason Westerners called African music primitive when it actually employed complex polyphonic or contrapuntal rhythmic effects.[19] In the music, singing, and functionality of the music, African music differed aesthetically from European music, Jones felt, and the fact that in language and music "the African tradition aims at circumlocution rather than exact definition"[20] meant that African-American music like the blues, a combination of African and European elements, would draw partially on these African elements to create a new music from "a new race."[21]

The approach that Jones took is important because he presented, as Langston Hughes said, "new and highly provocative conclusions bolstered by both history and sociology."[22] Still, Jones's writings on Africa and the blues were not highly systematic examinations of particular influences, though he did include a number of suggestions about influences. Rather, he seems to have been intent on making general conclusions that are reasonable and insightful, if not fully explored, and his book remains an important contribution to the literature of the blues, more of which will be discussed later.

Paul Oliver, in *Savannah Syncopators: African Retentions in the Blues,* found that previous anthropologists, critics, and jazz authorities agreed that "Africanisms of a kind have persisted in American Negro folk music and jazz,"[23] but that there was generally a lack of particularization as to what section of Africa should be studied and a refusal by these anthropologists and jazz critics to recognize the blues as more than a precursor of jazz. With a thorough grounding in this previous scholarship, Oliver proceeded to do his own research and collecting in Africa in order to compare his African research with what he found in his research in blues in America. Oliver argued in contrast to the exclusive emphasis of the influence of rain forest cultures on African-American music by people like Melville J. Herskovits. Oliver asserted the influence of the Savannah cultures further inland from the West African forest cultures. The widespread prevalence of string-dominated music in the Savannah argues for the influence of that music on blues, which, Oliver demonstrated, employs instruments, performing techniques, and vocal sounds similar to those of the Savannah. He felt, because of the suppression of drumming among slaves in North America, that the caste of professional musicians known as *griots* of the Savannah region had the advantage in facilitating the survival of their stringed musical traditions in America. Oliver's musical assumptions were buttressed by the existence in Savannah stringed music of blue notes, flattened thirds and sevenths, and diatonic, heptatonic, and pentatonic scales, all of which are found in the blues; and by linguistic, physiological, genetic, and historical evidence that argues for a link between Savannah peoples and African-Americans.

Oliver's challenges to the work of previous anthropologists drew the response of Richard Alan Waterman, and, when Waterman died in the midst of the exchange, David Evans joined the debate with Oliver, pointing out that non-stringed Savannah instruments have no counterparts in African-American folk music, challenging Oliver's parallel between the *griot* and the bluesman as well as his genetic arguments, and asserting that Oliver's examples of American words derived from African languages are from the Gullah dialect of Georgia and South Carolina coast and islands, an area of little blues activity. Finally, Evans found that there are African *influences* but not retentions in the blues, if Oliver meant to refer to purely African instruments, lyrics, and the like.[24] Oliver countered that non-stringed Savannah instruments may have their counterparts in jazz, thus strengthening his argument for Savannah roots. Arguing that, for example, *griot* caste-marriage practices would have been suppressed with all the other marital customs of Africans, Oliver nonetheless pointed to the frequent marriage of blues singers into other blues-singing families as one example of a number of similarities between *griots* and bluesmen. In regard to the slang words, Oliver pointed out that David Dalby, professor of African languages at the School of Oriental and African Studies at London University, verified that three-quarters of the specifically Negro words known to blues collectors are of Savannah origin; and Oliver cited the support of geneticists who back up his discussion of genetic drift.[25] Finally, Oliver's on-the-spot research and citations of support from current anthropological and linguistic critics argue for the correctness of his findings, though he certainly recognizes the need for discussion and further research. The informed challenges of Evans help provide the type of discourse needed to get to the root of the question of African connections.

Oliver's is the pioneering research in the blues field, and the exchanges between him and Waterman and Evans provide useful explorations of a complex issue. Subsequent works in the field have been neither as substantial nor as broad, but they seem to reach the same conclusions generally. In *Deep Blues,* Robert Palmer found that "Black American music as it was sung and played in the rural South was both a continuation of deep and tenacious African traditions and a creative response to a brutal, desperate situation."[26] Samuel Charters's *The Roots of the Blues: An African Search* showed that West African music and blues sound very little alike: the structures of melodies and types of accompaniments differ; the melodic integration between voice and guitar present in blues is not present in African music; and the blues strophe, rhyme, and controlled line lengths differ from the African. What *is* similar is the *way* of singing and playing, and the rhythmic texturing.[27] It is certainly true that African music rarely sounds like African-American blues; those rare instances when they do sound similar, as in Laura Boulton's 1930s recording of a "War Song" by a member of the nomadic Tuareg peoples of the Timbuktu regions, only serve to highlight the rarity and underscore the important point that the blues indeed borrow much from European music as well.[28] Finally, we might summarize the influence of what Robert Farris Thompson has called the "ancient African organizing principle of song and dance"[29] on African-American music, including blues:

> *The dominance of a percussive performance style* (attack and vital aliveness in sound and motion); *a propensity for multiple meter* (competing meters sounding all at once); *overlapping call and response* in singing (solo/chorus, voice/instrument—"interlock systems" of performance); *inner pulse control* (a "metronome sense," keeping a beat indelibly in mind as a rhythmic common denominator in a welter of different meters); *suspended accentuation patterning* (offbeat phrasing of melodic and choreographic accents); and, at a slightly different but equally recurrent level of exposition, *songs and dances of social allusion* (music which, however danceable and "swinging," remorselessly contrasts social imperfections against implied criteria for perfect living).[30]

It is clear, then, that a number of professional scholars and aficionados have worked at establishing a concrete connection between African and African-American music. Much of the most important and specific work got under way in the late 1940s and proliferated in the fifties, sixties, and seventies. Langston Hughes never really addressed himself extensively to the influence of African on African-American music. Rather, at those times when he discussed the influence of Africa on American music, he confined his remarks to general statements and impressions that took advantage of none of the anthropological or ethnomusicological work that was being or had been done. In *Black Magic: A Pictorial History of the Negro in American Entertainment,* he and Milton Meltzer wrote of the "syncopated beat which the captive Africans brought with them,"[31] the implantation of which in America "began with the hand-clapping, feet-stomping, drum-beating rhythms (related, of course, to the rhythms of the human heart), that Africans exported to our shores in the fifteenth century."[32] Hughes related the drumbeat of Africa with jazz in America, calling attention, in his narration for the Folkways LP *The Story of Jazz,* to the drum playing at New Orleans's Congo Square as a link between Africa and jazz.[33] Many years before that recording, he had already made an implicit connection: In "The Negro Artist and the Racial Mountain," he called jazz "the tom-tom of revolt against weariness in a white world."[34] The Africa that he wrote about in "Afro-American Fragment" in 1930 was, indeed, for him, "So long, / so far away,"[35] and he described himself as "only an American Negro—who had loved the surface of Africa and the rhythms of Africa."[36] That love of surface and rhythms did not spur him to investigate closely the influence of Africa on jazz or blues. Presumably, since he stated that "behind jazz is always the blues"[37] and that the music of jazz artists like Louis Armstrong is imbued with the blues,[38] Hughes felt that the blues, too, were influenced by the rhythms of Africa, but he never made an explicit statement to that effect. He came close in an article about Memphis Minnie, published in the *Chicago Defender,* in which he described the rhythm she was playing as "as old as Memphis Minnie's most remote ancestor," but the visions her music evokes are of "Louisiana bayous, muddy old swamps, Mississippi dust and sun, cotton fields, lonesome roads, train whistles in the night, mosquitoes at dawn and the Rural Free Delivery that never brings the right letter,"[39] not of Africa. The section of *The Big Sea* dealing with his trip to Africa is silent about jazz or blues, and in a letter to Carl Van Vechten dealing with a native jazz band in the Cameroon in Africa and a boy named George, who shipped with him to Africa, and who made up his own blues, Hughes did not seize on the opportunity to make a connection.[40] Perhaps "The Blues I'm Playing," published in *Scribner's Magazine* in 1934, comes closest to making the connection. A female pianist, Oceola Jones, who resists the efforts of her white patron to make her reject Harlem and jazz, would play the blues at Bricktop's in Paris: "In the blues she made the bass notes throb like tom-toms, the trebles cry like little flutes, so deep in the earth and so high in the sky that they understood everything."[41] Hughes was not an historian, anthropologist, or ethnomusicologist; he was a poet. He did not seem to be interested in exploring the African backgrounds of the blues in any systematic, scientific way, primarily because he understood that America was the environment of the blues.

2

We must recognize that the music of Africa did not proceed unmediated into forming the blues. Epstein pointed out that "the evidence makes it clear that African music and dancing not only were transported to the New World but also persisted there for generations."[42] She described the acculturation of African musical elements as reflected in the music of slaves in America up to the Civil War, and Paul Oliver described the various folk and popular elements that made up, influenced, and existed alongside the blues in the post-Civil War era.[43] Experts like the Lomaxes, Middleton, Charters, Oster, Oliver, and Evans agreed that field hollers were a major influence on the development of the blues style, and some have maintained that work songs, too, were contributors, though much less so. Epstein found few references to field hollers before the Civil War, though, of course, references to work songs were abundant. While she felt that it is impossible "to document a specific worksong's origin in Africa and its persistence in the New World,"[44] Leroi Jones asserted that the words of African work songs, calling attention to the gods bringing rain and the beauty of the ancestors, would have little meaning to slaves forced to labor in a foreign land, so the work songs changed, although the words, syntax, and rhythm of Africa remained in varying degrees.[45]

Therefore, while we might say that the influence of African work songs on African-American work songs was inevitable, the full extent of specific influence is difficult, if not impossible, to discern. The work songs, though, were group-labor songs, highly rhythmic and heavily accented. They coincided with the swing of an axe or the blow of a hammer, helping workers to maintain a groove and keep up their output. A large number of work songs recorded in the twentieth century suggest that the songs could be either improvised or traditional; that they dealt with a number of themes but were primarily about love or the hard work itself; and that the lyrics were often loosely connected units that, despite their avowed intention of establishing a working rhythm to ensure production, expressed important emotions and ideas in a neo-African style that demonstrated an identity separate from forced labor in a foreign, supposedly democratic society.

The field holler, sometimes called an "arwhoolie," "field cry," "field blues," or "over and over," has, like the work song, no instrumental accompaniment. However, the field holler is an individual song that, it has been suggested, came into being when the demise of the larger plantations broke up the work forces and put individual farmers in the fields singing their own songs to and for themselves as they labored. Jeff Titon called the style "freely decorative,"[46] while David Evans felt that field hollers tend to be "very loosely structured, highly embellished, and rhythmically free, often consisting of falsetto whooping or hollering with no words or a very minimal text."[47] The field holler was found by Sam Charters to be "closely related to African music, most closely to the praise songs and the individual men's songs of the West African tribes."[48] Therefore, the field hollers sung in this country, if they had an influence on the blues singer, might well establish a link to Africa in terms of their relation to such praise songs. The field hollers recorded in this century, if they accurately reflect those of the late nineteenth century, do seem to have influenced the style of the blues singer. Son House and Willie Brown certainly sang their hollers and blues in a similar manner, though it must be pointed out that both had recorded blues previous to these recordings.[49] Beyond recorded evidence, a number of blues singers, Son House and Bukka White among them, have stated the blues started from singing in the fields, and singers like Texas Alexander, Rambling Willard Thomas, Skip James, Blind Lemon Jefferson, and Peg Leg Howell have all been described as being heavily influenced by field hollers in their vocal styles. In fact, Paul Oliver saw Howell's blues as representing "the transition from old songs, work songs and ballads, to blues," during a period that saw the decline of the old songs and the growing dominance of blues. David Evans, in "Folk and Popular Blues," supported Oliver's theory that " 'the field holler vocal was combined with one of the common harmonic accompaniment patterns of the blues ballad' to mold the blues form,"[50] so the connection between these individual work songs, these hollers, and the blues is indeed very close. They were the last step of African-American music before the blues themselves emerged in the arena of folk music to provide, as Leroi Jones said, both "a more formal music" in its stanzaic structure and "a more liberated music" in the freedom it offered in the range of subjects.[51] That imposition of form and granting of freedom may well find its most meaningful expression in the ability of the blues to express the harsh limitations of this world while helping to transcend them.

Langston Hughes knew of the influence of work songs and field hollers on the blues, though he didn't write about them in an extensive way and, not being a Southerner, was not surrounded by them every day. In *The First Book of Jazz,* Hughes commented on the earlier songs: "A hundred years ago there were croons, work songs, and field hollers—a kind of musical cry—whose melodies had a blues sound. To these tunes, road workers or cotton pickers put whatever words came into their minds. They sang out of their personal thoughts or sorrows."[52] On the Folkways LP *The Story of Jazz,* he developed a scenario for the creation of the blues which places their origin in the fields:

> Maybe one hot day a man was working in a rice field when a song came into his head, then out of his mouth. A song, with words, perhaps like this:
>
> > O the sun is so hot
> > And the day is so doggone long.
>
> Then when he couldn't think of anything else right away to go with it he repeated the same line:
>
> > Yes the sun is so hot
> > And the day is so doggone long.
>
> But by that time maybe he had a new thought, so he sang:
>
> > And that is the reason
> > I'm singing this doggone song.
>
> Something like that must have happened the day the first blues was born. . . . Perhaps thousands of blues were made up in this way in the fields or on the levees, to relieve the monotony of working, to express some thought passing through the speaker's mind, or just for fun.[53]

These words were written, however, long after his blues poems of the 1920s and 1930s. Hughes's earliest blues efforts and his earlier writings on the blues rarely mentioned the field hollers and work songs. Indeed, in "Songs Called the Blues," published in *Phylon* in 1941, Hughes called the blues "songs of the black South, particularly the city South,"[54] though in the same essay, he described the "Dupree Blues" as "one of the newest authentic Blues to come up out of the South, by way of the colored boys in the government work camps,"[55] implicitly placing the blues alongside work songs. Of course, "Dupree Blues" was not a new song in 1941: Odum and Johnson had published it in *Negro Workaday Songs* in 1926, and it had been recorded in 1930 by Willie Walker and in 1935 by Georgia White—to whom Hughes referred as a girl who carried on "the old tradition of blues in the folk manner."[56] It is hard to imagine that Hughes did not see the connection between work songs and field songs and the blues, but he did not make much explicit connection between them in his writing until he began writing his histories of jazz in the fifties.

One suggestion of the connection comes in "Don't You Want To Be Free?," published in *One Act Play Magazine* in 1938, where Hughes created two "inverted" blues stanzas that are sung by external voices as slaves are led to and sold on the auction block:

> Cook them white folks dinner,
> Wash them white folks clothes,
> Be them white folks slave-gal,
> That is all she knows.
> Be them white folks slave-gal,
> That is all she knows.
>
> Whip done broke his spirit,
> Plow done broke his back.
> All they wants a slave, that's all,
> When a man is black.
> Nothin' but a slave, that's all,
> If a man is black.[57]

Hughes's employment of these blues stanzas in the slavery section of his play emphasized his ideas about the presence of the blues spirit and feeling in slavery times as related to the harsh work that limited the lives of the slaves and helped force them into an inferior social status. The stanzas also represent an inversion of the standard twelve-bar blues pattern in the repetition of the third and fourth lines as opposed to the first and second. It was a peculiarly effective way of emphasizing the social message of the stanzas by repeating that point, not what led to it. It is as if the echo of that line is the echo that is heard throughout the lives of African-Americans, or the one that should be heard, expressing the bitterness that might urge them into action. That is, of course, the major thrust of the play, which ends like Odets's *Waiting For Lefty* of three years earlier in its call to "Strike, Strike, Strike!" with the words "fight, fight, fight!"[58] It should be pointed out, however, that Gates Thomas collected a version of "C. C. Rider" around 1920 that uses a repeat of the second line of the stanza rather than of the first, so there is a precedent for the inversion that Hughes uses.[59] Hughes may not have been familiar with Thomas's work, but he might have heard some similar blues verse firsthand.

Hughes's play also features a sequence of lyrics, sung while people are hoeing in a field, which are somewhat like the levee camp hollers recorded by Son House and Willie Brown. Hughes wrote:

> When the cotton's picked
> And the work is done
> Boss man takes the money
> And we get none.[60]

House sang:

> I done walked this old levee
> 'Til my feet got numb
> If you see Mister Charlie ask him
> Did his money come.[61]

The similarity is clear, though the latter benefits from a sardonic irony lacking in Hughes's lines. Six pages later, Hughes begins dealing with the blues explicitly. Hughes, then, recognized the sequence of development and makes implicit the development of slavery songs and field hollers into the blues in his play—a connection that theoretically would have been even more explicit in performance.

In essence, Hughes's knowledge of the connection between African music, work songs and field hollers, and the blues seemed to be general and unsystematic during the early years of his writing, though he was by no means being false or misleading. He was more concerned with the artistic use rather than the scientific examination of his heritage. Only later, when he began writing his prose, non-fiction histories of jazz, did he strive to present a more complete picture than was necessary in his poetry. As a poet of the city, a poet of Harlem, Hughes did not find a frequent place in his poetry and fiction for the songs of the fields.

3

We know, of course, when the blues first emerged on commercial phonograph records, but it is impossible to say when the first blues was sung. Gates Thomas collected something very like a blues song in tune and lyric in south Texas in 1890, and W. C. Handy, who "heard the crude singing of the Negro" during his years in Mississippi and who "carried water for the men who worked in the rock quarry and carried water for the men who worked in the furnaces," printed blues songs that he heard as early as 1890 in his collection *Blues: An Anthology*.[62] In fact, the recollection and collection of blues songs began in the 1890s and by the turn of the century became more frequent, as people like Ma Rainey, W. C. Handy, Gates Thomas, Howard W. Odum, Will Thomas, W. Prescott Webb, and John A. Lomax all reported the existence of blues songs before their appearance on phonograph records.[63] David Evans, citing this period as a time of the "coming to maturity of the first generation of blacks born out of slavery," has suggested why the blues emerged at this time:

> This was certainly an appropriate time for young blacks to create the blues, those songs of uncertainty and tension, for they had been brought up in a world of problems and enormous difficulties without the experience of an older generation to fall back on. The attitudes of older blacks were a response to slavery, and their songs reflected this in large part. Slavery was brutal and oppressive, but it offered the black a well-defined role as an anonymous member of a slave society whose basic needs would be taken care of by his master. Post-Reconstruction "freedom," in contrast, offered black people economic independence, individualism, industrial life, and the chance for a greater expression of love and family responsibility. It also, however, left blacks educationally and economically unpre-

pared to cope with this new responsibility and sense of individualism and with the economic competition of industrial life.[64]

The blues, then, represented an adaptation of older instrumental and vocal techniques (which responded to one kind of oppressive system) to a new kind of music, one that responded to the unique problems posed by the new oppressive system and provided an appropriate way of expressing these problems.

Many people have attempted to define and analyze the blues, and their interpretations of what the blues are and do sometimes clash with each other. There is some truth in what the writers say, but their attempts to make their pronouncements absolute can be their downfall. Some say all blues are sad. Others claim that they are happy. This one says they are political; that one, apolitical. The blues, it is said, are a personal expression. No, comes the reply, they express the values of the group. Dramatic dialogues. Self-catharsis. Audience catharsis. Dance music. Devil music. Truth. The truth is, the blues *can* be all of these things. Just as we would not suggest that Hemingway and Faulkner were trying to do the same thing in the same way in their short stories, so we would not insist that all blues performers had the same philosophy, intent, technique, or ability. As with Victor Cousin's belief that systems of philosophy are not false but incomplete, so it seems here. The task is simply to unite these incomplete systems, to show that the blues can do a number of things in a number of ways. They have a depth and breadth that reflect a range of emotion, experience, and imagination, so all blues should not be treated as if they are the same.

The blues have sometimes been defined through the musical form itself because of the predominance of two types, the eight-bar and twelve-bar blues, in which each stanza lasts eight or twelve bars respectively. (Musical examples of eight-bar and twelve-bar blues will be given later when blues texts are compared to Hughes's poems.) The actual length of the stanzas is often somewhat looser than this, since a musical passage or vocal line may be shortened or extended at will to produce, for example, a seven- or thirteen-and-a-half-bar blues. Harold Courlander is correct in stating that "the blues stanza framework *tends* toward eight or twelve bar blues,"[65] and we must remember that this tendency may vary frequently, sometimes as a result of the emotional involvement of the singer whose feelings urge self-expression in a freer manner than a strict format would allow, or whose audience is responding to a particular passage that is then extended for their benefit. Of course, some blues performers have what the classically trained musician would call bad timing, meaning that they simply do not or cannot follow strict rules about timing, which creates problems for those people who perform with them. John Lee Hooker would be an example of a musician who uses the form in a free manner; Smokey Hogg seems to have bad timing. Hooker seems to extend his phrases, to take his time and let things flow as they may; Hogg seems jagged, disjointed, switching directions abruptly.

Still, the tendency toward eight- and twelve-bar stanzas, particularly in the folk-blues, provides a strong framework for blues performance. There are, of course, other blues stanza forms, like the sixteen- or thirty-two-bar stanzas, but these are mostly the creation of popular blues composers whose work will be discussed later. Suffice it to say here that W. C. Handy, one of the first and most famous blues composers, based his blues material on blues like the twelve-bar song he heard performed by a black quartet in Florence, Alabama, in 1890, and the eight-bar song he heard in St. Louis in 1892:

> I walked all the way from Old East St. Louis
> And I didn't have but one po' measly dime.[66]

The words of a blues song can be as loose within their own structure as the music is within its own confines as well. In the eight-bar blues, like the one printed above, the two lines take roughly four bars each to complete. Twelve-bar blues generally consist of one thought or statement repeated, and a third line which resolves or extends the repeated thought in some way (*AAB*). The two *A*'s here refer to the rhyme of the repeat line, which is an identical rhyme, and the *B* to the rhyme of the third line, which is a different word that rhymes with the *A* lines. Janheinz Jahn saw this statement-and-response element of the blues as being African, and identified a "blues logic in which the response line either expands, illuminates, justifies, explains or gives grounds for the statement line, or presents the antithesis of it."[67] However, it is difficult to imagine what else the response *could* do besides accomplish one of these purposes; and indeed, though Jahn argued to the contrary, the examples of European poetry altered to fit into the blues stanza form which he offered to show how they violate "blues logic" in fact *do* fit into one of these categories.

Additionally, it seems that in the earliest years of blues performing, an *AAA* pattern consisting of the same thought repeated three times was common. Henry Thomas, a Texas songster, was in his fifties when he recorded between 1927 and 1929 certain ballads, minstrel songs, reels, folk tunes, and songs derived from work songs that reflected an era of music predating the compositions of the younger blues singers being recorded. His "Texas Worried Blues" followed the *AAA* pattern:

> The worried blues
> God, I'm feelin' bad.
> I've got the worried blues
> God, I'm feelin' bad.
> I've got the worried blues
> God, I'm feelin' bad.[68]

In a blues song like this, then, there is no call-and-response at all in the lyrics, though the interplay between music and lyrics might be termed a call-and-response. The greater variety of the *AAB* stanza and its wide distribution on phonograph records seems to have established that pattern as the dominant one. There are other ways to provide lyrics for the twelve-bar stanza, such as the use of a refrain like the one in Jim Jackson's monumental hit, "Jim Jackson's Kansas City Blues":

> I woke up this morning, feeling bad
> Thought about the good time I once have had
>
> *Refrain:*
> I'm gonna move to Kansas City
> I'm gonna move to Kansas City
> I'm gonna move to Kansas City
> Honey, where they don't allow you.[69]

The variations in eight-bar and twelve-bar blues stanzas will be discussed more fully in the section dealing with Langston Hughes's individual poems.

Some of the best work being done with blues lyrics most recently relates to the work of Milman Parry and Albert Lord. John Barnie, referring to the theory of oral-formulaic composition propounded

first by Parry and Lord, quite rightly found either the line or the
half-line to be the basic textual unit of the blues, asserting that this
unit is accentual and "based on a comparatively free patterning of
stressed (´), halfstressed (\`), and unstressed (^) syllables."[70] The
singer is then free to change the wording of his lines from performance to performance, even within the same performance, as long
as he adheres to an established accentual pattern that works with
the music. As Scarborough wrote in 1925, "a Negro in his singing
can crowd several syllables into one note, or expand one syllable to
cover half-a-dozen notes. The exigencies of scansion worry him but
slightly."[71] Thus, no unit like the foot in poetry controls the line.
Rather it is often the half-line, which sometimes may expire with
the breath of the singer, in a short emotional burst, or the complete
thought of the entire line that is the unit of the blues, and the
ethnopoetic transcription of a blues lyric attempts to reflect the
appropriate unit when rendered on the printed page, along with
other individual characteristics of the vocal performance.[72] However, because the appropriate context of the blues lyric is oral
performance, the ethnopoetic rendering is a weak substitute for
that performance though it is better than the rigid renderings that
capture none of the rhythm or flow of the blues. In fact, some lyric
transcriptions eliminate repeating the second line and place "(x2)"
in back of the first line to indicate repetition, despite the fact that
there may have been some textual variation. Still, some ethnopoetic transcriptions, like Eric Sackheim's rendering of Son
House's "The Jinx Blues," fracture the half-line unit into three
separate lines and then two separate lines in the repeat:

> Well I got up this morning
> Jinx all around
> Jinx all around
> 'Round my bed
> I say I got up this morning
> With the jinx
> All 'round my bed.[73]

Thus the idea of the half-line as a unit suggests that a line is sung in
two parts, when in fact it may be multisectioned, as House sings in
the above selection in order to emphasize the pervasive presence of
the blues. There are, of course, basically two parts to both the first

four lines and the next three lines, but there is also another structure, a restructuring of the half-line, that helps produce the dramatic effect.

The way a blues singer makes up blues songs is one concern in Titon's *Early Downhome Blues*. To explain, in part, the way the blues are generated, Titon used the formulaic substitution systems generated by Parry and Lord to discuss the production of Serbo-Croatian epic singers. Phrases like "I woke up this morning" or "I'm going away, babe" occur frequently in blues lyrics, though the phrasing of the line may be slightly different and the resolution individual. Titon discussed the former in some of its various permutations, and the same kind of discussion applies to the many lyrics that discuss leaving in relation to time, location, and purpose:

> I'm goin' away babe and it won't be long.[74]

> Now, Lord, I'm goin' back down South
> Man, where the weather suits my clothes.[75]

> Well, babe,
> Goin' away to leave you by yourself.[76]

> I believe, I believe, I believe I'll go back home.[77]

> I'm leavin' here, mama, don't you want to go?[78]

Titon saw the widespread use of phrases like this as a parallel to Parry's song formula: "a group of words which is regularly employed under the same metrical conditions to express a given essential idea."[79] He also agreed with Michael Taft's transformational-generative grammar approach to blues lyrics, finding a deep structure for such blues lyric families helpful in discerning how blues texts are created. In essence, the formulas allow the singer to draw on established thoughts or phrases in the oral tradition, but the singer must adjust the lyrics to fit his subject matter, syntax, location, audience, and purpose. The tradition and the individual talent combine to create variations in blues texts.

There are some problems with Titon's comparisons between composition in Serbo-Croatian epics and blues. Parry wrote about his own collection of oral texts that had been made with the idea "of obtaining evidence on the basis of which could be drawn a series of generalities applicable to all oral poetries."[80] However, this did not mean that the formula was a component of all oral poetry. Indeed, as David Bynum pointed out in *The Daemon in the Wood,* Parry's "Test of Orality" was limited by Parry in its application to "texts from traditions of long, metrical, presumably sung, fabulous narrative, or *epos.*"[81] Albert Lord, in *The Singer of Tales,* did not find length to be a criterion of epic poetry (though the poetry he discussed was generally longer than a blues song), and he felt that oral narrative poetry included "all story poetry, the romantic and historical as well as the heroic."[82] However, despite the fact that length would not be a factor, the criterion of narrative creates a problem. Blues is primarily a lyric poetry, though it can sometimes be narrative, and Parry, though recognizing a phrasal repetition in " 'lyrical-elegiac' and 'encomiastic' ("praise") poetry, riddles, and such manifestly non-epic poems as *Christ and Satan,"* deliberately excluded such material from his discussions of formulaic style.[83] And besides referring to narrative in discussing formula, the repeated and systematic usefulness (as opposed to mere repetition) of a phrase must be apparent for the phrase to be a formula:

> For the oral poet who sings long, traditional, fabulous narrative, the ideas prescribed in the tradition summon certain conventional phrases to mind according to the metrical moment; and when the Singer repeats those phrases, as he must, in a system with other phrases which have the same metrical value and which are enough alike in thought and words to leave no doubt that the poet who used them knew them not only as single phrases but also as phrases of a certain type, then we have to do with the formulas of oral composition.[84]

The blues singer, as we have said, is not constrained by a "metrical moment," nor does he often repeat phrases like "woke up this morning" or "I'm going away, babe" in the same song the way Homer repeats, for example, "rosy-fingered dawn." There is not a *systematic* use of a phrase within one given text in the blues that would allow the song text to fit the Parry-Lord criteria for formulaic composition.

Still, as Parry hoped, his forays did provide useful generalities for oral poetries. Titon's attempt to find formulas in blues texts does call attention to important common phrases and repetitions that emphasize needs, desires, expectations, and responses common to the singers of blues songs and their audiences. The frequent repetition among blues singers of "I'm going away, babe" in some form suggests a pervasive need for escape or for finding something better. The repetition of the phrase having to do with getting up in the morning suggests a desire for some type of new beginning, though the phrase is many times qualified by the realization that the morning is only *another* beginning in a continuing cycle.

Robert Johnson employed the phrase in just such a way, establishing in the opening line of "I Believe I'll Dust My Broom" not only a new beginning and resolve to act but also a textual pattern that he exploits very well in the first lines of each of the following stanzas:

> I'm gonna get up in the morning
> I believe I'll dust my broom.[85]

Besides using the variation on "woke up this morning" to indicate the beginning of his resolution to act on his situation, Johnson uses the phrase as the beginning of his song, which is, perhaps, one of the ways he intends to deal with his problem. Creating and performing a song is, after all, an action—not a violent action, but an action. And if it does make people feel good rather than arousing them to violence, it does so very often by reminding them about the bad times in a way that evokes laughter. Each of Johnson's subsequent stanzas also begins with the pronoun "I" and indicates some type of decisive attitude or action:

> I'm gonna write a letter
> Telephone every town I know.
>
> I don't want no woman
> Want every downtown man she meet.
>
> I believe,
> I believe I'll go back home.
>
> And I'm getting up in the morning
> I believe I'll dust my broom.
>
> I'm gonna call up China
> See is my good girl over there.

The stanzas variously, and resolutely, accept and reject the woman, depicting beautifully the conflicting emotions involved in lovers' arguments, indicating that in fact the new day and new attitude can be part of a revolving cycle of days and attitudes. It is interesting that four of Johnson's twenty-nine different recorded songs begin with some variation on the phrase "woke up this morning." However, because they are four separate texts, any discussion would be of a repetition and not a formula.

It is perhaps most fruitful when trying to define the blues to go to the blues performer for an answer. In lyrics, the blues singer employs a number of different strategies in describing the blues. The singer may describe how he got the blues:

> I done walked these old blocks, got to go buy me some shoes,
> I done walked these old blocks, mama, got to go buy me some
>   shoes,
> That's the reason why Mr. McTell got the blues.[86]

> I got the blues for my baby, she got the blues for, I say me,
> Blues for my baby, she's got the blues for me,
> But I can't see my baby and she can't see me.[87]

He may discuss how the blues work on his mind:

> I woke up this morning with the blues three different ways,
> I woke up this morning with the blues three different ways,
> Had two minds to leave you, only one to stay.[88]

The blues are so pervasive that any situation can become a kind of blues, and the singer can discuss the characteristics of that kind of blues:

> Backwater blues done caused me to pack my things and go,
> Backwater blues done caused me to pack my things and go,
> 'Cause my house fell down and I can't live there no more.[89]

> I got the railroad blues, got boxcars on my mind,
> I got the railroad blues, got boxcars on my mind,
> And the girl I'm loving, she sure done left this town.[90]

The blues may be compared with something:

> You know the blues ain't nothing but a lowdown shaking, low
>   down shaking, aching chill,

I say the blues is a lowdown old aching chill,
Well if you ain't had 'em, honey, I hope you never will.[91]

Did you ever feel lonesome, just to hear your good man's name?
Did you ever feel lonesome, just to hear your good man's name?
If the jinx is upon you, the blues fall like showers of rain.[92]

Or it may be personified:

Blues jumped a rabbit, run him one solid mile,
Blues jumped a rabbit, run him one solid mile,
The rabbit sat down and cried like a natural child.[93]

Now my blues got at me, Lord, run me from tree to tree,
Now my blues got at me and run me from tree to tree,
You should have heard me begging "Mr. Blues, don't murder
   me."[94]

The singer may discuss how bad a certain kind of blues is:

I got the blues so bad I stagger when I'm sleep,
I got the blues so bad I stagger when I'm sleep,
My brains are dark and cloudy and my mind's gone to my feet.[95]

Or he may discuss how the particular kind of blues would affect
others:

If the fishes in the water had my blues they'd die.[96]

He may discuss how to get rid of the blues:

Whiskey straight will drive the blues away.[97]

People, if you hear me humming on this song both night and day,
People, if you hear me humming on this song both night and day,
I'm just a poor boy in trouble trying to drive these blues away.[98]

He may even plead with the blues to help him:

Good morning, Mr. Blues, Mr. Blues I come to talk with you,
Good morning, Mr. Blues, Mr. Blues I come to talk with you,
Mr. Blues I ain't doing nothing and I would like to get a job from
   you.[99]

But finally, the blues may be just omnipresent, all pervading, inherent in everyday life:

Well it's blues in my house from the roof to the ground,
Well it's blues in my house from the roof to the ground,
And it's blues everywhere since my good man left town.

Blues in my mailbox 'cause I can't get no mail,
Says blues in my bread box, 'cause my bread got stale,
And there's blues in my bed 'cause I'm sleeping by myself.[100]

The singer may demonstrate either a resistance to the blues, or a powerlessness to overcome the blues and die:

I got the blues, but too damn mean to cry,
Oh, I got the blues, but I'm too damn mean to cry.[101]

Blues you made me roll and tumble, you made me weep and sigh,
Lordy, Lordy, Lordy,
Blues you roll and tumble, you made me weep and sigh,
Made me use cocaine and whiskey but you wouldn't let me die.[102]

Or he may see it as the secular part of his consciousness doing battle with the spiritual:

Oh in my room, I bowed down to pray,
Oh I was in my room, I bowed down to pray,
Say the blues come along and they drove my spirit away.[103]

These examples, drawn from the work of both males and females, heterosexuals and bisexuals, folk, vaudeville, and semi-professional blues singers, and from a range of geographical locations, demonstrate the blues singer's penchant for defining blues with a situation, treating it not as an abstract idea, but a concrete event. And the interviewed blues performer does not often define the blues as particular chord structures or lyric patterns either, as Big Bill Broonzy explained:

For me to sing the blues that I learned in Mississippi I have to go back to my sound and not the right chords as the musicians have told me to make. . . . the real blues is played and sung the way you feel and no man or woman feels the same way everyday.[104]

The most essential element of the blues is the feeling that derives from a lifestyle and a particular situation—something that has happened to the singer or someone else, or that has been imagined as possible, or that has been imagined to reflect a deeper truth about the life of the singer, though the situation is not literally possible.[105]

Interviews with blues singers generally yield the same responses, concentrating on situations. The recordings collected by Alan Lomax in the 1940s and released on the LP *Blues In the Mississippi Night,* though masked by Lomax to suggest that they had been recorded after a country dance when they had actually been recorded in New York City, yielded interesting responses. Though the speakers' names were hidden supposedly to protect them from possible repercussions for speaking honestly, all three were instantly recognizable. The guitarist Natchez (Big Bill Broonzy) responded to a question about the blues:

> Some people say that the blues is a cow want to see her calf, but I don't say it like that. I say it's a man that's got a companion, and she turns him down. And things like that happens, you know. And that's where I gets the blues from—when I want to see my baby and want to see her bad and something happens, I can't find her. And that gives me the blues.[106]

Sib (Sonny Boy Williamson) answered with more personal remarks:

> Well, I tell you, it really worries me just to think. I used to have a sweet little girl, you know, named Estelle, you know, and we used to go to school together and we naturally grew up together—in other words, I wanted to love her, and asked her mother for her, and whereat she turned me down. And that caused me to sing the blues. . . . Well, her parents thought I wasn't the right boy for her, you understand, and wouldn't make her happy and everything, and so they turned me down, and then I got to sitting down thinking, you understand, and then I thought of a song, and I started to drinking and then I started to singing.

Leroy (Memphis Slim) interjects succinctly: "The blues started from slavery." Most blues performers define the blues by offering examples of social situations as these three did, from a general, personal, or societal perspective.[107]

These approaches are reflected in the definitions imposed on blues by various folklorists, anthropologists, creative artists, and aficionados. Dorothy Scarborough found that the blues expressed

"Negro reactions to every concept of elemental life."[108] Howard W. Odum and Guy B. Johnson wrote that the blues expressed the Negro's "gloomy moods in song,"[109] especially, as Johnson later wrote, "the wail of the despondent Negro lover."[110] Charles S. Johnson, writing of the music's influence on the "new racial poetry," saw the blues as a reflection of Negro peasant life:

> "The Negro" of popular conception is not the educated person of Negro blood; he is the peasant, the dull, dark worker, or shirker of work, who sprawls his shadow over the South and clutters the side streets of northern cities. These are the forgotten lives that thread about within their circles, who run the full scale of human emotions without being suspected of feeling; who, like the hopelessly deformed in body face futility and abandon themselves to their shallow resources before they begin to live. They are not known, and yet no life is without its beauty. Who would know something of the core and limitations of this life should go the blue *Blues*.[111]

Like these writers of the 1920s, subsequent commentators have held to the idea that the blues reflect the secular side of the life of the poor black laborer, dealing especially with male-female relations but with a good deal more as well: work, raising children, hunger, politics, war, automobiles, various kinds of sexuality, dancing, good times—even trips into outer space—and most of the gaps in between.

There have been a number of attempts to categorize the subjects dealt with in blues lyrics. Stanley Edgar Hyman listed five pervasive themes in blues music. The categories, though occasionally abstract and vague, do hint at the type of breadth possible in blues lyrics:

Leaving/travel/journey
Dramatic self pity
Compensatory grandiose fantasy
Abuse and bawdry
Cynicism[112]

These categories, of course, offer much latitude for the blues singer, so the stereotypical limitations perceived in the blues as a genre have no basis in fact. The pertinent question is *how* it deals with these themes, or rather, what are the blues supposed to accomplish or represent in dealing with these themes? The question is complicated by the number of settings in which the blues exist. The earliest commentators on the blues, people like Odum and Johnson, the Lomaxes, Scarborough, and Sterling Brown, wrote of the degeneration of the folk blues once the blues craze precipitated recording of popular blues in the twenties. David Evans, in *Big Road Blues: Tradition and Creativity in the Folk Blues*, differentiates between folk and popular blues, finding that the folk blues "are generally found in the southern countryside and small towns and that their music and lyrics tend to be traditional" while the popular blues "are generally found in cities and larger towns" and "tend to be less traditional, more original, and more self-conscious, factors that make them better suited to mass media or stage presentation."[113] Folk blues are also likely to be sung either unaccompanied or accompanied by a banjo, guitar, fiddle, harmonica, or piano, or some makeshift instrument like a jug. Many bluesmen have reported that they fashioned a primitive string instrument by sliding a piece of metal or glass along a wire that was attached to a wall. Music can be made exuberantly and skillfully on a variety of everyday objects—what better example of blues in everyday life than in the performing of blues to the scraping of a washboard? Folk blues are local, sung for a limited audience of family and friends, and draw on local events, favorite motifs, and musical techniques that emphasize a common oral tradition and experience among the listeners. They are played by nonprofessional musicians for the enjoyment of others and themselves. Money is not the motivation; the blues songs are there in the environment, and they accomplish what needs to be accomplished. The singer may tease or signify, criticize or brag, or whip out a fast piece for dancing. The songs contribute to the life and health (good or bad) of the community itself by affirming the common experiences of community members. Of course, because there are different dominant motifs, musical influences, and performers in various areas, the category "folk blues" encompasses a variety of different blues styles; the blues of Mississippi, Texas, and Georgia, for example, are all distinctly different from each other, as recorded examples demonstrate.

The many different types of blues styles are often subcategorized by blues researchers of geographical location and historical time period. For example, based on the recordings of folk blues performers during that period and the recollections of contemporary blues performers, the early Texas blues style—from about the 1880s to the 1930s—differed from the Mississippi blues style of the same period. Blues researcher Sam Charters has attributed the difference in style to the difference in environments of Mississippi and Texas:

> There was little of the oppressive plantation life of the Mississippi delta to shape the Texas blues. . . . In some Mississippi counties the Negro population is more than eighty percent of the people living in the county. . . . At its highest point, just after the Civil War, the colored population of Texas was less than thirty percent of the state's still sparse growth. . . . This has not meant that life has been easier for colored men and women in Texas. . . . But it has meant a less isolated, less confined life than the brutal society of Mississippi.[114]

Charters felt that this environment in Texas produced less local competition; therefore, traditional elements like slave songs and work songs were not displaced but were carried over into the blues performed by early twentieth-century Texas blues performers like Henry Thomas, Willard "Ramblin'" Thomas, and Texas Alexander. As time went on, brilliant original artists, artists who were nonetheless thoroughly familiar with traditional elements of the blues, contributed to the development of a blues style less crowded and insistently rhythmic than the type of style generally identified with many Mississippi blues artists, though admittedly there is variety among Mississippi blues artists. Charley Patton of Ruleville, Mississippi, certainly differed from Skip James of Bentonia or Mississippi John Hurt of Avalon. In the late 1930s and early 1940s, the general style performed by artists like Jefferson (who was almost too idiosyncratic to be copied, with his single-string figures set off against a jagged bass beat) combined with the recorded styles of Lonnie Johnson, Scrapper Blackwell, and jazz guitarists like Django Reinhardt and Charlie Christian. At that point Texan T-Bone Walker, who had recorded in a rural Texas style in 1929, adapted this single-string tradition and molded it into an urban style performed in the company of a larger ensemble. This style was, in turn, an influence on the post–World War II school of Memphis guitarists, among them B. B. King. Therefore, a blues style is based on a particular time, location, environment, and the interaction of elements in that environment, on the rise of a dominant local figure and, after the blues were recorded, on the introduction, via the phonograph, of various elements not normally associated with that area. What should be apparent is that no large geographical area had absolutely and exclusively one style, though there might be common characteristics; the styles were often dynamic and in transitional phases, and were forged out of a complex interaction of elements. It is best to listen to recordings of various blues artists based on these different variables to be more aware of the wide variety present in the blues—a supposedly limited genre.

Because the folk blues are performed in such a community or party-like setting where the events of the moment may be reflected in the words of the oral tradition, they often seem disjointed, diffuse, even aimlessly wandering. Scarborough found this looseness to be characteristic of much "Negro" folk song; her conclusions about the minds that create the songs are racist:

> ... There is sometimes little connection between the stanzas. The colored mind is not essentially logical, and the folk-song shows considerable lack of coherence in thought. Unrelated ideas are likely to be brought together, as stanzas from one song or from several may be put in with what the singer starts with, if they chance to have approximately the same number of syllables to the line. Even that requirement is not held to. . . .[115]

W. Prescott Webb published an article in 1915 dealing with an eighty-stanza song by a black singer named Floyd Canada, but Webb, too, had trouble with the structure of this folk blues, which he named "The African Iliad":

> The song tells no connected story, any more than the ruins of Rome tell a story, or the grave of an American Indian, with its bones, arrowheads, beads, and pottery, tells a story; but a story may be drawn from it,—the story of the modern negro. . . . while the song has little narrative unity, it has a certain unity of subject matter. Pervading nearly every line is a spirit of restless wandering,—the *Wanderlust* and desire for a long freight on which to ride away from trouble.[116]

Unfortunately, Webb's comparison of the song with ruins and graves prevented him from considering the possibility that it had some kind of unity that was not immediately apparent, and Webb set about piecing together parts of the song in his article as seemed logical to him: he selected thirty-five stanzas and grouped them under the headings "The Wanderlust and the Long Freight Train," "Home and Mother," "Love," "Marriage and Domestic Troubles," and "Trial, Death at the Hands of the Law, and Final Will." Canada's prodigious effort certainly would have been important and fascinating had it been reported intact; however, Webb's need for an order he understood relegated over half of the stanzas to oblivion, and put those that were reported in an order that tells us more about Webb than Floyd Canada.

The seemingly unsystematic progression of blues stanzas has been explained in a number of ways. The singers have been said to have thrown together verses in a haphazard manner, to have sung the verses in a stream-of-consciousness style, and to have followed a loose, associative, nonlogical progression. Samuel Charters compared the latter to the jarring juxtapositions of modern poetry, a comparison that suggests not the bluesman's familiarity with Pound and Eliot but a similarity of artistic imagination:

> In many of the blues which use arrangements of verses to develop emotional attitudes there is often a power of suggestion in the juxtaposition of verses that seem to have little relationship. This poetic technique has been used by several modern poets as a conscious artistic device, and it gives to the blues singers the same technical control over their material. They use it most often to compress their idiom, to imply, with the juxtaposition of verses, an association of events that would take several verses to explain and would lose the dramatic effect in the explanation.[117]

David Evans seems to have agreed with Charters, feeling that contrast and ambiguity are central to the nature of folk blues, and the presence of seemingly contrasting lyrics is simply a reflection of the conflicting imperatives of the lives of African-Americans. They are part of "the truth," "a truth based in universal human experience or at least a kind of experience that was known to the singer and audience."[118]

It is likely that all of these explanations have had some validity at one time or another for various blues singers. Different versions of the same song might in fact result from the use of a different strategy based upon the performance context. For example, the entrance of a former girlfriend at some function might prompt the blues singer to "cut" the old partner by interjecting a stanza about fidelity that had previously not been in that particular song. Or, if the loss was a sad one for the singer, he might interject a plea for understanding. If such a person does not enter, then the song might take a different direction. Therefore, a folk-blues aesthetic must take into consideration not only the singer's characteristic employment of material but the context of performance as well. In Zora Neale Hurston's *Mules and Men,* for instance, the singing of a tribute to Ella Wall takes on a new—and antagonistic—significance in light of the hard feelings between Ella, Big Sweet, and Lucy, since the three were spoiling for a fight.[119] The song might be the same, but the reason for singing it and the way it is sung are different. Part of the beauty of the oral tradition is this plastic nature, the looseness, freedom, and adaptability which makes such "equipment for living," to use Kenneth Burke's phrase, infinitely useful because of its response to nuances. The changeable nature of folk blues, then, is not a liability, but a strength. Folk blues breathe with the people who sing them.

One of the problems with the differentiation between folk and popular blues is that the line of demarcation is not always distinct. The first recorded blues was *written* by black music-store owner Perry Bradford and sung by "Mamie Smith, contralto," initiating a rage for composed blues that were folk-influenced but performed in a more refined style that drew on vaudeville and musical hall forms and techniques. This kind of blues, often called, confusingly, "classic" blues but more appropriately termed "vaudeville blues," was launched by the mass media and, as such, aimed at economic profit. The blues were actually first launched for popular mass consumption in the print media, with Hart Wand's "Dallas Blues" and W. C. Handy's "The Memphis Blues" in 1912. Handy, a prolific composer of the blues, discussed the origins of his interest in the blues:

> It was my good fortune to live for two years in the state of Mississippi and to hear the crude singing of the Negro down there. I also had experiences in my hometown, Florence, Alabama, where I carried water for the men who worked in the furnaces, who always sang

when they worked. I heard bits of songs that they sang. Something like this:

Ay-Oh

Ay-Oh-Ooh

I wouldn't live in Cairo.[120]

Handy's description of his experience sounds very much as if it comes from an interested outsider, someone remote from the black "peasants" and laborers who helped create the blues, and, indeed, he did seek to "improve" and impose order on the folk blues he heard. After all, he had gone to Wilberforce University to study theology, sang his way to St. Louis with a quartet, and had been the head of a minstrel band that toured the U.S., Cuba, Canada, and Mexico, playing classical music as well, so his experiences took him far outside the folk environment. And though he had known poverty and hard times—indeed he claimed to have written "St. Louis Blues" at a time when his music brought him "to sleep on the levee of the Mississippi River, on the cobblestones, broke and hungry"[121]—he also possessed a sophistication that influenced him to work on "improving" the folk music that he told Dorothy Scarborough was so essential to his compositions:

> Each one of my blues is based on some old Negro song of the South, some folk-song that I heard from my mammy when I was a child. Something that sticks in my mind, that I hum to myself when I'm not thinking about it. Some old song that is part of the memories of my childhood and of my race. I can tell you the exact song I used as a basis for any one of my blues. Yes, the blues that are genuine are really folk-songs.[122]

But Handy looked at the folk songs as source material for the creation of something bigger and better, such as in Langston Hughes's words, "great ballets, great sonatas, and great new forms still unevolved."[123] In other words, Handy adopted the white folk-lorists' approach to folk song as a survival from the past *and* the commercial approach to folk songs as material to be mined and transmuted into something more respectable and grand. Handy also found folk songs commercially exploitable since he had his own publishing company and with Harry Pace founded the Black Swan record label. As Chris Albertson pointed out, the "better class," upwardly mobile, middle-class Northern blacks distinctly looked down on the blues, so an attempt was made to "raise up" the blues to their level, though, inevitably, they wouldn't accept the blues.[124]

Of course, one of the problems Handy had to surmount was how to musically transcribe elements of blues that are extremely difficult to notate because of the slides, slurs, growls, and other features involved. In addition, he had to place those features in a more sophisticated setting that wasn't too incongruous. Martin Williams has compared Handy's approach to that of ragtime, and discussed his characteristic attempts to transcribe the blues successfully:

> In some ways, Handy's approach was more formal even than ragtime's. It was also perhaps a bit arty. He took indigenous blues melodies, made them regular, harmonized them, and evolved a system in which the "bent" tones of the blues "scale" . . . could be imitated by putting the third and seventh notes of the scale in minor. He built several of these melodies into often splendidly organized multithematic compositions on the model of rags. Even in Handy's somewhat fussy approach, rhythmic variety, "breaks" (suspension of a stated pulse), and passion were captured.[125]

And it was Handy's kind of arranged blues that was most often sung by the vaudeville blues singers whose "comparatively wide range of material . . . and the debt they owed to the tent shows and the vaudeville stage"[126] revealed their commercial ambitions. The debt may have been musical or visual—elaborate costumes that were copies or burlesques of the outfits worn by opera prima donnas—but it was indeed a debt owed very dearly by many of the singers classed as vaudeville blues singers.

Of course, we shouldn't generalize about the oversophistication of vaudeville blues singers. In the rush to record female blues singers after Mamie Smith's success, singers of varying talent and sensibility were recorded. Ma Rainey, who traveled the tentshow circuit through the South from around 1904, doing blues, comedy skits, dance routines, and ballads, sang the blues so feelingly that, as Sterling Brown reported, "she wouldn't have to sing any words; she would moan, and the audience would moan with her. . . . Bessie was the greater blues singer, but Ma really *knew* these people; she was a person of the folk; she was very simple and direct."[127] And Bessie Smith, though she did sing some pop-blues material, sang with the low-down authority of someone who represented, as Carl Van Vechten wrote about a 1926 performance of hers, "the true folk-spirit of the race," who "sings Blues as they are understood and admired by the coloured masses."[128] These singers were not necessarily slick professionals remote from the roots of the blues. No matter how classically trained their accompanists were, no matter how many trumpets, clarinets, trombones, and drums they added to replace the primarily stringed accompaniment to the folk blues, no matter how many songs they sang from the pens of blues composers like Handy, Andy Razaf, and Clarence Williams, or how much they were hyped as "hot mamas" and vamps in the popular press, some of the vaudeville singers still composed their own blues and retained the spirit, if not the setting, of the folk blues. The "overnight converts from pop music who learned the form but lacked the feel of the blues idiom"[129] were there, but so were the real blues singers. And if vaudeville blues were sometimes contrivedly smutty, as some contemporary converts claimed about such songs as "I Want Plenty Grease in My Frying Pan" or "You Had Too Much," or sentimental in the melodramatic manner of pop songs, a good many were honest and lively as well.

Another problem with the idea of popular blues is that once the popularity of the vaudeville blues was established in the 1920s, record companies began casting about for other kinds of blues, eventually getting to folk-blues performers like Sylvester Weaver, who recorded guitar solos in 1923, and Barrelhouse Ed Andrews, Daddy Stovepipe, and Papa Charlie Jackson in 1924.[130] But did these singers cease being folk-blues artists now that they were being distributed by mass media? Did they quit serving the interest of a small community and change their songs to suit commercial interests? For one thing, the phonograph record could take all kinds of blues artists, and some of their spontaneous additions to songs, out of the environment from which they derived, creating a totally different context for the music.[131] For another, recordings fixed the text of the performance so a song would be heard as unchanging, its length determined by the amount of space on a phonograph record. Further, the monetary incentive that replaced other incentives of the folk-blues performer might prompt the recorded singer to capitulate to the suggestions of recording executives, or to be smothered by the unnatural atmosphere of the recording studio, or to search for more commercially viable material and change the nature of his compositions. David Evans's study of the seventy-five recordings made by Blind Lemon Jefferson between 1926 and 1929 suggests that Jefferson, touted by Paramount Records as "a real old-fashioned blues singer,"[132] increasingly recorded more original thematic blues as opposed to the traditional, nonthematic blues of his earliest recordings.[133] It seems, then, that the production of blues for popular mass consumption, even by folk-blues performers, had an effect on the nature of the blues song. The effect varied from performer to performer, from significant to minimal, but it was definitely there. And it was not always negative. A blues song lasting two-and-a-half to three minutes has little chance to wander or become repetitious, as a song recorded in the field might, so it could actually gain a focus and conciseness that could be lost in a longer composition. Of course, the folk-blues singer might have expected some material gain from his performance—free food for playing at dances and suppers, rewards for playing for the white folks, etc.— but he could not have garnered the fame and *potential* monetary remuneration available to the recorded blues singer, nor the artifact that would allow him to sit back and listen to himself perform. In turn, phonograph records of blues purchased by folk-blues performers or made popular by wide disbursement could affect the repertoires of folk-blues singers as well—songs by big-selling artists like Bessie Smith and Blind Lemon Jefferson could be found in the repertoires of many folk-blues artists. Thus, the distinction between folk blues and popular (semi-professional, professional, and vaudeville) blues can sometimes be unclear. What is needed is a relative scale: performers may be said to *tend* toward folk or popular blues, based on the various criteria discussed above, but the judgments are often subjective.

The effect of commercial imperatives on the aesthetic of the folk-blues singer, which interested people like Scarborough, Odum and Johnson, and Sterling Brown initially, was not explored meaningfully by interested scholars in the 1930s through the 1950s. Folklorists "were mainly content to document the blues through fieldwork, and investigations into folk and commercial interaction were either not made or not reported."[134] This disdain for examining commercial blues recordings was perhaps influenced by the purist bias of Newman I. White, who had a distaste for any blues song "tainted" by commercialism, an attitude clearly present in his 1928 publication of *American Negro Folk Songs*,[135] though Guy B. Johnson had also lamented in 1927 that "the production of blues today is like the production of Fords or of Ivory Soap."[136] White felt that the blues were dying out, and he did not lament the death. Not until the late 1950s would the interaction between the blues and commercialism be studied in any depth; however, it is not possible to discern absolutely what the specific effects of that interaction were (and are).

With the introduction of other urban blues styles, such as the so-called "Bluebird beat" fostered by Lester Melrose in Chicago, the range of popular blues became even broader.[137] The Northern city was a different environment from the Southern farm, and the definition of the blues was further expanded by the concerns of the record-buying public, the demands of city life, and the joints and taverns in which the blues performers worked, increasingly accompanied by bands with three pieces or more. But despite all the modernization, all the developments in technology, and the range of influences that have affected the blues, folk blues are still being played—and recorded—today, primarily in rural areas.

4

There are a number of conflicting ideas about what the blues and the blues performer are and what they represent. The conflict, of course, arises from each individual's attempt to impose order on the blues based on personal philosophies and aesthetics, and the problem is, once again, that the blues can, in fact, represent a number of different ideas and philosophies. They may be at moments pessimistic or optimistic, personal or communal, angry or happy, protesting or resigned, analytical or casually unselfconscious. The task of discovering what they are and represent will force generalities that must ignore or dismiss as insignificant exceptions to those generalities. Defining the blues is a subjective task at bottom, one that must be approached carefully and sensitively.

Odum and Johnson wrote in the 1920s that in the blues "the negro was . . . expressing his gloomy moods in song,"[138] and Johnson later added that the "original" blues "may be thought of as the wail of the despondent Negro lover."[139] It was a common assumption that the blues are autobiographical laments, expressions of sadness that, in the expression, make the singer feel better because he is letting out his emotions and, in addition, make the listeners feel better as well. B. B. King, discussing audience responses, feels that when he sings the blues, "the whole song may not be about the person, but there are certain things in it that they will recognize that have happened to them or some of their friends, and when this happen, then they feel it."[140] Memphis Slim, among many other interviewed blues singers, agreed that the blues give consolation: "When I have troubles, blues is the only thing that helps me."[141]

The difference in interpretation among the critics, though, is imbedded in the question of *why* the singer feels better and *why* the song has a cathartic effect on the audience. Odum and Johnson, in enumerating the characteristics of the blues, insist that there is a strong strain of self-pity in the blues:

> A third characteristic of the blues is the expression of self-pity. Often this is the outstanding feature of the song. There seems to be a tendency for the despondent or blue singer to use the technique of the martyr to draw from others a reaction of sympathy. Psychologically speaking, the technique consists of rationalization, by which process the singer not only excuses his shortcomings, but attracts the attention and sympathy of others—in imagination, at least—to his hard lot.[142]

Thus Odum and Johnson suggested that the blues singer feels a weakness or inferiority in himself, perhaps even has a slight contempt for himself, and, as a person separate from his audience, seeks to reintegrate himself into the group by evoking sympathy for his inadequacies. The bluesman becomes the pitiful and pessimistic underdog, seeking to mask his defeat in the half-truths of his songs. The blues are, for Odum and Johnson, the defensive attitude of a weak person. David Evans, though not nearly so critical of the blues singer, still feels that the blues "reflect an attitude that, despite all of one's efforts, things are not likely to get much better in the long run."[143] The blues are sung, for Evans, with the spirit of struggle but the expectation of defeat. The blues are pessimistic, laced lightly with optimism, in Odum and Johnson's case the optimism of a pitiful person, in Evans's, the optimism of an ultimately resigned person.

Most other critics are not as hard on the blues and the blues singer as Odum and Johnson. In fact, some see the struggle about which Evans writes as a victory in itself. Richard Wright discussed the spirit of the blues in the 1960 introduction to Paul Oliver's *Blues Fell This Morning:*

> Yet the most astonishing aspect of the blues is that, though replete with a sense of defeat and down-heartedness, they are not intrinsically pessimistic; their burden of woe and melancholy is dialectically redeemed through sheer force of sensuality, into an almost exultant affirmation of life, of love, of sex, of movement, of hope. No matter how repressive was the American environment, the negro never lost faith in or doubted his deeply endemic capacity to live.[144]

For Wright, the vitality of the blues affirms African-American life and beauty and the belief in the strength of the individual and the group to not only survive, but thrive. The art of blues singing is, thus, an exaltation of separateness and an expression of pride. Blues singer Johnny Shines spoke of his pride in the blues and himself in an interview with Mark Humphrey:

> (Everybody thinks of) bluesmen as bein' stupid, illiterate, not able to think for himself, that's why he's singing these dirty, low-down songs. They don't realize that THEY'RE the one that's STUPID because they been taught that these songs was dirty, they was filthy, they was no good. . . . I tell you what, by the white man's own method he's degraded his own self because he made himself the weaker one. He said, "If there's one drop of your blood in my veins, then I am what you are." But what about all of this one-third of it makes him what I am, what about the two-thirds that he have? It didn't make him what he is. So that tells me that I'm three times as strong as him. . . . I'm the one wearin' the crown, even though it don't show.[145]

Bessie Smith expressed pride in her singing and her rejection of pretentious white society as well. Her response to actress Fania Marinoff Van Vechten's insistence on a kiss before Bessie left Van

Vechten's opulent party was, "Get the fuck away from me. . . . I ain't never heard of such shit,"[146] an act of defiance perhaps fueled by alcohol, but not initiated by it. Bessie did not like pretension, nor did she patronize whites about their attempts to sing the blues. She told Langston Hughes, "The trouble with white folks singing blues is that they can't get low down enough,"[147] a sentiment echoed by many a black blues artist who exhibited pride and expressed the superiority of the black singer in the blues field. As with Shines, here "low down" means high above.

Janheinz Jahn, too, saw the blues not as an expression of pain and unhappiness but akin to the African concept of the assertion of a life force: "The blues are sung not because one finds oneself in a particular mood but because one wants to put oneself into a certain mood. The song is the Nommo which does not reflect but creates the mood. And this mood is melancholy only from the romantic point of view current since the time of the abolitionists."[148] Thus, the blues are, for Jahn, an *action* and not a reaction. The problem with Jahn's assertion is that if the blues are based in some element of African-American experience, then they are at some point a reaction. The question of primary emphasis is important here. Are they mainly reaction or action? The fact that a blues singer may continue to sing a particular blues long after the situation that spawned it has been resolved suggests that action (and, probably, the need for a broad repertoire to perform) is the primary motivation. The assertion of creativity and power outlasts the fleeting mundane event. Kimberly Benston underscored this point in viewing the blues singer as a tragic figure who "understands his dilemma and is articulate about it," and who "takes action in his own way, defies destiny every time he sings the blues."[149] Thus the assertiveness of the blues demonstrates, as Larry Neal believes, that the blues "celebrate life and the ability of man to control and shape his destiny."[150] It is not an economic or political control over destiny, but a control over personal outlook and expression that defies the economic and political. Ralph Ellison would disagree with this assessment, asserting that though the blues do offer a means of transcending life's agonies, they "provide no solution, offer no scapegoat but the self."[151] They are, as part of African-American folklore, a way of announcing "the Negro's willingness to trust his own experience,"[152] offering hope but not control.

One way for someone to control and shape his own destiny is to assert both personal and community pride and values. Most commentators have seen the blues as a reflection of at least a segment of the African-American population—the values of the secular, lower-class African-American—though some, like Larry Neal, have seen the blues singer not as "a sobbing, alienated artist," but "the voice of the community, its historian, and one of the shapers of its morality."[153] Others, like A. X. Nicholas, feel that the blues singer "articulates the for-real emotions and experiences of the world-wide community of black and oppressed peoples (read 'majority')...."[154] Beyond that, Nicholas feels that "the blues will be the shoulders upon which the new culture," a communist society in which the people are in command of the art, will stand.[155] Neal and Nicholas, though, ignore the fact that the blues have been and are openly rejected by many members of the African-American middle and upper classes and religious community, and are, in fact, unknown to many oppressed peoples around the world, though some of these might be familiar with the blues through phonograph recordings. For Nicholas, apparently, those who reject the blues are not experiencing "for-real emotions" but are self-alienated, which, of course, is not necessarily true. When Houston A. Baker says that the blues offer "a phylogenetic recapitulation . . . of species experience,"[156] he is right in that the blues reflect African-American experience, but wrong in suggesting that they reflect the experiences and attitudes of *all* African-Americans.

The question of the blues singer's relationship to his community (either local or national African-Americans) raises the question of the singer's relationship to his song as well. Is the blues singer expressing his own troubles, those of his community, or some combination of the two? Rod Gruver challenged the idea of blues as autobiographical expression, suggesting that the blues are dramatic monologues; Jeff Titon countered that autobiography itself can be imaginative literature as well, so the distinction is not so clear; Dennis Jarrett felt that there is a fictional self (the bluesman) separate from the singer-composer who has a "generic personality," a traditional person who embodies the concerns of his audience.[157] Perhaps Titon and Jarrett are correct in their belief that there are imaginative elements to the role of the bluesman. But "the bluesman," as opposed to the songwriter, is not a *fictional* self; he is a social self as opposed to a private self. The social self is outwardly directed, intent on communicating and entertaining and taking his place among the members of his community/audience, and so he puts on a face to greet those he meets. He is The Bluesman, a person from whom certain attitudes and ideas are expected, a position he must live up to. Blues singer-pianist Pigmeat Jarrett, for example, is very quiet in his private life, but he becomes a shouting, signifying bluesman when he sits down to play. And the blues singer may be singing about someone else's problems in the first person. Says B. B. King, "I've seen many people hurt, homes broken, people killed, people talked about, so today I sing about it."[158] So the singer may be singing about something that happened to himself or someone else he knows, or he may even be making up events that did not happen. S. I. Hayakawa may feel that the blues are realistic, exhibiting "a willingness often absent in popular songs, to acknowledge the facts of life,"[159] but there is a great deal of fantasy in blues lyrics as well. None of these approaches necessitates the creation of another self; in fact, there is difficulty in identifying *which* is the *fictional* self and which is the *real* self. It may be more appropriate to speak of *private* and *social* selves.

There is also a question whether the singer or the song expresses anger or protest at societal conditions for African-Americans. In James Baldwin's *Blues For Mister Charlie,* "white liberal" Parnell's surprised response to the rage and hatred in Meridian's voice prompts Meridian to respond: "You've heard it before. You just never recognized it before. You've heard it in all those blues and spirituals and gospel songs you claim to love so much."[160] Leroi Jones used the voice of Clay in *Dutchman* to suggest the disdain and hatred present in the music of Bessie Smith: ". . . Old baldheaded four-eyed ofays popping their fingers . . . and don't know yet what they're doing. They say 'I love Bessie Smith.' And don't even understand that Bessie Smith is saying 'Kiss my ass, kiss my black unruly ass. . . .' If Bessie Smith had killed some white people she wouldn't have needed that music."[161] Messages were certainly there, even if whites didn't recognize them. Big Bill Broonzy discussed the blues as a masking of feelings of social protest:

I've known guys that wanted to cuss out the boss and he was afraid
to go up in his face and tell him what he wanted to tell him, and I've
heard them sing those things—sing words, you know, back to the
boss, just behind the wagon, hooking up to the horses or something
or another. Or the mules or something. And then he'd go to work
and go to singing and say things to the horse. You know, horse, make
like the mule stepped on his foot. Say "Get off my foot, goddamn it,"
or something like that you know, and he meant he was talking to the
boss.[162]

Memphis Slim added, "Yeah, blues is kind of a revenge." It seems,
then, that black song, including the blues, can express anger and
encoded protest. Scarborough suggested in 1925 that black folk
song contained encoded protest, writing that "politicians and
statesmen and students of political economy who discuss the Negro problems in perplexed, authoritative fashion, would do well to
study the folk-music of the colored race as expressing the feelings
and desires, not revealed in direct message to the white."[163]

In *The Poetry of the Blues*, Sam Charters found that protest is
not prevalent in the blues: "The blues does not try to express the
separateness of Negro life in America. Protest is only a small thread
in the blues."[164] Charters felt that the blues depicts day-to-day life
without overtly protesting against the prejudice and oppression of
the socioeconomic system as a whole. However, as we have already
said, the blues can be seen as the embodiment or dramatization of
the separateness of Negro life in America. In a general sense, social
protest can be made by a black person either complaining about
social status, situation, life-style, and social institutions, or asserting his ability to overcome inequities and extend his power.

Those in power certainly seem to perceive complaints as threats,
and therefore a form of protest. The blues contain examples of
direct protest against the white man and the system, whether white
critics wish to acknowledge them or not.[165] Some early scholars
actually accused folklorist Lawrence Gellert of falsifying his material because of the high incidence of protest material he collected.
The problem was simply that the relationship between white collector and black subject often prevented the black subject from
singing the protest songs. When John A. Lomax prodded Blind
Willie McTell for songs about hard times for blacks, a very uncom-
fortable McTell said he didn't know of any and that poor whites

had it as hard as blacks in the South.[166] Of course, the *blues* songs that Gellert collected do not have the same amount of social protest as the other types of songs. Titon suggested that this protest is missing because the recordings of the vaudeville blues singers and blues composers helped fix the themes of blues songs, and that "the formulaic process of blues composition makes it difficult to ascribe to the singer the ability to censor lyrics at will,"[167] so the presence of the black blues singer in the white-owned-and-run studio had little effect on the censorship of lyrics. However, it seems that a formulaic process of blues composition might indeed make it very easy for the blues singer to substitute, and thus censor himself, though the substitution may be an encoding that expresses the same idea. Titon also cited an interview with Lazy Bill Lucas during which Lucas said that "he had never known of a racial protest code in blues songs, for blues was about the troubles men and women have getting along. But he affirmed overt and encoded protest in conversation, stories, sayings and folksongs other than blues."[168] Paul Oliver feels that these blues of lost love are "a vehicle for protest . . . a sublimation of frustrated desires" directing aggression against "a mythical common enemy, the 'cheater.' "[169] However, a bluesman like Lucas seems to have no *conscious* knowledge of such a code or any belief that it exists, when confronted with such an idea. Additionally, a sublimation of racial hostility "performs a negative role in the black community, feeding fantasies and diverting energy into forms (including art) which allow racial injustice to continue."[170] One possible answer is that the blues protest in a positive way, by asserting black pride and awareness and by fostering both a black tradition and creativity in an environment that seeks to obliterate such positive feelings and actions. Surrealist Franklin Rosemont saw blues as "a desperate search for language: not for the language stolen from their ancestors, or for the language to which they are still not allowed full access, but for a new, exalted and *secret* language which takes shape dreamily in primordial gestures and cries."[171] This creative expression is itself a revolt against authority and the conventional and makes the black blues singer automatically a representative of protest and revolt by virtue of his existing and performing. And, theoretically, the audience understands this idea, either consciously or unconsciously. Thus, the blues and the blues singer embody protest and revolution as they embody the separateness of blacks in the U.S. Michael Haralambos, in *Right On: From Blues to Soul in Black America,* saw the blues as coming into being in response to the Jim Crow system that passively accepted and therefore reinforced that system, but that thesis is based on a few examples of blues lyrics and on analysis that does not consider the points made above.[172] If the blues began to be displaced by soul music in the early 1960s, it was not a result of its lack of relevance to blacks, but because of the record industry's emphasis on the teenage listener as opposed to the adult black.

It is obvious that there are a variety of attitudes toward the blues and the blues performer, and that a simple, comprehensive approach that explains what the blues are and do cannot be applied to all blues. However, it is necessary to set Langston Hughes's ideas about the blues against the attitudes expressed by others in order to establish a clearer picture of how he felt about the blues. We must examine his claims for them, the limitations he imposed on them, and the ways he used them in his poetry.

5

From his letters, essays, autobiographies, and recordings, it is easy to see that Langston Hughes had exposure to various kinds of blues, especially in the years leading up to the publication of his first two volumes of poetry. Because the blues he heard in his earliest years influenced Hughes to write the kind of blues poems that he did, a survey of his experiences with blues and blues performers will make it easier to establish Hughes's primary interests and concerns, giving us insight into the ideas he expressed about blues in his prose and the effects of his understanding of the blues tradition on his poetry.

Hughes apparently heard the blues for the first time in Kansas City, sixty miles east of his home with his grandmother, Mary Langston, in Lawrence, Kansas, during one of the two summers he spent with his mother before he was twelve years old.[173] In "Jazz as Communication," published in the *Langston Hughes Reader,* Hughes stated that "it was fifty years ago, the first time I heard the Blues on Independence Avenue in Kansas City,"[174] suggesting that Hughes was somewhere around six years old at the time of his first exposure to the blues. In 1964 Hughes wrote that the scene was "on a Charlotte Street corner" near his uncle's barbershop.[175] This discrepancy in street location could, of course, be accounted for by the fact that Hughes was writing about an event years after the fact, but it could also be significant that Hughes said that he had first heard the blues on Independence Avenue, since the blues in fact helped free him from more consciously "literary" verse and moved him toward vernacular expression. Speaking in 1959, Hughes discussed the impact of those early blues:

> At any rate, when I was a kid in Kansas City very often I used to hear the blues. There were blind guitar players who would sing the blues on street corners. There were people plunking the blues on beat up old pianos. That was of course before the days of the jukebox and the radio. In those days, almost everybody who could afford to have a piano had one, and played them in their homes. And so you heard a lot of music. Well, at any rate, I was very much attracted to the blues. I remember even now some of the blues verses that I used to hear as a child in Kansas City. And so I, in my early beginnings at poetry writing, tried to weave the blues into my poetry.[176]

Hughes recalled these as the days of live blues, of blues on the street corners and in the homes, of blues as part of the landscape and environment. In fact, Hughes remembered a specific performer and song:

> . . . I remember a blind guitar player moaning to the long eerie sliding notes of his guitar.
>
> > I'm goin' down to de river,
> > Take my rockin' chair,
> > Yes, down to de river,
> > Rock in my rockin' chair,
> > If de blues overcome me
> > I'm gonna rock on away from here.[177]

These were the traditional folk-blues singers and songs discussed earlier which formed a backdrop for his later poetry. In fact, in *The Big Sea* Hughes reported that his "The Weary Blues," which won him his first poetry prize, "included the first blues verse [he'd] ever heard way back in Lawrence, Kansas, when [he] was a kid."[178] The contradiction in location is probably not important: it was the same general area of the country, and whether he heard the blues first in Lawrence or in Kansas City, it is most important that he heard them.

The blues verse in "The Weary Blues:"

> I got de weary blues
> And I can't be satisfied.
> Got de weary blues
> And can't be satisfied.
> I ain't happy no mo'
> And I wish that I had died.[179]

is very close to the "Texas Worried Blues" recorded by songster Henry Thomas in 1928:

> The worried blues
> God, I'm feelin' bad.
> I've got the worried blues
> God, I'm feelin' bad.
> I've got the worried blues
> God, I'm feelin' bad.[180]

The crude blues of an older man like Thomas, who was fifty-three when he first recorded in 1927, were probably the kind Hughes heard in his Kansas childhood. It is important to place that tradition in order to understand the presence of the blues in that area and the way it sounded. Lawrence is in northeast Kansas on the Kansas River, approximately sixty miles west of Kansas City, now connected to Oklahoma, Missouri, Kansas, and Texas by U.S. 69 and I70 and the Santa Fe, Rock Island, and Missouri-Kansas-Texas railways. Indeed, Henry Thomas, at a 1929 recording session, recounted his experiences hopping the Texas and Pacific and "Katy" (MKT) lines in his "Railroading Some," going from Texas through Kansas City and on to Chicago, a route that had been open to passengers, migrants, and hoboes for years.[181] The blues were not new to the area: it was in a small Missouri town in 1902 (the date of Hughes's birth) that blues singer Gertrude "Ma" Rainey reportedly first heard blues music,[182] and Kansas City blues shouter Big Joe Turner, roughly a contemporary of Hughes, recalled leading around blues singers on the streets in the late teens and early twenties, and hearing the crude banjos, gas pipes, and water jugs that were used as instruments.[183]

These early blues, often sung unaccompanied, or accompanied by a guitar, piano, or makeshift instruments, were in Kansas City set in a milieu of varied musical idioms—ragtime, jazz, orchestral music—which produced the "loose, lithe, resilient orchestral jazz style to which the city gives its name."[184] This orchestral type of blues emerged in the teens and flowered in the era of 1925 to 1942, when larger ensembles touring the Southwest played blues in arranged form.[185] Thus, during his childhood and in his visits back home, Hughes heard not only the loosely arranged folk blues but, most likely, these other idioms and various combinations of a more arranged and sophisticated nature. Ross Russell discussed the nature of the Kansas City style:

> Kansas City style began as a grass-roots movement and retained its earthy, proletarian character to the end. In the beginning it was plain, rather stiff and crude, but aggressively indigenous, and colloquial. It drew from two main sources, folksong and ragtime. From folksong—with its grab bag of country dances, field hollers, ballads and work songs—and from the blues—both the old country blues and the newer urban blues Kansas City extracted much of its material. In its early stages Kansas City jazz might have been described as a folksy, raggy, blues-saturated dance music.[186]

What ultimately emerged in 1925–42 was the ensemble Kansas City blues style, "big city blues, but with a country, earthy feeling,"[187] that helped catapult to success Big Joe Turner, Pete Johnson, Jay McShann, Mary Lou Williams, and Count Basie, among others.

In fact, Hughes claimed that jazz led him to explore the roots of jazz, the blues: "I sort of went backwards from an interest in jazz to an interest in the folk roots of jazz. I went backwards from jazz to the blues—Blues really are the basis of jazz—and to the spirituals, the great Negro folk songs of the "saved" period. And, having tried to write poems in the syncopated rhythms of jazz, I then began to try to write poems in the folk idiom of the blues and the spirituals."[188]

Thus, although Hughes may have heard the blues very early on, it was an interest in jazz that spurred him to consciously attempt to understand what they were and how he could use them in his own poetry. This emphasis is particularly important, because it suggests that Hughes approached the folk blues through city jazz and the attempts of jazz musicians to develop the folk material in their own manner and turn it into something more refined, without losing the folk spirit.

Hughes went to Chicago in 1918, following his sophomore year in Central High School, "to join his mother, who, again separated from his stepfather, was now working as a cook for a lady who owned an exclusive millinery shop in the Loop."[189] Here again, he came upon the blues: "And in Chicago in my teens, all up and down State Street there were blues, indoors and out, at the Grand and the old Monogram theaters where Ma Rainey sang, in the night clubs, in the dance halls, on phonographs."[190] Georgia Tom Dorsey, who went to Chicago from Georgia in 1916, met people like Jimmy Blythe, a smooth pianist who flirted with boogie-woogie in his 1924 recordings. Upon his arrival in Chicago, Dorsey served as an accompanist for a number of singers at Paramount Records, as well as for Erskine Tate and Dave Peyton, orchestra leader at the Grand Theatre. Dorsey stated that there "wasn't much the blues then,"[191] that ragtime was big, but he responded affirmatively to a question about hearing street musicians there: "I knew a couple of blind fellows were pretty good, guitar players on the street. But I can't remember what they did or what they played. And a fellow there called himself Casey Jones, he was there when I came here. He had some chickens. He rode around on a little cart, and he would play the accordion, or it wasn't a guitar—he played something, and these chickens would dance for him."[192] Again it seems that there was a mixture of folk blues and a more sophisticated blues, but Hughes recalled specifically only Ma Rainey, the vaudeville blues singer whose diamonds, elaborate clothes, and sets never obscured her roots in the folk blues. Dorsey, who accompanied Rainey, said she got to Chicago around 1922—later than the date Hughes gave—and she made her first recordings in December 1923, shortly before appearing at the Grand in 1924.[193]

In 1921 Hughes was in New York and took a week to get acquainted with Harlem before his classes began at Columbia. Between then and 1923 when he sailed for Africa, he had numerous opportunities to sample Harlem musical life: "It was Harlem's Golden Era, that of the twenties. I was nineteen when I first came up out of the Lenox Avenue subway one bright September afternoon and looked around in the happy sunlight to see if I saw Duke Ellington on the corner of 135th Street or Bessie Smith passing by, or Bojangles Bill Robinson in front of the Lincoln Theatre, or maybe Paul Robeson or Bert Williams walking down the avenue."[194] Hughes's memory is at least partially faulty again, since Ellington didn't come up to Harlem from Washington, D.C., until 1923,[195] and Bessie Smith, though touring for some time, was not associated with Harlem or New York City.[196] Hughes was correct, though, when he described the preponderance of pianists he encountered and the way they played: ". . . Harlem in the twenties with J. P. and J. C. Johnson and Fats and Willie the Lion and Nappy playing piano—with the Blues running all up and down the keyboard through the ragtime and the jazz."[197] These were indeed *not* blues players but ragtime and jazz players like stride piano king James P. Johnson, his rival, Willie "The Lion" Smith, and their pupil Fats Waller.[198] The music was not folk blues but a hot hybrid of blues, ragtime, and cosmopolitan fever that was making the city jump to a different tune. Harlem was to become Hughes's city, and its music a big influence on him, but though it later got a greater injection of purer blues, it was not a place where folk blues were the predominant music.

In 1923 Hughes shipped out for Africa on the SS *Malone*, but the blues were on board with him, returning to the land that helped shape them. Carl Van Vechten published in 1925 a portion of a Hughes letter that discussed a shipmate:

Did you ever hear this verse of the blues?
I went to the gipsy's to get mah fortune tol'.
I went to the gipsy's to get mah fortune tol'.
Gipsy done tol' me Goddam yore unhard-lucky soul.

I first heard it from George, a Kentucky colored boy who shipped out to Africa with me—a real vagabond if there ever was one. He came on board five minutes before sailing with no clothes—nothing except the shirt and pants he had on and a pair of silk socks carefully wrapped up in his shirt pocket. He didn't even know where the ship was going. He used to make up his own Blues—verses as absurd as Krazy Kat and as funny. But sometimes when he had to do more work than he thought necessary for a happy living, or, when broke, he couldn't make the damsels of the West Coast believe love was worth more than money, he used to sing about the gipsy who couldn't find words strong enough to tell about the troubles in his hard-luck soul.[199]

In *The Big Sea* Hughes wrote that he and George became good friends, and George's stories, jokes, dancing, and singing must have provided a good transition from the life that Hughes was attempting to leave behind when he threw all of the books that he had had at Columbia over the rail of the SS *Malone*. If Hughes was a bit reserved and apprehensive about his trip, the wandering, free-spirited, uninhibited George was certainly not. At Horta, Hughes and George went ashore and consumed a bottle of cognac:

> George smashed the cognac bottle against the wall of a blue house and said: "I wants to holler."
>
> "George, don't you holler right here on the main street," I cautioned.
>
> George said: "This town's too small to holler in, but I got to holler anyhow." And he let out a tremendous "Yee-hoo-ooo!" that sent children rushing to their mothers' arms and women scurrying into doorways.[200]

This was the kind of naturalness, spontaneity, and lack of inhibition Hughes identified in the "low-down folks." It seems significant that George launched into his exuberant yell by "christening" a *blue* house, symbolizing the important place the blues had in his emotions, both happy and sad (as Hughes reported in the letter to Van Vechten). His blues were not just doleful, but absurd and lively as well. He sang blues for the moment as he lived for the moment, providing Hughes with an important, close glimpse of the blues singer and his blues. George was a person sloughing off inhibitions, just as Hughes tried to leave a part of his former life behind by tossing his books overboard.

In 1924 Hughes found himself working in a nightclub called Le Grand Duc, in Paris, having returned to New York from Africa and shipped out again. Interest in American jazz in Europe began shortly after World War I, spurred by visits by the Original Dixieland Jazz Band and Will Marion Cook's Southern Syncopated Orchestra to London in 1919,[201] and by a number of African-American musicians. They found the atmosphere in Europe better than that which they encountered at home, and settled there to play at places like Le Grand Duc, sometimes alongside European jazz players. Hughes described a jam session at Le Grand Duc, where Palmer Jones presided. Jones "knew a great many old blues and folk-songs like 'Frankie and Johnny' and 'Henrico'" and "would occasionally sing one or two of those songs for the guests, inserting off-color lyrics if the crowd was that kind of crowd."[202] Two of the guests, Cricket Smith and Frank Withers, had recorded together with Mitchell's Jazz Kings in 1922, and Buddy Gilmore had recorded as well.[203] But it was in these after-hours jam sessions that they really got down to the blues:

> Blues in the rue Pigalle. Black and laughing, heart-breaking blues in the Paris dawn, pounding like a pulse-beat, moving like the Mississippi!
>
> > Lawd, I looked up and saw a spider,
> > Goin' up de wall.
> > I said where you going, Mister Spider?
> > I'm goin' to get my ashes hauled!
>
> Through the mist of smoke and champagne, you laughed at the loneliness of a tiny little spider, going up a great big wall to get his ashes hauled. And the blues went on.
>
> > I did more for my good gal
> > Than de good Lawd ever done.
> > Did more for my good gal
> > Than de good Lawd ever done.
> > I bought her some hair—
> > Cause de Lawd ain't give her none.
>
> Play it, Mister Palmer Jones! Lawd! Lawd! Lawd! Play it, Buddy Gilmore! What you doin' to them drums? Man, you gonna bust your diamond studs in a minute!
>
> > Is you ever seen a
> > One-eyed woman cry?
> > I say, is you ever seen a
> > One-eyed woman cry?
> > Jack, she can cry so good
> > Just out of that one old eye.[204]

Hughes was literally a poor boy a long way from home. The blues expressed his loneliness, his desire to get in touch with his people and himself again, his hope, determination, and pride in people who accomplish what they can as well as they can despite limitations, even if it is *crying*. These were jazz musicians, but they were digging deep into their blues roots to express the blues that stayed with them wherever they went. These were memories of something they had all felt before, perhaps were still feeling, even if they were a long way from home. Hughes wrote that after he heard the Palmer Jones band playing, he "began to put the syncopated rhythms of jazz" into his poetry.[205]

When Hughes went back to Washington later that same year, he exulted in the unpretentious blacks along Seventh Street, laborers with no pedigrees who "played the blues, ate watermelon, barbecue, and fish sandwiches, shot pool, told tall tales, looked at the dome of the Capitol and laughed out loud."[206] Interestingly, Hughes followed this description immediately with:

> I listened to their blues:
>   Did you ever dream lucky—
>   Wake up cold in hand?[207]

This suggests that there is an implicit political protest in such a lyric, which refers to male-female relationships, and that the exuberance of these people should not be mistaken for innocence or ignorance. These people inspired Hughes to try to write poems like their songs: ". . . gay songs, because you had to be gay or die; sad songs, because you couldn't help being sad sometimes. But gay or sad, you kept on living and you kept on going. Their songs, those of South Street—had the pulse beat of the people who keep on going."[208] When Alain Locke arranged a poetry reading by Hughes before the Playwriter's Circle in 1927 in Washington, a blues pianist accompanied him, bringing Hughes the artist and blues music one step closer together, even though Hughes felt that the piano player was "too polished." He suggested to his Knopf editor that they ought to get "a regular Lenox Avenue blues boy" to accompany him at his reading in New York.[209] Poetry and performance were fast approaching one another, fueled by Hughes's observations of blues and what they meant in their appropriate—oral, performed—context. Most of the poems that Hughes wrote directly under the influence of this Washington environment did not appear in print until the publication of *Fine Clothes to the Jew* in 1927.

Shortly after this volume appeared, and after he read at Fisk, Hughes joined Zora Neale Hurston in New Orleans on her journey back to New York, and the two collected black folklore on the way. In New Orleans, Hughes lived on Rampart Street among many transients who enjoyed fish fries and drank home brew, and he recalled listening to Blind Lemon Jefferson, Lonnie Johnson, and Ma Rainey on the Victrola and to an occasional "wild" guitar player who came in off the street to perform for drinks. The area was an important source of material for Hughes: "In Baton Rouge and New Orleans I heard of the blues verses I used later in my short stories and my novel."[210] Any poor black neighborhood might include blues performers, but New Orleans, because of field recordings made by Okeh in 1924 and 1925, Columbia during 1926–28, Victor in 1927, and Vocalion in 1928,[211] might have been expected to have more than its share of aspiring recording artists. It would be difficult to speculate who Hughes might have heard, but judging from the material used in his prose, he must have heard some excellent blues. He also heard blues on his way back to New York via Tuskegee, where he and Hurston lectured on writing, and Macon, Georgia, where he met Bessie Smith.[212] These are the early scenes of Hughes's encounters with the blues, and they are the most important in terms of his blues poetry. Of course, Hughes continued to listen to the blues after this time, but he had formulated his ideas about the blues in the 1910s and 1920s.

It should be apparent from this discussion of Hughes's exposure to the blues up through the year he published his second volume of poetry, one that was criticized for its "low-life" content, that a consideration of the influence of the blues on Hughes's poetry must take into account the various *types* of blues he encountered. He had heard the blues in the country and in the city, in the South and in the North, in America and abroad, on the street, in house dives and theaters. He had heard folk blues, vaudeville blues, and recorded blues, and blues influenced by jazz, ragtime, and the Broadway stage. Generally, it seems as if Hughes was looking at the folk-blues singers in their environment, as a resource, as part of a folk past, or as part of a common past being lost to upwardly mobile blacks who were being trained away from their roots. Hughes seems to have looked at the blues *with* the jazz, ragtime, and vaudeville-influenced blues performers, perhaps because they were all using the blues for something else—to create either a different kind of music or, as in Hughes's case, poetry. Hughes discussed just this point in 1926 in his famous article "The Negro Artist and the Racial Mountain": "Our folk music, having achieved world-wide fame, offers itself to the genius of the great individual American composer who is to come."[213] But for Hughes, the poet was even a bit more of an outsider. In a letter to Mary Owings Miller published in *Contemporary Poetry* in 1943, he outlined briefly the poet's purpose: "I feel, in a sense, that the function of the poet is to interpret not only his own people to the rest of the world but to themselves."[214] This means that the poet must get both inside *and* outside of his people—a difficult task since once you begin thinking from a distance, the thought processes have changed. Hughes indicated his confusion about his position as an artist when he mused about whether he was a "folk-person" or not. It is likely that his doubts centered around his looking at the folk as subjects and history as well as part of his community. Nonetheless, his exposure to various types of blues affected the way he defined the blues and discussed the people he considered to be the best blues singers; it affected his poetry and fiction as well.

Although Hughes wrote frequently about the blues over his entire career, it was not as a professional folklorist or critic but as a casual essayist or commentator, so his discussions of the blues are not comprehensive, systematic explorations of the varied aspects of the blues. Of course, the blues have garnered much more recognition and close analysis since the mid-1950s, thirty years after Hughes's initial commentaries, and it is not fair to expect Hughes to have anticipated extensively the more recent critical developments among professional folklorists, musicologists, anthropologists, critics, and aficionados who have some historical distance from and perspective on the blues of the twenties and thirties. Hughes was for the most part consistent in the views on the blues he expressed in his non-fiction commentary from the 1920s to the 1960s, though some of the books he edited in collaboration with others may have been affected by the input of the collaborators. However, it is important to place Hughes's ideas on the blues in the context of the other views already surveyed to get a sense of his strengths, limitations, and perspective, and to set the backdrop for the analysis of his poems.

In a letter to Van Vechten published in *Vanity Fair* in 1925, Hughes described the blues as incredibly melancholy songs:

> The Blues always impressed me as being very sad, sadder even than the Spirituals, because their sadness is not softened with tears, but hardened with laughter, the absurd, incongruous laughter of a sadness without even a god to appeal to. In "The Gulf Coast Blues" one can feel the cold northern snows, the memory of the melancholy mists of the Louisiana lowlands, the shack that is home, the worthless lovers with hands full o' gimme, mouths full o' much oblige, the eternal unsatisfied longings.[215]

Hughes echoed these sentiments in his review of W. C. Handy's *Blues: An Anthology* in *Opportunity* in 1926:

> The folk blues are pictures of the life from which they come, the life of the levees, of the back alleys of dissolute streets, the red light districts and the cabarets of those with not even a God to look to. They are a long ways removed from the expectancy and faith of the spirituals. Their hopeless weariness mixed with an absurdly incongruous laughter makes them the most interesting folk songs I have heard. Blues are sad songs sung to the most despondent rhythm in the world. . . .[216]

In these instances, Hughes saw the blues as sad songs that were even sadder because of the bitter laughter they sometimes evoked. He did not describe the songs as possibly therapeutic in any way for the singer or audience, nor did he depict the laughter as a celebration of blackness or common African-American experience; and he did not refer to any good-time blues that eschewed despondency for celebration of something like the return of a loved one. Later, in 1966, Hughes wrote in *The Book of Negro Humor* that "there is always something in the blues that makes people laugh, or at least smile,"[217] but Hughes didn't explicitly identify there what that *something* is. He did use the blues lyric "I'm laughin' to keep from cryin'" as an epigraph, and that seems to be related to "the will to live" in the songs that come out of "black, beaten, but unbeatable throats."[218] Of course, Hughes had written of the resistance of "the low-down folks" to American standardization in

"The Negro Artist and the Racial Mountain," praising them for their individuality and willingness to let black artists express themselves as they wished. The songs seemed to reflect their satisfaction with their identities and their unwillingness to capitulate culturally. So, though the blues were sad songs, they were the sad songs of proud and wise people, and the mixture of laughter and tears demonstrated their vivacity, wisdom, and determination. However, this idea was implicit in Hughes's earliest discussions of the blues. Later he stated the idea explicitly.

In fact, Hughes felt that black music put people in touch with themselves and the universe, that it united the internal and external. He used a blues lyric to exemplify his point, suggesting that the blues moved to a kind of natural rhythm and life-pulse, that they were a giver of strength:

> Like the waves of the sea coming one after another, always one after another, like the earth moving around the sun, night, day-night, day-night, day-forever, so is the undertow of black music with its rhythm that never betrays you, its strength like the beat of the human heart, its humor and its rooted power.
>
> > I'm goin' down to de railroad, baby,
> > Lay ma head on de track.
> > I'm goin' down to de railroad, babe,
> > Lay ma head on de track—
> > But if I see de train a-comin',
> > I'm gonna jerk it back.[219]

Thus the alternating despair and hope of the blues, the tears and laughter, are like the eternal rolling of the waves under the alternating light and darkness of time, and the indomitable spirit of the human heart beats through it all, accepting it as it comes, sometimes despairing but never giving up. Such tenacity seems to be related to the theory propounded by Jahn that the blues are an assertion of *Nommo* or life force, that the despair articulated is in the service of the hope expressed either in words or in the black musical performance itself.

Hughes described that musical performance—the structure to which the lyrics were sung—in a very general way that does not suggest that he knew as much about it as he did about various stanzaic patterns: "The *Blues,* unlike the *Spirituals,* have a strict poetic pattern: one long line repeated and a third line to rhyme with the first two. Sometimes the second line in repetition is slightly changed and sometimes, but very seldom, it is omitted."[220] In 1962 Hughes repeated the "railroad" lyric mentioned above in a discussion of the difference between blues and spirituals, calling the song a folk blues remembered from his childhood that followed the standard twelve-bar musical form.[221] Noting that the blues are almost always sung by individuals in contrast to the group approach to spirituals, Hughes classified the blues as masculine or feminine in theme: ". . . the men's blues are almost always about being out of work, broke, hungry, maybe a long ways from home, no ticket to get back. In other words, they're sort of economic blues. The women's blues, on the other hand, are almost always about love. Very often a woman will be singing about some man who's gone off and left her before she's ready for him to go, or something like that."[222] It is an unfortunate distinction Hughes made. First of all, love is the primary subject of most blues, not just those sung by women, and female singers could certainly sing economic blues, too. Vaudeville blues perhaps fixed an image of the female lamenting the loss of her man, but there were the vamps, wild women, and independent women, too, so Hughes overgeneralized in limiting the female blues as he did.[223] There are also, as we have pointed out, more subjects treated in blues than Hughes suggested, and a greater variety of stanzaic forms than he indicated here. Perhaps in the interest of being concise Hughes generalized a bit too much. As a lover of vaudeville blues, he was certainly aware of other stanzaic forms, and of blues both shorter and longer than twelve bars—this is in fact reflected in his poetry as well. Hughes was describing the most common form, not the variety of forms, but in doing this he was doing a disservice not only to the blues but to his own poetry as well.

In fact, Hughes often seemed to demonstrate a preference for the city, and especially vaudeville blues singers. He reinforced his suggestion that the blues were city songs in "Songs Called the Blues," his review of Handy's *Blues: An Anthology,* where he wrote that the blues "are songs of the black South, particularly the city South."[224] This definition reflects not only Hughes's preference for the blues of the city, but also his view of himself as a city person or city artist and not the "primitive" his patron Charlotte Mason wanted him to be. In the same review he discussed the spirit of the blues in terms of "The Gulf Coast Blues." Recorded in 1923 by Bessie Smith, this song was a vaudeville blues with a sixteen-bar introduction written by pianist-composer Clarence Williams, though it did draw on some folk-blues elements.[225] Additionally, Handy's anthology reprinted Handy arrangements and originals alongside blues composed by Clarence Williams and even George Gershwin. The blues were being transferred to a different, alien environment: the printed page and the Broadway stage.

Hughes explained and perhaps defended his preference for city blues songs in "Jazz as Communication":

> I'm not a Southerner, I never worked on a levee. I hardly ever saw a cottonfield except from the highway. But women behave the same way on Park Avenue as they do on a levee: when you've got hold of one part of them the other part escapes you. That's the Blues.

> Life is as hard on Broadway as it is in Blues-originating land. The Brill Building Blues is just as hungry as the Mississippi Levee Blues. One communicates to the other, brother! Somebody is going to rise up and tell me that nothing that comes out of Tin Pan Alley is jazz. I disagree. Commercial, yes. But so was Storeyville, so was Basin Street. What do you think Tony Jackson and Jelly Roll Morton and King Oliver and Louis Armstrong were playing for? Peanuts? No, money, even in Dixieland. They were communicating for money. For fun, too—because they had fun. But the money helped the fun along.[226]

Hughes was, of course, correct in saying that one can get the same kind of blues anywhere, but the blues of the country and the blues of the city certainly sound different, and the city money not only created a different purpose but sometimes compromised the musicians' integrity. Louis Armstrong made some strictly commercial recordings during his career. The question is, can he be faulted for making money when he needed it? One cannot simply live on artistic integrity—not if one is playing for a living. And that was often the difference between country and city musicians, between folk and professional musicians.

Over the years in his prose Hughes often named blues performers that he preferred or considered the best. A look at lists of these names indicates Hughes's blues aesthetic and enables us to make judgments about what Hughes was trying to accomplish in his poetry. The lists consist always of recorded blues singers and, when Hughes was not aided by an assistant editor or writer, include primarily vaudeville or sophisticated blues singers.[227] Bessie, Mamie, Clara, and Trixie Smith are named most often, along with Ma Rainey, who shows up slightly fewer times. These are all vaudeville blues singers, though they can be differentiated by their approach to the blues. Ma Rainey brought the work songs and folk blues of the deep South to her music, and she could moan like a chain-gang lifer watching his wife walk up the road with another man. Bessie Smith, too, had these deep roots, and, learning in part from Rainey, she used her flexible and powerful voice to sing a vocally brash and pyrotechnically superior brand of blues that gave her the status of a legend. On a good day Clara Smith, billed the "Queen of the Moaners," could moan low down enough to bury a coffin, but she could not match Ma's melisma and glissando effects, and Bessie surpassed her in their duets. In general Clara's voice was lighter than Ma's and Bessie's, but not so light as that of Mamie, who had a pop voice that leaned toward blues, rather than a blues voice that leaned toward pop. Trixie, too, had a voice that was lighter and sweeter than those of Ma, Bessie, and Clara, a voice not as parched in the fields or as aged in alcohol—or as aesthetically successful in the studio. She was much more likely to hit a note in closer proximity than work with it as the others would do, sliding up and down.

Other female vaudeville singers mentioned by Hughes include Victoria Spivey and Chippie Hill, Midge Williams, a singer with Louis Armstrong's band, and Gladys Bentley, a powerful singer who recorded in 1928 and 1929 with white jazz guitarist Eddie Lang and who imitated a trumpet vocally on several of those recordings.[228] Georgia White, whom Hughes called a carrier of "the old tradition of the blues in the folk manner,"[229] was a strong blues and boogie-woogie piano player and a good singer who was comfortable with both urban Chicago blues and the vaudeville blues tradition, but she was by no means a folk-blues performer. One of the best that Hughes named, Memphis Minnie, recorded Memphis country blues alone, in duet, and with the Memphis Jug Band; she sang hard group Chicago blues, and, toward the end of her career, some pop blues as well. However, her reputation rests on her earlier efforts—her commercially recorded blues that demonstrate a firm grounding in rural folk blues but also a real feel for the brash blues emerging in Chicago in the 1930s and 1940s. By the time Hughes wrote about her in 1943 she had been a successful recording artist for fourteen years and was firmly established in the tough city style.[230]

Interestingly, in 1940 Hughes named Lonnie Johnson as "perhaps the finest living male singer of the blues,"[231] and listed Johnson almost as often as the vaudeville blues singers. Johnson probably appealed to Hughes because he was versatile: he performed field-holler blues with "Texas" Alexander; his own urban blues; vaudeville blues with Victoria Spivey, Clara Smith, and Georgia White; pioneer jazz guitar duets with Eddie Lang; jazz sides with The Chocolate Dandies, Louis Armstrong, Johnny Dodds, Duke Ellington, Jimmy Noone, James P. Johnson, and Clarence Williams; and ballads and pop songs during a recording career that lasted from 1925 to the late 1960s.[232] Johnson was perhaps the most successful sophisticated blues singer and guitarist in the history of the blues, a man whose smooth voice and rapid and subtly nuanced guitar playing maintained that spark of the folk blues that many sophisticated singers lacked. His success was probably due to his melismatic singing and playing. Along with his smooth vocals he often slid up to notes very plaintively, and his single string playing was vocally based as well. The entire effect was very smooth though often remarkably plaintive in his slow blues, and adventurous but basic on his fast notes. Johnson is perhaps the perfect correlative for what Hughes wanted to do—to encompass, absorb, and transcend the various kinds of blues and jazz, to emerge as someone distinctive and superior, but to remain anchored in the folk idiom.

Later in Hughes's career, when Hughes was assisted in his editing and writing about the blues, his lists expanded to include artists pushed to the forefront by the folk music revival, like Sonny Terry, Brownie McGhee (who played "Gitfiddle" on Broadway in *Simply Heavenly*), and Josh White; revitalists like Claire Austin, Odetta, and Barbara Dane; contemporary rhythm and blues singers like Charles Brown, Louis Jordan, Dinah Washington, and Lavern Baker; and important blues and boogie-woogie figures like Leroy Carr, Tampa Red and Georgia Tom, Pinetop Smith, Albert Ammons, Pete Johnson, Meade Lux Lewis, Professor Longhair, and

T-Bone Walker. The lists became fuller, more representative of various styles, as Hughes's purpose changed and he felt the influence of his collaborators. Since the bulk of Hughes's blues poetry was completed before these final lists were compiled, their importance for his work may not be as great as the artists named in his earlier published articles. However, the changes do indicate either that Hughes was expanding his knowledge of the blues field or that he was able to express himself more fully. It is likely that it was the former, since Hughes was becoming increasingly interested in the historical development of African music as a popular historian and more attuned to the developments of the blues as they began expanding into the white markets. After all, there was always a great variety in the folk blues and in the recorded blues of the 1920s and 1930s, as another black poet, Sterling Brown, demonstrated in his discussions.[233]

Perhaps Hughes's novel *Not Without Laughter* (1930) exemplifies his preference. In it, Aunt Hager calls the musician, Jimboy, "the devil's musicianer"[234] as a blues singer, but admires his renditions of religious songs. Jimboy's wife, Annjee, thinks he is a great big kid, meant to play, but also a John Henry type who tries to outwork everyone. He is certainly a type of the wandering bluesman, irresponsible, but also someone who brings spirit and good times with him when he comes. In fact, he is more of a spirit or a repository of songs than a fully developed character. The real hero of the novel is Aunt Hager's daughter Harrietta, an intelligent high school girl who works at the country club and who likes to dance and have fun. She and her mother fall out over Harrietta's lack of interest in Christianity, and they separate when they can't express their feelings about wanting to be back together again after Harrietta has run off with the circus. In the end, though, Harrietta Williams, "The Princess of the Blues," makes a triumphant appearance at the Monogram Theatre on State Street in Chicago. Using her intelligence and her love of the type of songs Jimboy sang, she has become a successful commercial vaudeville blues singer and a racially proud businesswoman; she can now provide her nephew Sandy with the money to go back to school and get an education rather than skipping school to run an elevator to help pay the rent. Through intelligence, hard work, and racial awareness and pride (like the vaudeville blues singers, she drew on the folk roots of the blues—Jimboy—for her material and spirit), Harrietta has "built herself up" and is now able to provide for future generations. It is a black, middle-class view of success combined with an embracing rather than a rejection of racial heritage, a combination of the spirit of the secular (her music) and the spirit of the religious (her unselfish charity in helping Sandy), that makes Harrietta the hero in Hughes's book.[235]

Hughes created a similar type of hero in "The Blues I'm Playing" in the character of Oceola Jones. White patron Dora Ellsworth attempts to buy black pianist Oceola Jones away from black music, Harlem, and her boyfriend, supporting Oceola while she studies with noted classical pianists in Europe and sleeps and lives with Ellsworth. Oceola finally rejects art for art's sake (in favor of art for life's sake) and the aesthetic values of Ellsworth to play her own blues. Hughes encapsulates the artistic conflict brilliantly in the final blues lines of the story:

> O, if I could holler
> sang the blues,
> > Like a mountain jack,
>
> > I'd go up on de mountain
> sang the blues,
> > And call my baby back.

"And I," said Mrs. Ellsworth rising from her chair, "would stand looking at the stars."[236]

The lyrics of this blues song were mass-disseminated in Leroy Carr's monumentally popular 1928 recording, "How Long—How Long Blues." His song in turn probably derived from Ida Cox's 1925 recording of "How Long, Daddy, How Long" (both of which were eight-bar blues) or Ma Rainey's "Mountain Jack Blues" of 1926 (a twelve-bar blues), though this lyric was probably traditional.[237] Oceola demonstrates her brilliant technique in the classical idiom and even achieves some success at it, but ultimately rejects Mrs. Ellsworth's insistence on Oceola's sublimating her emotions in order to live life as it ought to be lived. The blues lyric, then, is her emancipation proclamation, her break with attempts to "train" her too far away from her roots, though at least at one point she accepted the training—for the money it brought her, as well as the experience. While Harrietta uses her folk roots to make herself financially successful and help her family, Oceola rejects the idea that her "promise" must be realized in a field that is disconnected from (and disconnects her from) her family and community, and from herself.

Hughes's exposure to the blues was fairly broad, but his own urban preference and his Harlem headquarters helped predispose him to vaudeville and professional blues, both of which were rooted in varying degrees in the folk-blues tradition. As a creative artist, Hughes was much like the blues composer or professional musician in seeking to draw on his folk roots not only out of pride and the need for individual artistic freedom but, sometimes, for economic reasons as well. For these reasons he did not reject more commercially oriented blues but sought to use the characteristics of those kinds of blues to express one part of the city side of the blues. Some part of the folk blues lived on not only in the more sophisticated blues, but "in the air" as well. Hughes's great comic character, Jesse B. Simple, discussed Ma Rainey: "I will not deny Ma Rainey, even to hide my age. Yes, I heard her! I am proud of hearing her! To tell the truth, if I stop and listen, I can still hear her. . . ."[238] Hughes wanted to capture the blues in the air, in whatever climate it existed, and he put much of his stopping and listening to work in the variety of blues poems that he wrote.

NOTES

1. "Blue" and "Blue Devils," *OED*, Compact ed. (1981), 944–45. See also "Blue" and "Blues" in Bartlett Jere Whiting, *Early American Proverbs and Proverbial Phrases* (Cambridge, Mass.: Belknap Press, 1977), 37–38.

2. Franklin Rosemont, Preface, *Blues and the Poetic Spirit,* by Paul Garon (London: Eddison Press, 1975), 7.

3. David Evans, "Africa and the Blues," *Living Blues,* no. 10 (1972): 27.

4. See H. E. Krehbiel, *Afro-American Folksongs* (New York: G. Schirmer, 1914); Paul Oliver, *Savannah Syncopators: African Retentions in the Blues* (New York: Stein and Day, 1970), 102. Ernest Borneman, *An Anthropologist Looks at Jazz* (New York: Jazz Music Books, 1946); Rudi Blesh, *Shining Trumpets: A History of Jazz* (New York: Knopf, 1958), 25–46; Marshall Stearns, *The Story of Jazz* (New York: Oxford University Press, 1958), 3–64; Harold Courlander, *Negro Folk Music U.S.A.*

(New York: Columbia University Press, 1963); Gunther Schuller, *Early Jazz* (New York: Oxford University Press, 1968), 3–62.

5. Alan P. Merriam, "African Music," in *Continuity and Change in African Cultures*, ed. William R. Bascom and Melville J. Herskovits (University of Chicago Press, 1959), 72, 85.

6. Dena J. Epstein, *Sinful Tunes and Spirituals* (Urbana: University of Illinois Press, 1977). See Melville J. Herskovits, *The Myth of the Negro Past* (Boston: Beacon Press, 1958); Melville J. Herskovits, *The New World Negro* (Bloomington: Indiana University Press, 1966); Richard Alan Waterman, "African Influence on the Music of Americans," in *Acculturation in the Americas*, ed. Sol Tax (University of Chicago Press, 1952), 207–18; Richard Alan Waterman, " 'Hot' Rhythm in Negro Music," *Journal of the American Musicological Society* 1 (1948): 4.

7. Alan Lomax, "The Homogeneity of African-American Musical Style, in *Afro-American Anthropology*, ed. Norman E. Whitten, Jr., and John F. Szwed (New York: Free Press, 1970), 197.

8. Alan Lomax, "Song Structure and Social Structure," *Ethnology* 1 (1962): 449.

9. Lomax, "Song Structure and Social Structure," 448.

10. Janheinz Jahn, *Muntu: An Outline of the New African Culture* (London: Faber and Faber, 1961), 219.

11. Ibid., 217.

12. John S. Mbiti, *African Religions and Philosophy* (Garden City, N.Y.: Anchor Books, 1970), 1.

13. Alan Dundes, Introduction to "Residual African Elements in the Blues" by Janheinz Jahn, in *Mother Wit From the Laughing Barrel*, ed. Alan Dundes (Englewood Cliffs, N.J.: Prentice Hall, 1973), 97.

14. Mbiti, *African Religions*, 15.

15. Janheinz Jahn, *A History of Neo-African Literature* (New York: Grove Press, 1968), 172.

16. Ibid.

17. Leroi Jones, *Blues People* (New York: William Morrow Paperbacks, 1963), x.

18. Ibid., 17.

19. Ibid., 24–25.

20. Ibid., 31.

21. Ibid., 7.

22. Langston Hughes, as quoted in jacket notes to Leroi Jones, *Blues People*.

23. Paul Oliver, *Savannah Syncopators: African Retentions in the Blues* (New York: Stein and Day, 1970), 17.

24. David Evans, "Africa and the Blues," 27–29.

25. Paul Oliver, "Echoes of the Jungle?" *Living Blues* 13 (1973): 29–32. Oliver draws on research by Lorenzo Turner and David Dalby in his discussion of African roots for such terms as "juke," "jive," and "Bobo" (*Savannah Syncopators,* 93). Robert Farris Thompson, in *Flash of the Spirit: African and Afro-American Art and Philosophy* (New York: Random House, 1983), 104–5, discusses "jazz," "funky," and "goofer" etymologies, tracing their origins to Africa, particularly to Ki-Kongo words and concepts. See also Lorenzo Dow Turner's *Africanisms in the Gullah Dialect* (University of Chicago Press, 1949).

26. Robert Palmer, *Deep Blues* (New York: Viking, 1981), 39.

27. Samuel Charters, *The Roots of the Blues: An African Search* (New York: Perigree Books, 1981), 119–26.

28. Laura C. Boulton, *African Music: Rhythm in the Jungle,* recorded 1930s, Victor 78 RPM set, 86A.

29. Thompson, *Flash of the Spirit,* xiii.

30. Ibid.

31. Langston Hughes and Milton Meltzer, eds., *Black Magic: A Pictorial History of the Negro in American Entertainment* (Englewood Cliffs, N.J.: Prentice-Hall, 1967), 4.

32. Ibid., 5.

33. Langston Hughes, Narration, *The Story of Jazz,* Folkways FJ 7312, n.d.

34. Hughes, "The Negro Artist and the Racial Mountain," 308.

35. Langston Hughes, "Afro-American Fragment," in *Selected Poems* (New York: Vintage, 1974), 3.

36. Hughes, *The Big Sea,* 325.

37. Hughes and Meltzer, eds., *Black Magic,* 80.

38. Hughes, *The Story of Jazz.*

39. Langston Hughes, "Music at Year's End," *Chicago Defender,* 9 January 1943, in *Living Blues* 19 (1975): 7. "Blues In Stereo," in *Ask Your Mama* (New York: Knopf, 1961), 35–37, does juxtapose the blues and Africa by the use of commentary in the margins of the text.

40. Carl Van Vechten, "The Black Blues," *Vanity Fair* 24, no. 6 (1925): 86.

41. Langston Hughes, "The Blues I'm Playing," *Scribner's Magazine* 95, no. 5 (1934): 349.

42. Epstein, *Sinful Tunes,* 74.

43. Paul Oliver, *Songsters and Saints* (Cambridge: Cambridge University Press, 1984). As Oliver points out, it is important to remember that many of the artists of the 1920s and 1930s who are identified as blues artists today were in fact songsters with a vast repertoire of various kinds of songs. Blind Willie McTell, for example, performed religious, ragtime,

and pop songs as well as blues, and Charley Patton, dubbed by some "the founder of the Delta blues," "had a large repertoire of blues ballads, ragtime pieces, and songs derived from either white popular or rural white traditions" (John Fahey, *Charley Patton* [London: Studio Vista, 1970], 7). However, these artists seemed to play their blues like blues and their ragtime like ragtime. The exception is the East Coast blues artists who were generally influenced by the variety of styles included in that geographical area. Hughes recognized that some blues singers were songsters—Jimboy in *Not Without Laughter* was a songster himself.

44. Epstein, *Sinful Tunes,* 69.

45. Jones, *Blues People,* 18–21.

46. Titon, *Early Downhome Blues,* 137.

47. Evans, *Big Road Blues,* 27.

48. Sam Charters, *The Bluesmen* (New York: Oak Publications, 1967), 28.

49. See Robert M. W. Dixon and John Godrich, *Blues and Gospel Records 1902–1943* (Chigwell, Essex: Storyville Publications, 1982), 122, 340–41, for references to these artists' earlier recordings.

50. Oliver, *Songsters and Saints,* 251. Both the Oliver and Evans quotes are from this source.

51. Jones, *Blues Peoples,* 68.

52. Langston Hughes, *The First Book of Jazz* (New York: Franklin Watts, 1976), 18.

53. Hughes, *The Story of the Jazz.*

54. Langston Hughes, "Songs Called the Blues," *Phylon* 2, no. 2 (1941): 143.

55. Ibid., 145.

56. Ibid., 144.

57. Langston Hughes, "Don't You Want To Be Free?," *One Act Play Magazine* (Oct. 1938): 364.

58. Ibid., 393.

59. Gates Thomas, "South Texas Negro Work-Songs: Collected and Uncollected," in *Rainbow In the Morning,* ed. J. Frank Dobie (Hatboro, Pa.: Folklore Association, 1965), 160.

60. Hughes, "Don't You Want To Be Free," 368.

61. Son House, Fiddlin' Joe Martin, and Willie Brown, "Camp Hollers," *Son House: The Lengendary 1941–42 Recordings in Chronological Sequence,* Roots RSE 1, n.d.

62. Thomas, *South Texas Negro Work-Songs,* 160; W. C. Handy, *W. C. Handy Narrates and Sings His Immortal Songs,* Mark 56, 684, n.d.; W. C. Handy, *Blues: An Anthology* (New York, 1926; rpt., New York: Macmillan, 1972), 61, 206–7.

63. John W. Work, *American Negro Songs and Spirituals* (New York: 1940), 32–33; W. C. Handy, *Father of the Blues* (1941; rpt., New York: Collier, 1970), 78; Gates Thomas, 172, 177–79; Howard W. Odum, "Folk-Song and Folk-Poetry As Found in the Secular Songs of the Southern Negroes," *Journal of American Folklore* 24 (1911): 255–94, 351–96; Will H. Thomas, *Some Current Folk-Songs of the Negro* (Austin: Folklore Society of Texas, 1912), 9, 10, 12; W. Prescott Webb, "Notes on Folk-Lore of Texas," *Journal of American Folklore* 28 (1915): 291–96; John A. Lomax, "Self-Pity in Negro Folk Songs," *The Nation* 105 (July-Dec. 1917): 141–45; David Evans makes an excellent survey of this and other material in *Big Road Blues* (Berkeley: University of California Press, 1982), 32–39.

64. Evans, *Big Road Blues*, 40.

65. Harold Courlander, *Negro Folk Music U.S.A.* (New York: Columbia University Press, 1963), 126.

66. W. C. Handy, ed., *Blues: An Anthology*, 61, 206–7.

67. Janheinz Jahn, *A History of Neo-African Literature*, 167.

68. Henry Thomas, "Texas Worried Blues," *Ragtime Texas*, Herwin 209, n.d. [1928].

69. Jim Jackson, "Kansas City Blues," *Kansas City Blues*, Agram 2004, n.d. [1927].

70. John Barnie, "Oral Formulas in the Country Blues," *Southern Folklore Quarterly* 42, no. 1 (1978): 42. Parry and Lord's work will be discussed below. See notes 79 and 80.

71. Dorothy Scarborough, *On the Trail of Negro Folk-Songs* (Cambridge, Mass., 1925; rpt., Hatboro, Pa.: Folklore Association, 1963): 272. A. X. Nicholas is certainly wrong in his assertion that the blues are sung in iambic pentameter lines; see *Woke Up This Mornin': Poetry of the Blues* (New York: Bantam, 1973), 1.

72. See Eric Sackheim, ed., *The Blues Line: A Collection of Blues Lyrics* (New York: Schirmer Books, 1975), and Jeff Todd Titon, ed., *Downhome Blues Lyrics* (Boston: Twayne, 1981), for attempts at rendering blues lyrics on the page based on the way they are sung. Paul Oliver criticizes this ethnopoetic rendering of blues texts as if they were poetry by Williams or Cummings in his review of Titon's book in *Blues Unlimited* 144 (1983): 53.

73. Sackheim, *Blues Line*, 208. See also Titon's *Early Downhome Blues*, 68, for a transcription of Charley Patton's "Pony Blues" that also breaks the line into more than two parts.

74. Henry Thomas, "Bull Doze Blues," *Ragtime Texas* [1928].

75. Sonny Boy Williamson, "Down South," *Bluebird Blues*, RCA 518, 1965 [1938].

76. Big Joe Turner and Pete Johnson, "Roll Em Pete," *The Story of the Blues,* Columbia 30008, n.d. [1938].

77. Jack Kelly, "Believe I'll Go Back Home," in *Memphis Blues,* ed. Bengt Olsson (London: Studio Vista, 1970), 102.

78. Memphis Jug Band, "Going Back to Memphis," *The Jug Bands Vol. 1,* Collector's Classics 2, n.d. [1930].

79. Albert B. Lord, *The Singer of Tales* (1960; rpt., New York: Atheneum, 1965), 178.

80. Adam Parry, ed., *The Making of Homeric Verse: The Collected Papers of Milman Parry* (Oxford: Clarendon Press, 1971), 272.

81. David Bynum, *The Daemon in the Wood* (Cambridge: Harvard University Press, 1978), 7.

82. Lord, *The Singer of Tales,* 6.

83. Bynum, *Daemon,* 8.

84. Ibid., 12.

85. Robert Johnson, "I Believe I'll Dust My Broom," *King of the Delta Blues Singers,* Columbia 1654, n.d. [1936].

86. Georgia Bill (Blind Willie McTell), "Mr. McTell Got The Blues," *Blind Willie McTell: 1927–1949 The Remaining Titles,* Wolf WSE 102, 1982 [1927].

87. Barefoot Bill, "My Crime," *Alabama Country: 1927/31,* Origin OJL 14, n.d. [1929].

88. Charley Lincoln, "Depot Blues," *Kings on the Twelve String,* Gryphon GLP13159, n.d. [1928].

89. Bessie Smith, "Backwater Blues," *Nobody's Blues But Mine,* Columbia CG31093, 1972 [1927].

90. Yank Rachell, "T-Bone Steak Blues," *Missouri and Tennessee,* Roots RL310, n.d. [1929].

91. Son House, "The Jinx Blues," *Son House,* Roots RSE 1, n.d. [1942].

92. Ora Brown, "Jinx Blues," in *The Meaning of the Blues,* ed. Paul Oliver (New York: Collier Books, 1963), 334–35. [1926].

93. Blind Lemon Jefferson, "Rabbit Foot Blues," *The Immortal Blind Lemon Jefferson,* Milestone 2004, n.d. [1926].

94. Little Brother Montgomery, "The First Time I Met You," *Crescent City Blues,* Bluebird AXM2–5522, 1977 [1936].

95. Blind Willie McTell, "Dark Night Blues," *Kings of the Twelve String,* n.d. [1928].

96. Jaybird Coleman, "No More Good Water," *Alabama Country 1927/31* [1927].

97. Mississippi John Hurt, "Got The Blues, Can't Be Satisfied," *Mississippi John Hurt 1928,* Biograph BLP C4, n.d. [1928].

98. Walter Davis, "Worried Man Blues," in Oliver, ed., *The Meaning of the Blues,* 332.

99. Otis Harris, "Waking Blues," in Oliver, ed., *The Meaning of the Blues,* 333.

100. Merline Johnson, "Blues Everywhere," in Oliver, ed., *The Meaning of the Blues,* 332.

101. Howard W. Odum and Guy B. Johnson, *Negro Workaday Songs* (1926; rpt., New York: Negro Universities Press, 1977), 18.

102. Sara Martin, "Death Sting Me Blues," *Ida Cox,* BYG 529073, n.d. [1928].

103. Son House, "Preachin' the Blues," *The Mississippi Blues 1927–1940,* Origin OJL5, n.d. [1930].

104. Yannick Bruynoghe, *Big Bill Blues* (1955), quoted in *Living Country Blues* by Harry Oster (Detroit: Folklore Associates, 1969), 20.

105. Included in the last two categories are songs like Robert Johnson's "Me and the Devil" and Joe Williams's "Mr. Devil Blues," in which the devil himself is confronted by the speaker. The confrontation sometimes explains the singer's evil nature:

> Me and the Devil was walking side by side
> Me and the Devil, oooh, was walking side by side
> I'm gonna beat my woman until I get satisfied.

(Robert Johnson, "Me and the Devil," in *Robert Johnson, King of the Delta Blues Singers.*) At other times, the meeting explains the reason why the singer has the blues:

> Good morning Mr. Devil, I come here to chain you down
> Good morning Mr. Devil, I come here to chain you down
> Everytime I move you drag my rider down.

(Joe Williams, "Mr. Devil Blues," in *The Great Harmonica Players, Vol. 2,* Roots RL 321, n.d.) Johnson welcomes the devil and revels in his own satanic connections; Williams evokes the Devil either to reflect a deeper truth about the origin of evil nature or to rationalize his woman's weaknesses. Son House's "Jinx Blues," quoted earlier, is another example. Bessie Smith's "Black Mountain Blues," written by J. C. Johnson, describes a place where babies cry for liquor, birds sing bass, and people use gunpowder to sweeten their tea. The hyperbole greatly enhances the description of Black Mountain's reputation, allowing the singer to express both fear and admiration—both sides of "bad."

106. Big Bill Broonzy, *Blues In the Mississippi Night,* United Artists UAL 4027, 1959. The subsequent quotes by Sonny Boy Williamson and Memphis Slim are from the same recording. Langston Hughes mentioned

both Broonzy and Memphis Slim as notable blues performers in *Black Magic* (1967).

107. See Paul Oliver, *Conversation with the Blues* (New York: Horizon, 1965), David Evans *Big Road Blues* (Berkeley: University of California Press, 1982), and Barry Lee Pearson, *Sounds So Good To Me* (Philadelphia: University of Pennsylvania Press, 1984) for interviews with blues performers.

108. Scarborough, *On the Trail,* 272.

109. Howard W. Odum and Guy B. Johnson, *Negro Workaday Songs* (1926; rpt., New York: Negro Universities Press, 1977), 17.

110. Guy B. Johnson, "Double Meaning in the Popular Negro Blues," *Journal of Abnormal and Social Psychology* 22, no. 1 (1927): 12.

111. Charles S. Johnson, "Jazz Poetry and Blues," *Carolina Magazine* 58 (1928): 17.

112. Stanley Edgar Hyman, "The Folk Tradition," in Dundes, ed., *Mother Wit From the Laughing Barrel,* 46–56. A more extensive discussion of themes used in the blues will be taken up in chapter 3.

113. Evans, *Big Road Blues,* 3.

114. Samuel Charters, *The Bluesmen* (New York: Oak Publications, 1967), 166.

115. Scarborough, *On the Trail,* 272.

116. Webb, 292.

117. Samuel Charters, *The Poetry of the Blues* (New York: Avon, 1970), 40.

118. Evans, *Big Road Blues,* 58.

119. Hurston, *Mules and Men,* 157–59.

120. W. C. Handy, *W. C. Handy Narrates and Sings His Immortal Songs,* Mark 56, 684, n.d.

121. Ibid.

122. Scarborough, *On the Trail,* 265.

123. Langston Hughes, "Maker of the Blues," *Negro Digest* (Jan. 1943): 38.

124. Chris Albertson, *Bessie* (New York: Scarborough, 1982), 34.

125. Martin Williams, *The Jazz Tradition* (Oxford: Oxford University Press, 1983), 24–25.

126. Derrick Stewart-Baxter, *Ma Rainey and the Classic Blues Singers* (New York: Stein and Day, 1970), 7. Of course, some early singers of the folk blues had wide repertoires as well. See Paul Oliver, *Songsters and Saints* (Cambridge University Press, 1984), for a good discussion.

127. Sterling Brown, as quoted in Stewart-Baxter, *Ma Rainey,* 42.

128. Carl Van Vechten, "Negro 'Blues' Singers," *Vanity Fair* 26, no. 1 (1926): 106.

129. Albertson, *Bessie,* 36.

130. Folklorist Lawrence Gellert was recording noncommercial blues songs as early as 1924 in Greenville, South Carolina, and Robert Gordon was collecting recordings of black folk songs in North Carolina and Georgia around 1925–28. These recordings, and those of John and Alan Lomax in 1933 and afterward, were made after the first vaudeville blues recordings and in fact still may have been influenced by commercial blues recordings. See *Nobody Knows My Name: Blues From South Carolina and Georgia, 1924–32,* Heritage 304, 1984. Sylvester Weaver could well be discounted as a folk artist, owing to the relative sophistication of his playing, his accompaniments to Helen Humes, Virginia Liston, and Sara Martin, and, perhaps, his apparent role as talent scout for Okeh records. See *Smoketown Strut,* Agram 2010, n.d., for recorded examples of Weaver's music and transcriptions of music and lyrics, and *Living Blues* 52 (Spring 1982): 18–25 for a discussion of Weaver, Sara Martin, and Helen Humes and a Weaver discography.

131. Hughes recognized the problems the blues singer could have with the "piccolos" or juke boxes as well. In *Simply Heavenly,* act 1, scene 5, the blues singer-guitarist Gitfiddle complains, "Juke boxes is the trouble now, Miss Mamie. Used to be, folks like to hear a sure enough live guitar player. Now, I start playing, somebody puts a nickel in the piccolo, drowns me out." See *Five Plays By Langston Hughes,* ed. Webster Smalley (Bloomington: Indiana University Press, 1968), 137. Since the play was written and staged at a late point in Hughes's career, it demonstrates Hughes's (belated) concern with the negative aspects of commercialism in the blues.

132. Charters, *The Bluesmen,* 180.

133. Evans, *Big Road Blues,* 77.

134. David Evans, "Folk, Commercial, and Folkloric Aesthetic in the Blues," *Jazz Forschung* 5 (1973): 27.

135. See Newman I. White, *American Negro Folk-Songs* (Cambridge: Harvard University Press, 1928), 388–90.

136. Guy B. Johnson, "Double Meaning in the Popular Negro Blues," 12.

137. For a discussion of Lester Melrose and the Bluebird label, see Mike Rowe, *Chicago Breakdown* (London: Eddison Press, 1973), 17–25, and Robert Dixon and John Godrich, *Recording the Blues* (New York: Stein and Day, 1970), 78–103.

138. Odum and Johnson, *Negro Workaday Songs,* 17.

139. Johnson, "Double Meaning in the Popular Negro Blues," 12. The idea of blues as autobiographical songs has been asserted by Paul Oliver in *The Story of the Blues* (Philadelphia: Chilton, 1969), 30 ("blues singers

nearly always sing about themselves"), and by Ralph Ellison in "Richard Wright's Blues" in *Shadow and Act* (New York: Random House, 1964), 79 ("the blues is an autobiographical chronicle of personal catastrophe expressed lyrically").

140. Michael Haralambos, "Soul Music and Blues: Their Meaning and Significance in Northern United States Black Ghettoes," in *Afro-American Anthropology*, ed. Norman E. Whitten, Jr., and John F. Szwed (New York: Free Press, 1970), 375.

141. Memphis Slim, *Blues in the Mississippi Night*. There are instances of blues performers saying that singing the blues made them feel bad. In William A. Owens, *Tell Me A Story, Sing Me A Song* (Austin: University of Texas Press, 1983), 315, blues singer-pianist Grey Ghost sang a number of blues songs for Owens and then wished to stop: "Then the blues were on him, he said, and he did not feel like singing anymore." Most performers, though, do say that performing makes them feel better.

142. Odum and Johnson, *Negro Workaday Songs,* 20–21.

143. Evans, *Big Road Blues,* 19.

144. Richard Wright, Foreword, *The Meaning of the Blues,* ed. Paul Oliver (New York: Collier Books, 1963), 9. Wright's foreword is not always accurate. The five immediately apparent characteristics that he identifies—submerged guilt, passivity (allied to sex), lack of the theme of otherworldliness, lack of mention of the family, and lack of the home site in the blues—are not really characteristic of the blues. Ralph Ellison's jibe in "The World and the Jug" (*Shadow and Act,* 140–41) about Wright's knowledge of the blues probably stems from these inaccuracies. Ellison was very critical of Wright's knowledge of the blues, suggesting that Wright's blues composed for Paul Robeson and his introduction to Oliver's book reveal his ignorance. In fact, Ellison found the spirit of Hemingway's work to be imbued more with a feeling akin to the blues than was Wright's work. See Ellison, "The World and the Jug," 140–41. The Robeson recording of Wright's lyric, which also features the Count Basie Orchestra, was released on Okeh 6475. See Paul Oliver's *The Blues Tradition,* 160–61, for a transcription of the lyrics.

145. Mark Humphrey, "I Am the Backbone of America," *Living Blues* 23 (1975): 29.

146. Albertson, *Bessie,* 143.

147. Hughes, *The Big Sea,* 296.

148. Jahn, "Residual African Elements in the Blues," 102.

149. Kimberly Benston, "Tragic Aspects of the Blues," *Phylon* 36, no. 2 (1975), 166.

150. Ibid., 167.

151. Ralph Ellison, "Richard Wright's Blues," in *Shadow and Act,* 94.

152. Alfred Chester and Vilma Howard, "Interview with Ralph Ellison," in *Writers at Work, 2nd Series* (New York: Viking, 1965), 324.

153. Larry Neal, "Any Day Now: Black Art and Black Liberation," in *Black Poets and Prophets: The Theory, Practice and Aesthetics of the Pan-Africanist Revolution,* ed. Woodie King and Earl Anthony (New York: Mentor Books, 1972), 152–53.

154. A. X. Nicholas, Introduction, *Woke Up This Mornin': Poetry of the Blues,* ed. A. X. Nicholas (New York: Bantam, 1973), 2.

155. Ibid., 7.

156. Houston A. Baker, *Blues, Ideology, and Afro-American Literature* (University of Chicago Press, 1984), 5.

157. Rod Gruver, "The Blues as Dramatic Monologues," *JEMF Quarterly* 6 (1970): 28–31; Jeff Titon, "A Reply to 'The Blues As Dramatic Monologues,'" *JEMF Quarterly* 6 (1970), pp. 79–82; Dennis Jarrett, "The Singer and the Bluesman: Formulations of Personality in the Lyrics of the Blues," *Southern Folklore Quarterly* 42 (1978): 31–37. Ralph Ellison is among those commentators who have seen the blues as "an autobiographical chronicle of personal catastrophe expressed lyrically" ("Richard Wright's Blues," in *Shadow and Act,* 79), though the blues as group expression was something Ellison recognized as well.

158. Michael Haralambos, "Soul Music and Blues: Their Meaning and Relevance in Northern United States Black Ghettoes," in *Afro-American Anthology,* 374.

159. S. I. Hayakawa, "Popular Songs vs. the Facts of Life," in *Mass Culture,* ed. Bernard Rosenberg and David Manning White (Glencoe, Ill.: Free Press, 1957), 399. For fantasy in blues lyrics, see the earlier lyrics cited dealing with the devil.

160. James Baldwin, *Blues for Mister Charlie,* in *Contemporary Black Drama,* ed. Clinton F. Oliver and Stephanie Sills (New York: Scribner's, 1971), 266.

161. Leroi Jones, *Dutchman,* in *Contemporary Black Drama,* ed. Clinton F. Oliver and Stephanie Sills (New York: Charles Scribner's Sons, 1971), 229.

162. Big Bill Broonzy, *Blues in the Mississippi Night.* The following quote from Memphis Slim is from the same source.

163. Scarborough, *On the Trail,* 280.

164. Charters, *The Poetry of the Blues,* 12.

165. For examples of such protest, see Walter Davis, "Howling Wind Blues," *Think You Need a Shot,* Victor 731015, n.d. [1931]; Leadbelly, "The Bourgeois Blues," in *The Leadbelly Songbook,* ed. Moses Asch and Alan Lomax (New York: Oak Publications, 1962), 24; Casey Bill Weldon, "WPA Blues," *Red Hot Blues,* Earl 605, 1982 [1936]; Peetie Wheatstraw,

"Third Street's Going Down," in Paul Garon, *The Devil's Son-In-Law* (London: Studio Vista, 1971), 79 [1937]; Peetie Wheatstraw, "Working on the Project," *Kokomo Arnold and Peetie Wheatstraw,* Blues Classics 4, n.d. [1947]; Lightnin' Hopkins, "Tim Moore's Farm," *Lightnin' Hopkins, Early Recordings, Vol. 2,* Arhoolie 2010, n.d. [1949]; J. B. Lenoir, "Everybody Wants to Know" and "Eisenhower Blues," *J. B. Lenoir,* Chess 2ACMB 208, 1976 [1954, 1955]; J. B. Lenoir, "Shot on James Meredith" and "Born Dead," *J. B. Lenoir,* Crusade 1, n.d. [1960s]. These are not the only examples, but they are some outstanding ones. Some authors have suggested that Leadbelly had some help with "The Bourgeois Blues" and that he sang the song for his new folk audience (see Titon, *Early Downhome Blues,* 191), though neither suggestion means that Leadbelly did not agree with what he sang. Perhaps the term "bourgeois" is what seems out of place to those who doubt Leadbelly's authorship. Contact with people who used the term could have influenced Leadbelly to use it, but it is just another term for a middle-class mentality that Leadbelly would have had no trouble criticizing. Peetie Wheatstraw's "The Good Lawd's Children" does not specifically protest against white people, but against patronizing and duplicitous Christian charity. It is hard not to think of whites specifically, though, when hearing the lyrics. These are some "patriotic" blues songs as well. See, for example, Grey Ghost, "De Hitler Blues" in *Tell Me A Story, Sing Me A Song,* 309–10; Doctor Clayton, "Pearl Harbor Blues," *Pearl Harbor Blues,* RCA International 731045, n.d. [1942]; Sonny Boy Williamson, "Win The War Blues," *Sonny Boy Williamson, Vol. 3,* Blues Classics 24, n.d. [1944]. These, of course, deal with the World War II effort, which would directly affect the individual draftee as well. Bobo Jenkins's "Democrat Blues," *Country Blues Classics Volume 2,* Blues Classics 6, n.d. [1954] is a remarkable political blues.

166. "Monologue on history of the blues; monologue on life as maker of records; monologue on himself," *Blind Willie McTell: 1940,* Melodeon 7323, n.d.

167. Titon, *Early Downhome Blues,* 190.

168. Ibid., 224.

169. Paul Oliver, *Screening the Blues* (London: Cassell, 1968), 258.

170. Titon, *Early Downhome Blues,* 192.

171. Franklin Rosemont, "A Revolutionary Poetic Tradition," *Living Blues* 25 (1976), 20–23.

172. Michael Haralambos, *Right On: From Blues to Soul in Black America* (New York: Drake, 1975).

173. Faith Berry, *Langston Hughes: Before and Beyond Harlem* (Westport, Conn.: Lawrence Hill, 1983), 6. Berry discusses Hughes's early life with his grandmother, mother, and father, but does not bring up his

early exposure to the blues. Kansas City is the setting of Hughes's "Five O'Clock Blues," *Langston Hughes Reader,* 162–63.

174. Langston Hughes, "Jazz as Communication," *The Langston Hughes Reader,* 493.

175. Langston Hughes, "I Remember the Blues," in *Missouri Reader,* ed. Frank Luther Mott (Columbia, Mo.: University of Missouri Press, 1964), 152. Independence Avenue, a major thoroughfare which is in part U.S. 24, runs from Kansas City, Kansas, into Independence, Missouri, a suburb of Kansas City. Charlotte Street intersects Independence Avenue in Independence, Missouri.

176. Langston Hughes, *Langston Hughes Reads and Talks About His Poetry,* Spoken Arts 7140, 1959.

177. Hughes, "I Remember the Blues," 153. W. C. Handy described the "unforgettable" effect of a blues song that he heard in Tutwiler, Mississippi, describing the guitar playing as "the weirdest music" he had ever heard. See Oliver, *The Story of the Blues,* 26. The connection between Hughes and Handy will be explored more fully later.

178. Hughes, *The Big Sea,* 215.

179. Langston Hughes, "The Weary Blues," in *The Weary Blues and Other Poems* (New York: Knopf, 1926), 23–24.

180. Henry Thomas, "Texas Worried Blues," *Ragtime Texas* [1929].

181. Mack McCormack, jacket notes, *Ragtime Texas.*

182. John W. Work, *American Negro Songs and Spirituals* (New York: Bonanza Books, 1940), 32–33.

183. Jacket notes, *Have No Fear, Big Joe Turner Is Here,* Savoy 2223, 1977. The following quote is from the same source. *Lottie Kimbrough and Winston Holmes,* Wolf 114, n.d., presents recordings by two Kansas City blues performers of the nineteen-teens and twenties.

184. Nat Pierce, jacket notes, *Kansas City Piano,* Decca 79226, n.d.

185. Charles Keil, *Urban Blues* (University of Chicago Press, 1966, 61).

186. Ross Russell, *Jazz Style in Kansas City and the Southwest* (Berkeley: University of California Press, 1971), 321.

187. Nat Pierce, jacket notes, *Kansas City Piano,* Decca 79226, n.d.

188. Langston Hughes, *Poetry and Reflections,* Caedmon, 1640, n.d. Hughes and Bontemps include a section on "The Jazz Folk" in *The Book of Negro Folklore* (New York: Dodd, Mead, 1958), including primarily New Orleans musicians.

189. Berry, *Langston Hughes,* 16.

190. Hughes, "I Remember the Blues," 153.

191. Jim and Amy O'Neal, "Living Blues Interview: Georgia Tom Dorsey," *Living Blues* 20 (1975): 20. For recordings by Jimmy Blythe,

consult *Moods of Jimmy Blythe,* Whoopee 105, n.d. [1924–30], and *Pitchin' Boogie,* Milestone 2018, 1971 [1924–26].

192. O'Neal, "Living Blues Interview: Georgia Tom Dorsey," 21.

193. A number of other black female entertainers, among them Bessie Smith, Clara Smith, Ida Cox, Sara Martin, Ethel Waters, and Susie Edwards also appeared at the Grand. Either Hughes or Dorsey apparently mixed up the dates of Rainey's presence in Chicago. It is likely that it was Hughes, since he reports hearing the blues on phonograph records, and he wouldn't have heard that until 1920 or later.

194. Langston Hughes, "The Twenties: Harlem and Its Negritude," *African Forum* 1, no. 4 (1966): 12.

195. Michael Lipskin, Foreword, *Fats Waller,* by Maurice Waller and Anthony Calabrese (New York: Schirmer Books, 1979), xi.

196. John Godrich and R. M. W. Dixon reported in their discography *Blues and Gospel Records, 1902–1943* (Chigwell, Essex: Storyville, 1982), 657, that Smith recorded in early 1921 for Emerson in New York City. On 12 February 1921, the *Chicago Defender* carried an ad for this record, which John Hammond, Sr., claimed was released under the name of Rosa Henderson, according to Chris Albertson in the booklet to Columbia LP CG 33. However, no recordings are listed in *Blues and Gospel Records* as recorded by Rosa Henderson in 1921. Albertson also reported in the booklet that Bessie cut an audition record of "I Wish I Could Shimmy Like My Sister Kate" for Okeh, and in his book *Bessie,* that she auditioned for Black Swan in 1921. None of the test records have been recovered.

197. Langston Hughes, "Jazz as Communication," 493.

198. James P. Johnson accompanied a number of blues singers, including Bessie Smith, besides recording his own primarily ragtime and jazz compositions for commercial release and his 1938 Library of Congress recordings. J. C. Johnson was also an accompanist who recorded jazz and pop songs and some sides of blues interest with Lonnie Johnson. Willie "The Lion" Smith recorded many jazz sides over the years, and accompanied others as well, including Mamie Smith on her first six issued sides in 1920. Fats Waller is well known for his jazz, pop, and humorous tunes, but he too accompanied blues singers like Alberta Hunter, Hazel Meyers, and Maude Mills. All were professional musicians/composers/entertainers chosen as studio musicians for their sophistication and versatility.

199. Carl Van Vechten, "The Black Blues," *Vanity Fair* 24, no. 6 (1925): 86. Ma Rainey's "Southern Blues," reissued on *Queen of the Blues,* Biograph BLP 12032, n.d. [1923], contains a variant of this blues lyric.

200. Hughes, *The Big Sea*, 8–9.

201. Dan Morgenstern, jacket notes, *Django Reinhardt and the American Jazz Giants*, Prestige 7633, 1969.

202. Hughes, *The Big Sea*, 161.

203. Brian Rust, *Jazz Records 1897–1942* (New Rochelle: Arlington House, 1978), 1085–86.

204. Hughes, *The Big Sea*, 162–63. The lyric about the spider is repeated in the "Simple" story entitled "Jealousy" in *The Best of Simple*, 41. It was recorded by Tampa Red in 1929 as part of his "Uncle Bud," which is not so much a blues song as it is a pre-blues folk tune. See Tampa Red, *It's Tight Like That*, Blues Documents 2001, n.d. The second lyric about hair can be heard in Luke Jordan's 1927 recording "Church Bell Blues." See *Travellin' This Lonesome Road*, RCA International 1175, 1970. The "spider" and "one-eyed woman" verses are also included in Hughes's and Bontemps's *Book of Negro Folklore*, 394–95, and in *The Book of Negro Humor*, 99.

205. Hughes, *Langston Hughes Reads and Talks About His Poetry*, Spoken Arts 7140, 1959.

206. Hughes, *The Big Sea*, 209.

207. Ibid. Hughes is referring not only to blues songs but religious songs as well. Bessie Smith recorded a "Cold in Hand Blues" in 1925. See *The Empress*, Columbia 30818, n.d. Barbecue Bob recorded a version of the lyric in his "Barbecue Blues," included on *Chocolate to the Bone*, Mamlish 3808, n.d.

208. Hughes, *The Big Sea*, 209.

209. Milton Meltzer, *Langston Hughes: A Biography* (New York: Crowell, 1968), 111. Faith Berry also discusses Hughes's use of musical accompaniment in *Langston Hughes: Before and Beyond Harlem*, 73, stating that Hughes began to use musical accompaniment "wherever the opportunity arose."

210. Hughes, *The Big Sea*, 290.

211. Godrich and Dixon, *Recording the Blues*, 106.

212. Hughes, *The Big Sea*, 296.

213. Hughes, "The Negro Artist and the Racial Mountain," 308.

214. Langston Hughes, Letter to Mary Owings Miller, *Contemporary Poetry* (Autumn 1943): 4. In "Songs Called the Blues," *Phylon* 2, no. 2 (Summer 1941): 145, Hughes goes further: "I see no reason why great dances could not be born of the Blues. Great American dances containing all the laughter and pain, hunger and heartaches, search and reality of the contemporary scenes—for the Blues have something that goes beyond

race or sectional limits, that appeals to the ear and heart of people everywhere. . . ."

215. Carl Van Vechten, "The Black Blues," 86.

216. Langston Hughes, review of *Blues: An Anthology* by W. C. Handy, *Opportunity,* August 1926: 258.

217. Langston Hughes, ed., *The Book of Negro Humor* (New York: Dodd, Mead, 1966), 97. The two following quotations are from the same page.

218. Langston Hughes, "Songs Called the Blues," 143.

219. Hughes, *The Big Sea,* 209. Hughes also uses the lyric in "Don't You Want To Be Free?," *One Act Play Magazine* (Oct. 1938): 377.

220. Hughes, *Fine Clothes to the Jew,* 13.

221. Hughes, *Poetry and Reflections,* Caedmon 1640, n.d.

222. Ibid.

223. For some examples, see *Mean Mothers: Independent Women's Blues Vol. 1,* Rosetta 1300, 1980, and *Women's Railroad Blues,* Rosetta 1301, 1980. Of course, both albums also contain songs that fall under Hughes's definition as well.

224. Langston Hughes, "Songs Called the Blues," 143.

225. Bessie Smith, "The Gulf Coast Blues," *The World's Greatest Blues Singer,* Columbia CG33, n.d. [1923]. Smith actually sings that men have mouths full of gimme and hands full of much obliged. The lyric is normally sung the way Hughes reported it.

226. Langston Hughes, "Jazz as Communication," in *The Langston Hughes Reader,* 492. Hughes discusses the practicality of his own poetry in *The Big Sea,* 214–19. It earned him meals, prize money, valuable introductions, and a college scholarship. Vachel Lindsay, one of Hughes's early influences and benefactors, carried around a pamphlet entitled *Rhymes to Be Traded for Bread,* a practice that comes to mind as an obvious statement about the practicality of art. W. E. B. DuBois, in a 1922 editorial in *The Crisis,* bemoaned the fact that there was a feeling among "colored people" that "art should not be paid for" because the quester for beauty "should rise above paltry consideration of dollars and food." See *An ABC of Color* (New York: International Publication, 1969), 122. Hughes obviously agreed that art was not meant to drive away financial gain.

227. The sources of these lists include *The Big Sea,* "Songs Called the Blues," "Music at Year's End," "Shadow of the Blues," *First Book of Jazz,* "Langston Hughes: He Found Poetry in the Blues," "My Early Days in Harlem," "I Remember the Blues," "The Twenties: Harlem and Its Negritude," *Black Magic,* and Hughes's letters written to Arna Bontemps.

228. See the Discography for references to recordings by these singers. Hughes and Bontemps include "Southern Blues," obviously derived from Ma Rainey's 1923 recording (reissued on *Queen of the Blues,* Biograph BLP 12032, n.d.), in *The Book of Negro Folklore,* 391.

229. Hughes, "Songs Called the Blues," 144. *Georgia White Sings and Plays,* Rosetta 1307, 1982, reissues sixteen songs recorded between 1935 and 1941.

230. Memphis Minnie has had a number of LP reissues over the years and has come to rival Bessie Smith as a female blues artist among collectors. Two of her best reissues are *Blues Classics by Memphis Minnie,* Blues Classics 1, n.d., and *Memphis Minnie Vol. 2,* Blues Classics 13, n.d. Some of her later recordings, including pop blues, are reissued on *Gonna Take the Dirt Road Home,* Origin OJL 24, n.d.

231. Hughes, "Songs Called the Blues," 144.

232. See Godrich and Dixon, *Blues and Gospel Records 1902–1943,* 384–91. Johnson also played the harmonium, piano, kazoo, and violin, further demonstrating his versatility. I list a number of Lonnie Johnson albums in the Discography below. A variation of the first stanza of Johnson's "Hard Times Ain't Gone No Where," which is included on *The Blues of Lonnie Johnson,* Swaggie S1225, 1969 [1935], is printed among the random blues verses by Hughes in *The Book of Negro Humor,* 98. See my later discussion of Johnson's "Jelly Roll Baker," a lyric given on p. 42 of *The Book of Negro Humor,* in a section entitled "Just For Fun." A recording of Lonnie Johnson backing Louis Armstrong is part of *The Story of Jazz,* Folkways 7312, n.d., which is narrated by Hughes. Also included are a song by Ma Rainey, Meade Lux Lewis's "Honky Tonk Train Blues," and references to Blind Lemon Jefferson, Bessie Smith, Pine Top Smith, Albert Ammons, and Jimmy Yancey.

233. For Brown's remarks, see "Blues as Folk Poetry," in *Folk Say I,* ed. B. A. Botkin (Norman, Okla.: University of Oklahoma Press, 1930), 324–39; "Blues, Ballads, and Social Songs," in *Seventy-Five Years of Freedom* (Washington D.C.: Library of Congress, 1943), 17–25; "Spirituals, Blues and Jazz: The Negro in the Lively Arts," *Tricolor* 3 (1945): 62–70; "The Blues," *Phylon* 13 (1952): 286–92; "Negro Folk Expression: Spirituals, Seculars, Ballads and Work Songs," *Phylon* 14 (1953): 45–61. Hughes and Bontemps used "Blues as Folk Poetry" as the introductory essay to their blues section in *The Book of Negro Folklore,* 371–86, recognizing Brown's superior expertise in the field.

234. Langston Hughes, *Not Without Laughter* (New York: Knopf, 1930), 34.

235. Of course, the long-suffering and self-sacrificing Aunt Hager is a

hero as well. In a sense, Harrietta's aid to Sandy is a sort of reconciliation between Hager and Harrietta, since Hager's religious nature and Harrietta's secular ways had finally been brought together.

236. Langston Hughes, "The Blues I'm Playing," 351. As a point of interest, Linda Dahl quotes a *Down Beat* interview with Mary Lou Williams, with whom Hughes was familiar, in which Williams mentions a Kansas City pianist named Oceola. Unfortunately, Williams knew little else about this Oceola. Perhaps she was the inspiration for Hughes's portrait; perhaps not. See Linda Dahl, *Stormy Weather* (New York: Pantheon, 1984), 67.

237. Carr's original version, parts one, two, and three, has been reissued on *Leroy Carr 1928,* Matchbox MSE 210, n.d. A 1932 version, "How Long Has This Evening Train Been Gone," is on Collector's Classics CC50, n.d. Alberta Hunter, a vaudeville blues singer, recorded a "How Long, Daddy, How Long" in 1921, and Ida Cox, another vaudeville blues singer, recorded a version of the song in 1925. Cox's rendition has been reissued on *Blues Ain't Nothin' Else But,* Milestone 2015, n.d. Ma Rainey's version is included on *Ma Rainey,* Milestone M47021, 1974 [1928]. A stanza from "How Long Blues" is included in *The Book of Negro Folklore,* 396–97, with slight variations on Carr's words.

238. Langston Hughes, "Shadow of the Blues," *The Best of Simple* (New York: Hill and Wang, 1961), 168.

3

CREATING THE BLUES

1

Given Langston Hughes's extensive exposure to African-American folk music, it is not surprising that he decided to make use of the blues tradition in his secular poetry. There was literary precedent for the use of colloquial diction and folk material in twentieth-century American literature. Sterling Brown pointed out that the New Negro poets shared with the makers of the "New Poetry" in America the movement's "reaction against sentimentality, didacticism, optimism, and romantic escape" and "learned to shun stilted 'poetic diction,' to use fresher, more original language and to humanize poetry."[1] This outlook put them philosophically in line with groups like the Imagists who, led by Ezra Pound and F. S. Flint, aimed at renewal and concentration in contemporary poetry and sought to compose in the sequence of the musical phrase, not the metronome. Renewal for Hughes, however, meant looking into an African and a slave past, not into European history or "classic" Western literature, and the musical phrase was from African-American folk music, not from the classical music at which even Pound tried his hand.[2] So while Pound and Flint were working independently of Hughes and the New Negro poets, they still shared a common interest in revitalizing poetic diction, though they went about it in separate directions.

The writers of the Chicago Renaissance were even more important for Hughes, drawing as they did from Walt Whitman a "democratic" poetry (particularly attractive because democratic principles weren't applied to the treatment of African-Americans), a stated appreciation of the beauty and dignity of the common man, and a poetic line that moved poets out from underneath the foot of iambic pentameter. Hughes demonstrated his respect for Whitman, in fact, by editing a selection of Whitman's poetry for children and praising Whitman in articles like "Whitman: Negroes' First Great Poetic Friend."[3] Whitman helped Hughes realize that what was under the bootsoles of white America was the stuff of poetry as well.

In *The Big Sea,* Hughes acknowledged the influence of Chicago Renaissance writers like Carl Sandburg and Vachel Lindsay, both of whom could have provided models for the kind of poet Hughes wanted to be. In fact, early in his poetic development Hughes "began to try to write like Carl Sandburg."[4] In Sandburg's work Hughes found a vigorous colloquialism and energetic depictions of city life, as in "Chicago"; in Sandburg himself Hughes found a wandering hobo and balladeer, a writer of biographies, an autobiography, and children's books in addition to poems and articles. In short, Sandburg and Hughes both aimed for a breadth of expression, trying in a variety of genres to get their messages out. Sandburg's poetic influence can be seen in several poems in Hughes's first volume, *The Weary Blues,* most notably in "Proem" and "The Negro Speaks of Rivers."[5]

Vachel Lindsay, the poetic singer, uniter of poetry and chant, another wanderer and troubadour, likewise provided a poetic precedent for Hughes. By his use of music and his dramatic performances, even by his directions in the margins of a page as to how the poetry was to be performed (a modified version of which Hughes employed later in *Ask Your Mama),* Lindsay attempted to bring the artist, the poem, and the audience closer together and thus revivify poetry, as Hughes himself wished to do. Lindsay was also important to Hughes for the encouragement and impetus he gave Hughes's career after the busboy left three poems next to Lindsay's plate at the Wardman Park Hotel in 1925, though Lindsey gave more moral support than actual professional or financial assistance like that offered by Carl Van Vechten. The poems Hughes showed Lindsay, "The Weary Blues," "Jazzonia," and "Negro Dancers," were the first three poems after the "Proem" in *The Weary Blues,* and bore evidence of some of the alliteration, incidence of onomatopoeia, and exoticism found in Lindsay's verse.

Lindsay, in fact, recommended the "New Poetry" movement to Hughes in a 1925 letter and he warned Hughes of what factions, flatterers, and lionizers could do to ruin a poet, advising Hughes to rely on his own instincts as much as possible.[6] The success of poets like Sandburg and Lindsay, their reputations and publications in Chicago Renaissance poetry journals like *Poetry,* which also published some of Hughes's poetry beginning in 1926, must have at least encouraged Hughes to follow his instincts in using folk material such as the blues in his poetry, and in emphasizing oral communication and unaffected language that would take poetry out of polite parlors. This influence of Sandburg and Lindsay was not stronger than that of important artists like Paul Laurence Dunbar, Alain Locke, and James Weldon Johnson, all of whom had a more direct personal influence on Hughes, but we should not ignore Sandburg's and Lindsay's contributions to Hughes's self-confidence about his work.

If the Chicago Renaissance gave Hughes one precedent for opening the poetic gates to colloquial diction in his poetry, it was his sincere love of the blues and his pride in the African-American past, in African-American creativity, and in the "low-down folks" that spurred Hughes to employ the blues tradition in depicting the secular side of the soul of his people. However, another possible reason for Hughes's use of the blues should be recognized. As has been pointed out, Hughes was capable of ripping away the mask of romantic pretense about jazz musicians by pragmatically pointing out that jazz musicians played for money (in "Jazz As Communication"); he also recognized quite clearly (in *The Big Sea*) that his poetry could bring him financial rewards that he might not receive otherwise, in the form of meals, contacts, and a college scholarship. Practically speaking, then, Hughes certainly would have been shrewd enough to recognize that the blues craze of the 1920s might also extend to the poetry of an African-American who used the blues in his work. After all, if Mamie Smith could sell seventy-five thousand copies of "Crazy Blues" in one month, and if Jim Jackson could reputedly sell one million copies of "Jim Jackson's Kansas City Blues," might not a poet cash in on some of this popularity as well?[7] This is not to say that this was the only reason, or even the main reason, that Hughes drew on the blues tradition. After all, the audiences for blues records and for books of poetry were probably different. Still, Hughes must have recognized that his use of the blues might have a positive effect on his sales to book buyers who were also blues aficionados. Whites slumming in Harlem may have been particularly attracted to the blues poems, since it was what they considered the "primitive" music that brought them there.

One of the most important and obvious ways that Langston Hughes used the blues tradition, which is also the primary way critics used to identify Hughes's blues poems, was in his employment of musical and stanzaic structures. Although there is one predominant musical structure in the blues, the twelve-bar blues, there are other musical structures that predate, coexist with, or derive from it. Hughes was exposed to these structures in the various environments in which he found the blues, and he used these preexisting structures in a number of his blues poems, in some cases extending the structure of blues songs with original literary ideas. By comparing the structures of a variety of Hughes's blues poems to folk-blues examples and recorded examples by blues performers to whom Hughes referred at various points in his career, it is possible to gain a better idea of Hughes's use of both preexisting and original structures in his poetry. In some of his best "experimental" blues poems, Hughes used varied stanzas, line placement, and typography to convey both the spirit of the oral performance and a psychological or sociological complexity that stood up to such literary treatment on the page. He employed traditional twelve- and eight-bar stanzas, sometimes with his own literary touches, experiments with stanza patterns after the manner of the vaudeville composers, and free-verse poems with touches of the blues to give those poems an unmistakable blues quality.

The term "twelve-bar blues" refers to a musical composition with several basic (and variable) characteristics:

1. The composition is in 4/4 time (four beats to a measure).
2. The composition lasts or clearly tends toward the twelve measures or bars.
3. The composition tends toward a specific chord structure which, in its most rudimentary form and performed in the key of C, would consist of three basic or "implied" chords—C, F, and G— performed in a particular sequence. Techniques employed on various accompanying instruments provide a wide diversity

within these basic chord changes. A guitarist, for example, might employ various flatpicking or fingerpicking patterns and various chords that would make the performance more exciting. (Such a chord sequence, expressed in musical terms, follows or tends toward the following: four bars tonic/two bars subdominant/two bars tonic/two bars dominant/two bars tonic.)

4. The composition employs one of a number of basic stanzaic patterns or random slight variations on those patterns. Most common are stanzas consisting of one thought or line repeated three times (*AAA*); a thought or line sung once and followed by another line sung twice (*ABB*); two different thoughts or lines followed by a refrain (*AB* refrain); and, most commonly, one thought or line sung twice with a third line resolving the thought of the first two lines (*AAB*). In all cases the repetition of lines can be approximate—words changed, added, or omitted. The end words of the lines normally rhyme, and the line designations (*AAA, AAB, ABB*, etc.) should not be confused with a notation of the rhyme scheme.

Any discussion of the influence of blues rhythms and musical techniques on Hughes's blues poetry must necessarily take into account the fact that there has been no system of musical notation devised that totally captures the blues as they are performed. Because of the "bent" notes, slurs, pitch coloration, and melismatic effects in the blues, for example, conventional musical notation is inadequate; the music cannot be trapped behind the bars of a staff. In addition, visual representation of the music and the sung performance is no substitute for the experience of hearing the performance.

We can make the comparison between blues performances and Hughes's lyrics in a number of different textual and extratextual ways. Hughes himself made the comparison. His contacts with blues singers and performances throughout his life; his writings about the blues; the recordings of his blues poems to musical accompaniment either by himself or by people like "Big" Miller, Josh White, or Otis Spann (among others), sometimes under his direction; and, sometimes, his use of the word "blues" in poem titles or in the poems themselves (though this is not necessarily an indicator of the poem's "bluesiness") all underscore the fact that the blues were on his mind and that, in fact, blues music and blues lyrics provided models for his own blues poems. In addition, Hughes's writings about the blues indicate a general knowledge of the historical development of the blues, and the themes that he employs, the relationship between lines in his stanzas, and, sometimes, his interjection of words referring to instrumental sounds or audience responses (all of which will be discussed later) are all consistent with the blues tradition. Thus Hughes's potential use of such material; his intent to do so; the presence of blues content, theme, the half-line textual unit; and the audience response often evoked by the blues performance that he clearly wished for his blues poems suggest that indeed his blues poems are informed by the blues in a number of ways.

There are ways of approximating a blues performance, however inadequately, in order to suggest how a performed blues song resembles a blues poem by Hughes. The most basic way, one which will be employed most often here to provide the greatest number of people access to the comparison, involves placing the basic chord changes and the four beats to a bar present in 4/4 time in the appropriate location in relation to the lyrics as they are sung. Under this system, for a twelve-bar blues song there are twelve groups of four beats each. This means that a strict twelve-bar blues lasts forty-eight beats, and that each of the three thoughts lasts roughly sixteen beats (four bars). These beats are not spaced out evenly in the line in relation to the way the musical beats are counted out. Also, because there are only four beats counted out to the bar, nothing more complicated than quarter notes, which last one beat (four to a bar), are indicated in such a notation. That means that any sung or played note that lasts any shorter or longer than the strictly counted beat is not precisely notated here. An eighth note, for example, which lasts half as long as a quarter note (thus, one half of a beat), or a dotted quarter note, which lasts a beat and a half, do not receive specific attention, nor do any other variations from a metronomic regularity. This system focuses on the basic beats and the general way that the text fits into the four-beat bar.

The placement of the numbered beats in relation to the text, however, does convey some sense of the way the words are sung in relation to the bars. In such a notation, the further apart the numbered beats are spaced out over words in the text, the faster the group of words under each numbered beat are sung; the closer together the numbered beats are, the slower the corresponding words are sung. In other words, the number indicates generally where the beat falls in the text, and the words which have no number over them are sung in the spaces between beats.

In addition, at the end of the blues "line" or thought, there is often a section of music that is played after the sung text for that line has been completed. Thus in this system, at the end of the line there are numbered beats under which there are no words. Beyond that, the words of a line often begin on the fourth beat of the previous four-bar cluster. Therefore, the opening words of lines often begin on the fourth beat of a bar before starting the counting of the next four-bar sequence.

Under this system, anyone who knows three basic chords and can count four beats to the bar while reading the corresponding textual material can get a general idea of the way the line progresses. Tommy Johnson's twelve-bar "Lonesome Blues"[8] would be notated thusly under this system:

```
C
1     2    3 41 2   3      4     1234  123                      A
I woke this mornin' said my mornin' prayer
```

```
        F                           C
4 1        2    3 41 2       3 4    1  234  123                 A
I woke up this mornin' I said my mornin' prayer
```

```
                                    C
4 1       2    3        41   2  3 4  1     234  123  A
I woke up this mornin' babe I said my mornin' prayer.
```

Jeff Titon has attempted to render musically Johnson's vocal performance on this song,[9] and the attempt is useful for those who read music since it approximates the way the singer sings the lyrics. His notation, which makes use of symbols such as arrows to indicate pitched variations and crooked lines to indicate slurs to and from definite pitches, reveals one way that a singer might sing his lyrics to twelve-bar blues accompaniment:

Such a system can be applied to a number of Hughes's twelve-bar blues poems, though of course there are many variations on the way lyrics can be sung. For those who do not read music, and even for those who do, the best strategy is to listen to the blues recordings cited in note 8, above, to get a feel for the way the lyrics are sung. Then Hughes's blues poems can be read or sung in a manner approximating blues vocal performances.

Hughes was, of course, familiar with a variety of blues stanza patterns. Leadbelly, whom Hughes mentioned in his article "Songs Called the Blues" in 1940, recorded "Packin' Trunk Blues" using an *AAA* stanza:

> Sittin' down here wonderin' would a matchbox hold my clothes.
> Sittin' down here wonderin' would a matchbox hold my clothes.
> Sittin' down here wonderin' would a matchbox hold my clothes.
>
> I don't want to be bothered with no suitcase on my road.
> Don't want to be bothered with no suitcase on my road.
> I don't want to be bothered with no suitcase on my road.
>
> Now what would you do when your baby packin' up her trunk?
> What would you do when your baby packin' up her trunk?
> Now what would you do when your baby packin' up her trunk?
>
> Get you a half a gallon of whiskey and, and get on you a big drunk.
> Get you a half a gallon of whiskey and get on you a big drunk.
> Get you a half a gallon of whiskey and get on you a big drunk.[10]

Of course, Leadbelly seems to have taken the repeated line of an *AAB* stanza and sung it three times, and taken the resolution line (*B*) and made it into its own (*AAA*) stanza. Still, this is an example of the use of an *AAA* stanza by someone with whom Langston Hughes was familiar.

Despite Hughes's familiarity with the *AAA* stanza, he didn't publish any blues poems of his own that used this stanza form. As one of the editors of *The Book of Negro Folklore,* he helped choose for inclusion "Dink's Blues," reprinted from John and Alan Lomax's *American Ballads and Folk Songs.* This song included six *AAA* stanzas among the eleven *AAB* stanzas:

> Ef trouble was money, I'd be a millionaire. (× 3)
> Ef I gets drunk, wonder who's gwine carry me home. (× 3)
> I used to love you, but, oh, God damn you now. (× 3)
> De worry blues ain't nothin' but de heart disease. (× 3)
> When my struck sorrow de tears come rollin' down. (× 3)
> Ef I leave here walkin', it's chances I might ride. (× 3)[11]

Of course, one of the characteristics of the *AAA* stanza is that the repeated line can stand by itself as a complete statement, and perhaps *best* stands as a statement repeated three times because of the momentum and emphasis gained from a stanza that offers no line of resolution. However, Hughes apparently did not find such repetition useful for his own poetry, preferring, as did many recorded professional and vaudeville blues singers, an *AAB* stanza that provided more variation. It is likely that popular recordings assisted in getting rid of the *AAA* stanza by the examples they set. Perhaps Hughes felt that the three-line stanza was finally a failure in creativity, since he stated in his narration to *The Story of Jazz* that the repeat line in *AAB* blues was there to give the singer a chance to find a rhyming line. This is, of course, not necessarily the case, but it was possibly another reason why Hughes avoided the stanza.

The recorded *ABB* stanza turns up often in versions of "See See Rider," a blues of wide popularity that did not always stick to that stanza structure. As has already been pointed out, Gates Thomas reported a version of the song in "South Texas Negro Work Songs," and his version employs four *ABB* stanzas and a final *ABA* stanza. The opening verse is most famous:

> C. C. Rider, just see what you have done!
> You made me love you, now yo' woman's done come!
> You made me love you, now yo' woman's done come![12]

Ma Rainey's version, recorded for Paramount in 1924, starts with a sung introduction typical of many vaudeville blues, but her first verse uses the same *ABB* stanza:

> See see rider, see what you done done,
> Lawd, Lawd, Lawd,
> Made me love you, now your gal done come.
> You done made me love you, now your gal done come.[13]

Hughes used one *ABB* stanza in one of his blues poems, "Black Gal":

> Yet I ain't never been no bad one.
> Can't help it cause I'm Black.
> I hates them rinney yeller gals
> An' I wants my Albert back.
> Ma little, short, sweet, brownskin boy,—
> Oh, God, I wants him back.[14]

"Don't You Want to Be Free?" contains two *ABB* stanzas as well:

> Cook them white folks dinner
> Wash them white folks clothes,
> Be them white folks slave-gal,
> That is all she knows.
> Be them white folks slave-gal,
> That is all she knows.
>
> Whip done broke his spirit,
> Plow done broke his back.
> All they wants a slave, that's all,
> When a man is black.
> Nothin' but a slave, that's all,
> If a man is black.[15]

In "Black Gal," Hughes used what is roughly an *ABB* stanza to switch the emphasis from the self-pity of the first thought to the intense desire of the woman to have her man back. By changing the repeated lines from the hatred directed toward others to the love directed toward Albert, the speaker's *love* becomes more vivid and intense, and it also allows a reference to Albert's skin color—brown—into the poem. Since this is a major tension in the poem—the black woman losing a brown man to a yellow or light-skinned woman whose color might have been considered more desirable at the time because it was closer to white—its introduction in the black woman's statement of love and desire is particularly heartfelt and poignant. In "Don't You Want to Be Free?," along with the rare use of the *ABB* stanza, Hughes wrote a poem that, in its direct and overt protest against racism, is not typical of his blues poems. Perhaps Hughes chose this stanza form to make his message stand out even more, both by its departure from his norm and the emphasis it gives to a slave's existence, which is repeated in the final lines of each stanza. However, this type of stanza did not necessarily fit Hughes's published explanation of how the blues were thought up. That imitation, coupled with the benefits of other stanza types, may have been why he avoided the *ABB* stanza.

Another type of twelve-bar blues stanza consists of two lines followed by a refrain in every stanza. This type of stanza offers both variety (the first two lines) and repetition (the refrain), and the refrain is made more memorable by the repetition, facilitating a sing-along effect, as in "Jim Jackson's Kansas City Blues," which probably owed much of its monumental success to this feature:

> I woke up this mornin' feelin' bad,
> Thought about the good time I once have had.
>
> *Refrain:*
> I'm gonna move to Kansas City.
> I'm gonna move to Kansas City.
> I'm gonna move, baby, honey where they don't allow you.[16]

At other times, however, the refrain can be used to apply to a number of examples or incidents discussed in the lines previous to the stanzas, as in Memphis Minnie's "Nothing in Rambling":

> I was born in Louisiana, raised in Algiers,
> And everywhere I been, the peoples all say,
>
> *Refrain:*
> Ain't nothin' in ramblin', either runnin' around.
> Well, I believe I'll marry, ooh, ooh, Lord, and settle down.
>
> I first left home, I stopped in Tennessee,
> The peoples all beggin', "Come and stay with me."
>
> *Refrain:*
> Cause there ain't nothin' in ramblin', either runnin' around
> I believe I'll get me a good man, ooh, ooh, Lord, and settle down.

I walked through the alley with my hand in my coat,
The police start to shoot me, thought it was something I stole.

Refrain:
You know there ain't nothin' in ramblin', either runnin' around,
Well, I believe I'll marry, ooh, ooh, Lord, and settle down.

The peoples on the highway is walkin' and cryin'.
Some is starvin', some is dyin'.

Refrain:
You know there ain't nothin' in ramblin', either runnin' around.
I believe I'll get a good man, ooh, ooh, Lord, and settle down.

You may go to Hollywood and try to get on the screen,
But I'm gonna stay right here and eat these old charity beans.

Refrain:
Cause there ain't nothin' in ramblin', either runnin' around.
Well I believe I'll marry, ooh, ooh, Lord, and settle down.[17]

In this type of twelve-bar stanza, the first two lines are completed in four bars, leaving eight bars during each stanza to repeat the refrain. In the case of Memphis Minnie's song, that emphasizes the lesson she learned from being out on the road, and its sing-along attractiveness puts its "truth" into the mouths of those who are listening to (and singing along with) the song.

None of Hughes's blues poems used this twelve-bar stanza (though one of his songs does, to be discussed later), but he did reprint, in *The Book of Negro Humor*, a variant on the stanza in "Jelly Roll Baker":

> She said, Mister Jelly Roll Baker,
>   Let me be your slave.
> When Gabriel blows his trumpet
>   I'll rise from my grave
> For some of your jelly roll.
>   She said, I love your jelly roll!
> It's good for the sick
>   and it's good for the old.
> Can I put in an order
>   For two weeks ahead?
> I'd rather have your jelly
>   Than my home-cooked bread.

Mister Jelly Roll Baker,
  I love your jelly roll.
Mister Jelly Roll Baker,
  Your good jelly roll's
Like Maxwell House coffee,
  Good to my very soul!
Mister Jelly Roll!
Ow! She hollered,
Jelly Roll![18]

The version that Hughes prints seemed to be a variant of the song Lonnie Johnson recorded in 1942 for the Bluebird Company and later, under the same title, for King Records. Johnson's first stanza is substantially the same as Hughes's first eight lines above, but Johnson adds extra verses:

I was sentenced for murder in the first degree
The judge's wife called up and said, "Let that man go free."

Refrain:
"He's a jelly roll baker, he's got the best jelly in town,
He's the only man can bake jelly roll with his damper down."

Was in the hospital shot all full of holes
The nurse left a man dyin' and say "He's got to give the jelly roll."
"It's good old jelly," she says, "I love my good jelly roll."
She says, "I'd rather let him lose his life than to miss my good jelly roll."

Lady asked me who learned me how to bake good jelly roll.
I said, "Nobody, miss, it's just a gift from my soul."
Bake good jelly roll, mmm, that good old jelly roll.
She says, "I love your jelly roll, it do me good deep down in my soul."

She says, "Can I put in an order for two weeks ahead?
"I'd rather have your jelly than my home-cooked bread."
"I love your jelly roll, I love your good jelly roll."
"It's just like Maxwell House coffee, it's good deep down in my soul."[19]

In this blues stanza Johnson sings the first two lines in four bars and follows with a variable refrain that repeats the same general message—that the singer has a good jelly roll that the woman discussed in the first two lines of each stanza finds hard to resist. Though Hughes never wrote a twelve-bar blues poem that is comparable to Johnson's song, he did use a modulated or varied refrain in several of his blues poems (to be discussed later), and songs like Johnson's "Jelly Roll Baker" provided examples for Hughes to follow.

As noted earlier, the *AAB* stanza is the predominant stanza form in recorded blues, deriving most likely from the stanza "in which a single line was simply repeated once, twice, or even three times," sometimes with a refrain.[20] W. C. Handy reported hearing an *AAB* blues stanza in the Mississippi Delta in 1903:

> Boll Weevil, where you been so long?
> Boll Weevil, where you been so long?
> You stole my cotton, now you want my corn.[21]

Once the blues finally made it on phonograph records, this form, with its repeat line and response line, became the most popular, though the other stanzaic variations were still recorded.

Actually, the word "line" used to describe a repeated phrase can, as we have already discussed, be a misnomer, since the "half-line" is often referred to by some as the textual unit of the blues. The mid-line caesura, placed between bars 1 and 2 perhaps for rhythmic variation and textual emphasis, splits the "line" into two lines, and indeed Hughes seems to have recognized this characteristic by rendering his poems ethnopoetically on the page—that is, by splitting the "lines" into two lines and thus making the *AAB* stanza six lines long, with two lines to each letter. Thus, the lyric Handy reported would be transcribed:

> Boll Weevil,
> Where you been so long?
> Boll Weevil,
> Where you been so long?
> You stole my cotton,
> Now you want my corn.

By writing down his blues poems this way, Hughes attempted to bring more of the oral performance, the rhythms of the music and voice, into his poetry. His discussion of the shortness of the lines of his poetry on his *Poetry and Reflections* album hints at an economic advantage as well:

The very first poem that I sold was a jazz poem. It was a poem about the Charleston. . . . Well, this little Charleston poem of mine, and two others, I sent to a magazine called *Vanity Fair*. That was a very smart New York magazine at that time, and they bought these poems, and they paid me fifty cents a line. But my three poems were quite short and when I got the check and looked at it it wasn't very much money. So I thought to myself, well, from now on I'll cut all my poetic lines in half and make two out of them and get bigger checks. So now you understand when you see my poems having very short lines how I became aware of the value of shortening the line in poetry. Ha! Commercial reasons.[22]

These three poems, "To Midnight Nan at Leroy's," "Fantasy in Purple," and "Suicide," are not blues poems, though "To Midnight Nan at Leroy's" is a jazz poem that mentions the singing of a blues song:

> Sing your Blues song,
> Pretty baby.
> You want lovin'
> And you don't mean maybe.[23]

Significantly, this poem already has short lines throughout, indicating that in his blues and jazz poems the commercial reason for cutting his lines in half was added to an aesthetic imperative that influenced him to try to capture the nuances of oral performance. Sometimes the singer makes textual pauses in places that are unconventional in terms of how we might read a line, as in Peg Leg Howell's "Rock and Gravel Blues":

> Honey let's go to the
> River and sit down.
> Honey let's go to the
> River and sit down.
> If the blues overtakes us
> Jump overboard and drown.[24]

Hughes was aware of this occasional occurrence as well, employing a similarly placed break in "Hard Daddy":

> I wish I had wings to
> Fly like de eagle flies.
> Wish I had wings to

Fly like de eagle flies.
I'd fly on ma man an'
I'd scratch out both his eyes.[25]

In both cases, the breaking of the line momentarily suspends the thought and raises questions for the listener: Where does Howell want to go? For what does Hughes's speaker want wings, and what will that speaker do after she flies on her man? Although Hughes imitated an oral nuance here, the effect is amplified on the printed page, where the suspension of the line is both auditory *and* visual. This is a perfect example of a literary use that coincides with an oral characteristic.

The response line in the *AAB* blues stanza, like the response line in the *ABB* stanza, can serve a number of different purposes in relation to the repeat line, as Janheinz Jahn has pointed out. It can expand on it, as in this verse from Victoria Spivey's "Blood Hound Blues":

Well I broke out of my cell
When the jailer turned his back.
I broke out of my cell
When the jailer turned his back.
But now I'm so sorry,
Bloodhounds are on my track.[26]

Hughes employed a similar technique in "Suicide" in *Fine Clothes to the Jew*, where the response line expands on the woman's loneliness and discusses a possible reaction to the situation:

Ma sweet good man has
Packed his trunk and left.
Ma sweet good man has
Packed his trunk and left.
Nobody to love me:
I'm gonna kill myself.[27]

The response line can illuminate the repeat line, as in Blind Lemon Jefferson's "Pneumonia Blues":

Aching all over
I believe I got the pneumonia this time.
I'm aching all over
Believe I got the pneumonia this time.

And it's all on account of
That low down gal of mine.[28]

Hughes used the response line to illuminate in two stanzas of "Homesick Blues," where it explains why the bridge is "a sad song in de air" and why the speaker's heart is in his mouth:

De railroad bridge's
A sad song in the air.
De railroad bridge's
A sad song in de air.
Ever time de trains pass
I wants to go somewhere.

I went down to de station.
Ma heart was in ma mouth.
Went down to de station.
Heart was in ma mouth.
Lookin' for a box car
To roll me to de South.[29]

The response line can justify the repeat line, as in Bessie Smith's "Black Mountain Blues":

Black Mountain people
Are bad as they can be.
Black Mountain people
Are bad as they can be.
They uses gun powder
Just to sweeten their tea.[30]

Just as Bessie Smith justifies her statement about how "bad" Black Mountain people are, Hughes's speaker justifies his opening statement as well in "Love Again Blues":

My life ain't nothin'
But a lot o' Gawd-knows-what.
I say my life ain't nothin'
But a lot o' Gawd-knows-what.
Just one thing after 'nother
Added to de trouble that I got.[31]

Elsewhere, the response line might imply the antithesis or contradiction of the repeat line:

> Some people say them
> Overseas blues ain't bad.
> Some people say them
> Overseas blues ain't bad.
> It must not have been
> Them overseas blues I had.[32]

Hughes wrote of the false comments of others in "Evenin' Air Blues":

> Folks, I come up North
> Cause they told me de North was fine.
> I come up North
> Cause they told me de North was fine.
> Been up here six months—
> I'm about to lose my mind.[33]

The paradox of loving someone who mistreats you is itself subjected to a potential contradiction of *that* in the response line of "In a Troubled Key":

> Still I can't help lovin' you,
> Even though you do me wrong.
> Says I can't help lovin' you,
> Though you do me wrong—
> But my love might turn into a knife
> Instead of to a song.[34]

By employing these varying strategies in his response lines, Hughes not only remained faithful to the blues tradition, but he imitated the potential variety of what's often considered a limited form. When combined with his use of a number of different traditional and original stanza forms and placement of lines, some of which are still to be discussed, the effect is to demonstrate some of the diversity of which the blues lyric is capable.

Hughes also made use of an *ABC* twelve-bar stanza in "Only Woman Blues," and that type of stanza, though not especially common, was recorded by some blues performers. The sophisticated Lonnie Johnson was the kind of blues artist who would try this type of stanza, with its greater variety and rhyming challenge:

> He'll give you his money, he'll buy you clothes
> What else can a poor workin' man do?

You take his money and you waste it
On anybody you don't care who.
It's good while it lasts you
But it's all comin' home to you.[35]

Hughes, too, used this type of stanza in the opening of "Only Woman Blues" in *Shakespeare in Harlem:*

I want to tell you 'bout that woman,
My used-to-be—
She was de meanest woman
I ever did see.
But she's de only
Woman that could mistreat me.[36]

One reason Hughes used this stanza is the apparent eagerness of the singer to tell the audience about his woman, as stated in the first line. That desire to discuss the woman stems from her meanness—treated in lines 3 and 4—and her attractiveness to the speaker—treated in lines 5 and 6. The speaker's desire to discuss this paradox gives birth to the *ABC* stanza, just as in Johnson's song his sympathy for the working man, his disdain for the woman, and his predictions of what will happen to her generates an *ABC* stanza as well. It is obvious that Hughes was not simply trying to employ as many different stanzas as possible, but sought to use stanzas that served his purpose psychologically. Of course, there are numerous variations on these basic strategies for response lines in twelve-bar blues, both in the blues tradition and in Hughes's poems, and it seems that Hughes had an excellent idea of the possibilities open to him in terms of the relationship between the repeat lines and the response lines.

Collected as early as the twelve-bar blues was another popular blues music stanza, the eight-bar stanza. It has several characteristics:

1. The composition is in 4/4 time.
2. The composition lasts or clearly tends toward eight measures or bars.
3. The composition tends toward a specific chord structure, which, in its most rudimentary form and performed in the key of C, would consist of three basic or "implied" chords—C, F,

and G—performed in a particular sequence adapted to the eight-bar length.

4. The composition employs any number of basic stanzaic patterns; most often *AA, AB,* and *AB* with a refrain.

Odum reported a number of *AA* stanzas in the *Journal of American Folklore* in 1911, including a version of "Po' Boy Long Way from Home":

‖:Come here, babe, an' sit on you' papa's knee:‖
‖:You brought me here an' let 'em throw me down:‖[37]

Odum also printed a number of *AB* stanzas, such as "Long and Tall an' Chocolate to the Bone":

Well, I'm goin' to buy me a little railroad of my own,
Ain't goin' to let nobody ride but the chocolate to the bone.[38]

There are two basic ways that a chord progression can be applied to this type of stanza. One is simply to play the chords as in a twelve-bar blues, skipping the chord changes for the repeat line, as in King Solomon Hill's "That Gone Dead Train":[39]

```
        C
        1   2       3   4   1   2   3   4
        I'm goin' way down,

        1           2           3   4       1   2   3
        Lord, I'm gonna try to leave here today.

                    G               F
        4           1   2   3   4   1   2   3
        Tell me that's a mean old fireman

                            C
        4       1   2   3   4   1   2   3   4
        And that train is just that way.
```

The other chord structure is like the one used in the famous "Trouble in Mind" and in Lonnie Johnson's eight-bar blues "There Is No Justice":[40]

```
                C               G
                1   2 3   4     1       2   3   4
                Now they put me in the jailhouse
```

```
F
1       2       3   4   1   2   3
Twenty long years today,

        C
4       1       2   3
And it's drivin' me crazy

        G               F       C       G
4       1       2       3   4 1 234    123
I've got thirty more years to stay.
```

This type of musical setting has, in its most basic form, more chord activity than the one presented in King Solomon Hill's "The Gone Dead Train," but the stanza and line length are often very similar. Because of this, it is difficult to tell what kind of musical setting Hughes might have had in mind for his eight-bar blues; however, it is more important to realize that eight-bar blues like this existed, and that Hughes's four-line blues stanzas are not necessarily merely the result of typographical accommodation. So when Hughes wrote "Sylvester's Dyin' Bed,"[41] he probably had an eight-bar stanza in mind:

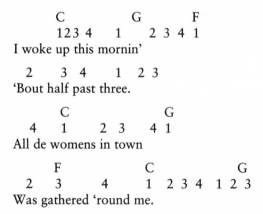

```
        C               G           F
        123 4       1       2   3   4   1
        I woke up this mornin'

        2       3   4       1   2   3
        'Bout half past three.

                C               G
        4       1       2   3   4 1
        All de womens in town

        F                   C               G
        2       3       4       1   2   3   4   1   2   3
        Was gathered 'round me.
```

These lines from Hughes's poem are not unlike some of the boastful East Coast blues like Blind Willie McTell's "Searchin' the Desert for the Blues," an eight-bar blues that uses this chord progression. Both poems and songs benefit from a quick lyric progression typical of a fast-talking boaster:

> You may search the ocean
> You might go cross the deep blue sea
> Honey, you'll never find
> Another hotshot like me.[42]

Among other poems, "Could Be," "Bad Luck Card," and "As Befits a Man" fit the same pattern. Hughes's "Reverie on Harlem River" is another of this type of eight-bar poem, but here he employed typography for dramatic effect in its last stanza:

> Did you ever go down to the river—
> Two a.m. midnight by your self?
> Sit down by the river
> And wonder what you got left?
>
> Did you ever think about your mother?
> God bless her, dead and gone!
> Did you ever think about your sweetheart
> And wish she'd never been born?
>
> Down on the Harlem River
>   Two a.m.
>   Midnight!
>   By your self!
> Lawd, I wish I could die—
> But who would miss me if I left?[43]

The first two stanzas of the poem build toward the final stanza, in which the singer describes how he has nothing and nobody left. The first four lines in the final stanza are actually a paraphrase of the first two lines of stanza 1, but in this stanza, lines 2, 3, and 4 are dramatically emphasized by the division of what was one line into three. The time and the singer's loneliness, perhaps even his exasperation, are captured in what could be regarded as an ethnopoetic type of rendering of an oral performance—we can "hear" the singer emphasizing these words. This is a literary use of typography in a traditional blues stanza, but again the literary and the oral coincide, with no violence done to either one. The relationship between the two lyric lines of the stanza is substantially the same as in the twelve-bar blues. There is no repeat (we need to be careful not to say that the repeat is lost, since it was not necessarily there in the first place) so there is neither the repetition nor the emphasis of the repeat line of the twelve-bar blues, but the stanzas move more quickly and, particularly when played quickly, this rapidity is heightened even more. Even without the music, this shorter reading time is obvious.

Another eight-bar blues pattern is the *AB* refrain pattern, used in Leroy Carr's famous "How Long—How Long Blues" and by Ma Rainey in "Daddy, Goodbye Blues," both from 1928. Titon transcribed Carr's vocal performance as follows:[44]

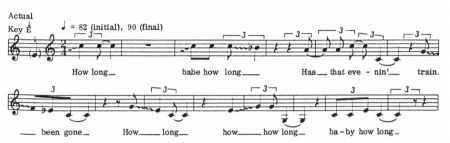

In our more basic system, Rainey's "Daddy, Goodbye Blues" is notated as follows:

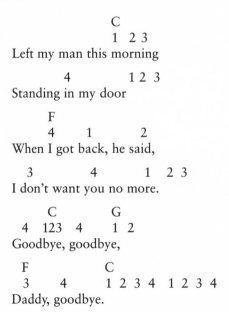

This type of eight-bar stanza functions the same way as the *AB* refrain twelve-bar stanza in terms of the relationship between the

AB lines and the refrain, generating familiarity with the refrain and making it almost a sing-along section of the song while anchoring the different stanzas in a dominant thought or idea.

The *AB* refrain stanza is the model for two of Hughes's best blues poems, "Southern Mammy Sings"[46] and "Same In Blues." The first of these begins with this stanza:

<pre>
                    C
                    1   2 3
       Miss Gardner's in her garden.

         4   1   2 3
       Miss Yardman's in her yard.

                           F
         4   1   2   3
       Miss Michaelmas is at de mass

            4   1 2 3 4
       And I am gettin' tired!

         C   G   F
         1234 1 2 3
         Lawd!

                    C
         4   1 2 3 4 1 2 3 4
       I am gettin' tired!
</pre>

However, Hughes altered the traditional stanza as it normally exists in the recorded blues songs of this type by changing the refrain in each stanza:

> The nation's they is fightin'
> And the nation's they done fit.
> Sometimes I think that white folks
> Ain't worth a little bit.
>   No, m'am!
> Ain't worth a little bit.
>
> Last week they lynched a colored boy.
> They hung him to a tree.
> That colored boy ain't said a thing
> But we all should be free.
>   Yes, m'am!
> We all should be free.

Not meanin' to be sassy
And not meaning to be smart—
But sometimes I think that white folks
Just ain't got no heart.
　No, m'am!
Just ain't got no heart.

Hughes closely integrated the *AB* lines and refrains of each stanza by making the refrain a clear repetition of the affirmation or denial of the central thought in the *AB* lines. The refrains are even more effective in the way that they change thoughts or suggestions from the *AB* lines into assertions in the refrains: "Sometimes I think that white folks / Ain't worth a little bit" becomes a definite assertion in the refrain, as do the words of the "colored boy" and the idea that white folks "ain't got no heart." The use of the negative in the refrains discussing white folks and the positive in the refrain discussing the "colored boy" underscores the negative feeling toward white violence and heartlessness and the positive reaction to assertions of freedom. Finally, by placing these assertions in a refrain, which normally makes the lines more memorable and prompts the audience to join in, the message is emphasized even more.

"Same In Blues" modulates the refrain in a similar way, though by its alteration of only one word it lends itself to an even closer comparison to the *AB* refrain patterns that influence the audience to repeat the refrain with the "singer":

I said to my baby,
Baby, take it slow.
I can't, she said, I can't!
I got to go!

　There's a certain
　amount of traveling
　in a dream deferred.

Lulu said to Leonard,
I want a diamond ring.
Leonard said to Lulu,
You won't get a goddamn thing!

　A certain
　amount of nothing
　in a dream deferred.

Daddy, daddy, daddy,
All I want is you.
You can have me, baby—
but my lovin' days is through.

    A certain
    amount of impotence
    in a dream deferred.

Three parties
On my party line—
But that third party,
Lord, ain't mine!

    There's liable
    to be confusion
    in a dream deferred.

From river to river,
Uptown and down,
There's liable to be confusion
when a dream gets kicked around.[47]

The three-line refrains are also emphasized typographically by italics, which separate them even further from the *AB* lines. This is probably done because they represent a kind of external, intellectual generalization on the various situations depicted in the *AB* lines. Stanza 1 suggests the infringement of the deferred African-American achievement of happiness, fulfillment, and freedom (the "American Dream") on the sexual relationship between two people. The woman's demand for a luxury item and the man's refusal in stanza 2 drives a wedge even further between the two of them. By this time it is becoming apparent that the "dream deferred" creates individual difficulties affecting their lives on social, sexual, and economic levels. In the third stanza, now that the female is ready for sexual action, the man says he is no longer capable, prompting a fourth stanza that euphemistically refers to the woman's lover as the third party on his party line. The fact that the "dream deferred" has brought these two people to this situation suggests that the third party, encroaching on the speaker's private property, might be the system that defers the dream as well as an actual lover. The last stanza emphasizes the confusion caused by the deferred dream and the resulting inability of the two people to coordinate their desires. That stanza breaks the previous pattern by eliminating the italicized refrain and by taking the words of the refrain from the previous stanza and integrating them into the *AB* lines. Thus, the stanza is completed—the thought is there—but it stops short of achieving the fullness of the pattern that had been established. This variation is peculiarly successful in communicating structurally what has been discussed in the words: that sometimes the system withholds things that should be given, that it causes an emptiness or lack that makes life precariously off-balance.

Twelve- and eight-bar stanzas are not always mutually exclusive in the same song. The previously mentioned "The Gone Dead Train" by King Solomon Hill contains eight-bar *AB* stanzas throughout except for the final verse:

> Mm, Mm
> I want to ride your train.
> I said look here engineer
> Can I ride your train?
> He said, "Look you ought to know this train ain't mine
> And you askin' me in vain."[48]

As the final stanza of a song the title of which emphasizes the inability to ride the train, this stanza is particularly effective. The first two lines indicate the singer's desire, punctuated by his moaning, to ride the train; the next two lines make the desire more dramatic by calling up a specific dramatic situation—the asking of an engineer for a free ride. The responses in the final two lines, then, are particularly disappointing to the singer, who has built up his longing in this climactic stanza through a subtly modulated repetition to his final letdown.

Hughes mixed eight- and twelve-bar stanzas in a similar way in "Lover's Return":

> My old time daddy
> Came back home last night.
> His face was pale and
> His eyes didn't look just right.
>
> He says, "Mary, I'm
> Comin' home to you—

So sick and lonesome
I don't know what to do."

Oh, men treats women
Just like a pair o' shoes—
You kicks 'em round and
Does 'em up like you choose.

I looked at my daddy—
Lawd! and I wanted to cry.
He looked so thin—
Lawd! that I wanted to cry.
But the devil told me:
Damn a lover
Come home to die.[49]

In this poem, Hughes italicized the third stanza in order to empha-size its difference—perhaps even to suggest that it is a performance. This stanza is different from the others in that it refers to a general "truth" rather than to the specific situation at hand. However, it maintains its similarity to the previous stanzas in that these three stanzas have an identical blues form and rhythm. The typography emphasizes the close relationship between personal experience and the general blues performance, between expression in the blues and the daily colloquial expression of the speakers. In addition, this italicized stanza indicates the woman's "second mind" about her "old time daddy," for whom some sympathy is built up in stanzas 1 and 2. The final stanza, a twelve-bar stanza in which the repeat line captures the sympathetic part of the woman's attitude, attempts to project her refusal to help her lover onto the devil by italicizing the "devil's" comments. That sympathetic attitude, related to the gen-eralized comments on the bad way that men treat women, is asso-ciated with the devil's denial of help. However, that association comes in a stanza in which, because of the expanded *AAB* form, the woman seems very sensitive and concerned. The earlier version of this poem made stanza 3 a twelve-bar stanza as well, but Hughes's use of that stanza really diminishes the impact of having the last stanza add two lines and the devil to help the woman resolve her feelings while presenting herself in as positive a light as possible. By mixing stanza forms and selective italicizing, Hughes subtly highlighted the woman's psychological state of mind and, thus, used the written word to assist the oral form.

Hughes used a similar structure strategy—writing eight-bar stanzas leading up to a final twelve-bar stanza—in "Black Gal" and "Little Green Tree," the latter titled "Little Green Tree Blues" when it was printed in *The Poetry of the Negro*. There it has slightly different wording and consists of three twelve-bar stanzas, differing from its publication in *One Way Ticket* and *Selected Poems:*

> It looks like to me
> My good-time days done past.
> There's nothin' in this world
> I reckon's due to last.
>
> I used to play
> And I played so dog-gone hard.
> Now old age is got me,
> Dealt me by bad-luck card.
>
> I look down the road
> And I see a little tree.
> Little piece down the road
> I see a little tree.
>
> Them cool green leaves
> Is waitin' to shelter me.
>
> O, little tree!⁵⁰

In this poem Hughes reduced what were twelve-bar stanzas to eight-bar stanzas, probably because he wished the length of his stanzas to reflect the speaker's sense of the fleetingness of his life and good luck. It might have been a good strategy to make these *ABB* stanzas, which would emphasize the speaker's dejection; however, since his dejection is not going to last either—he has the hope that the little green tree will shelter or comfort him—the eight-bar stanzas are most effective. The repeat line in the final stanza, then, emphasizes hope, which Hughes insisted was inherent in the blues, and yearning for hope, and the exclamation of the joy found in this sign of hope. Additionally, Hughes emphasized that hope by setting off the response lines from the repeat lines in stanza 3. Hughes worked very carefully with structure here. From the look of the poem on the page, the stanzaic pattern seems to be broken with line 13, thus placing the sighting of the tree with the despair of the first two lines. However, the *blues* pattern tells us that the pattern is broken with line 9, thus placing the sighting of the tree with the hope of the remainder of the poem. Therefore, Hughes found the perfect visual way of representing the despair and hope related to the sighting of the tree, which will presumably allow the speaker to finally take his rest. In *Selected Poems* the final exclamation is italicized, suggesting that it is more than just an individual hope of the singer in the poem, but perhaps the hope of *all* "blues people," including Hughes.

So Hughes worked on his blues poems with a knowledge of various traditional twelve- and eight-bar stanzas, but he added a number of his own touches. By mixing stanza forms, italicizing, and working with novel line placements in traditional stanzas, Hughes extended the blues tradition in his own literary way. These blues are thus sometimes structurally familiar and structurally novel simultaneously, mirroring some aspect of the theme of the individual poem.

In addition to the various twelve- and eight-bar stanzas, there are a number of other stanza forms employed in the blues, especially in the music of the vaudeville blues singers, who were influenced by the polished arrangements W. C. Handy made of the folk blues he heard in the South. Handy, who first heard the *AAA* form sung by Phil Jones in Evansville, Indiana, sometime around 1896, discussed how he took this form and created, for variation, an *AAB* stanza, as in "St. Louis Blues," and then went even further:

> I hate to see de eve'-nin' sun go down
> Hate to see de eve'-nin' sun go down
> 'Cause my baby, he done lef' dis town

To vary the pattern still further, and to avoid monotony in the music, I used a four line unit in the next part of the lyric.

> St. Louis women wid her diamond rings
> Pulls dat man roun' by her apron strings.
> 'Twant for powder an' for store-bought hair
> De man I love would not gone nowhere.[51]

In essence, these four lines form a sixteen-bar bridge (four bars per line) between two twelve-bar stanzas in Handy's song, and they represent one of the innovations of the vaudeville blues composers.

Sometimes there were sixteen-bar introductions to twelve-bar songs, as in Ma Rainey's 1924 recording of "Lucky Rock Blues":

> Feelin' kinda melancholy
> Made up my mind to go away.
> Have no time for faith, it's folly,
> Sometimes it helps [unintelligible] the way.
> To forget the man you love
> Although he may be mean.
> Goodbye, folks, I'm on my way,
> Way down to New Orleans.
>
> Goin' to New Orleans
> To find that lucky rock.
> Goin' to New Orleans
> To find that lucky rock.
> Tryin' to loose myself
> From this bad luck I've got.[52]

The first eight lines, which correspond to the four-line bridge in Handy's song, provide a conversational, almost narrative introduction to the twelve-bar blues stanzas which are the heart of the song. These eight lines are influenced by the vaudeville stage, more melodic and vocally crooned than moaned. Many of the vaudeville blues singers were backed by the best jazz musicians of the day, like Louis Armstrong, King Oliver, Joe Smith, James P. Johnson, Fletcher Henderson, Lovie Austin, and Coleman Hawkins, and during these introductory passages the playing of these jazz musicians was much more mannered and subdued than when the singer moved into the twelve-bar stanza. In "Lucky Rock Blues," for example, the musicians play mainly chords or the melody and harmony softly and tentatively behind Rainey, but the riff they play between the sung lines in the twelve-bar stanzas jumps up and down with the anticipation and excitement of finding the "lucky rock." This type of introduction was common in many vaudeville blues, though, of course, the vaudeville singers sang many eight- and twelve-bar blues without these additions.

Because vaudeville composers like Handy were exactly that—composers—they were constantly searching for new forms or new ways to use the old forms, to add newness or novelty to their compositions. So the vaudeville influence diversified the blues tradition, sometimes sweetening it, sometimes making it maudlin or stilted, and occasionally complementing it, providing varied stanzaic patterns that were departures from the traditional stanzas. The strains of jazz improvisation that sounded along with the often pop-influenced vocals frequently located the vaudeville blues in an urban and professional environment, even if they did draw in varying degrees on folk blues. This kind of diversity in the music of singers with whom Hughes was familiar must have in some way influenced him to work with varying blues stanza forms. At the very least, they provided a precedent for what Hughes was doing, especially since these vaudeville blues, which were first recorded in 1920, experienced peak recording years between 1923 and 1926, though they were still recorded for a number of years after 1926.[53]

Hughes greatly admired Handy's part in helping to disseminate and "legitimize" blues through polishing and publishing efforts,[54] especially in songs like "Memphis Blues" and "St. Louis Blues." Hughes called the latter "one of America's best-known popular songs all over the world."[55] In 1942 he called the song "the greatest American song written in our time," noting that it had been "heard around the world everywhere, played by dance bands from Constantinople to Melbourne, Cape Town to Seattle," and "performed by such artists as Bessie Smith, Bing Crosby, and Louis Armstrong."[56] Handy agreed with Hughes that "someday it [the blues] will be the basis for great ballets, great sonatas, and great new forms still unevolved."[57] Hughes's letters to and from Arna Bontemps are peppered with references to Handy, especially regarding the use of "St. Louis Blues" in "St. Louis Woman," a play by Bontemps and Countee Cullen (based on Bontemps's novel *God Sends Sunday*) for which Hughes wrote the libretto.[58] Handy, too, apparently admired Hughes, as Onwuchekwa Jemie pointed out, since Handy commented that Hughes's poem "Hope" said in four lines "what it would have taken Shakespeare two acts and three scenes to say."[59] In fact, Hughes wrote lyrics for Handy's "Golden Brown Blues," and the two collaborated with Clarence Muse on "Go and Get the Enemy Blues," a World War II–era effort. Hughes's admiration of Handy, coupled with his interest in vaudeville blues singers, resulted in a number of poems that seem to draw on the spirit of the composed blues of Handy and others like him. "Blue Monday" fits one type of sixteen-bar stanza pattern:[60]

1 2   3   4
No use in my going

1   2   3   4   1234 123
Downtown to work today,

4   1
It's eight,

2   3   41
I'm late—

2   3   4   1234 1234 1
And it's marked down that-a-way.

2   3
Saturday and Sunday's

4   1 2   3 4
Fun to sport around.

1 2   3
But no use denying—

4   1 2   3
Monday'll get you down.

4 1 2   3 4   1
That old blue Monday

2   3   4   1   234 1234
Will surely get you down.

Vaudeville blues singer Margaret Carter's "I Want Plenty Grease in My Frying Pan" has a similar structure:[61]

1   2   3   4   12 3
I need plenty grease in my frying pan

4   1   2   3 4 1 234
'Cause I don't want my meat to burn.

1   2   3   4 1   2   3
You know I asked you first to get me some lard

4   1   2   3 4 1   234
But it seems that you cannot learn.

```
  1     2  3  4    1
You know I use plenty grease

  2  3
Everyday

  4  1  2    3    4
But I ain't did no fryin' while

  1     2  3  4
You was away.

  1     2    3    4    1 2 3
I need plenty grease in my frying pan

  4    1       2   3   4  1  2 3 4
'Cause I don't want my meat to burn.
```

Each of the two works divides up into three sections and demonstrates a dependence between the groups of lines to explain the
entire meaning. Both also lead up to the final flat statement of fact,
though in Carter's performance the stanza is framed by the same
two lines. Carter's musical accompaniment includes a stop-time
section, at which time "the orchestra plays only one note in every
measure as background."[62] This occurs during the four-line middle
section, punctuating the message of those lines and preparing the
listener for the final message. Such an accompaniment is entirely
possible in "Blue Monday" as well. In fact, it would emphasize the
double meaning of the title of the poem. A Blue Monday party, a
regular event in many clubs even today, takes place after musicians
finish their regular jobs and congregate at a club late Sunday night
into early Monday morning to play for their own pleasure, sometimes continuing until late Monday afternoon. Such parties would
be good-time events for all musicians and patrons in attendance.[63]
Thus in one sense the "Blue Monday" of the title refers to all-night
good-timing—as the line in the middle section says, it is "fun to
sport around." On the other hand, if one were to do this and have
to go to work the next day, the weariness, hangover, or whatever
precipitated by late hours and riotous behavior would also surely
make it a Blue Monday. Both interpretations are dealt with in the
middle section and, if Hughes truly did have a stop-time chorus in
mind, it would be particularly effective.

Of course, we know that from very early in his career Hughes was attracted to the use of musical accompaniment to his works. Music helped animate the inanimate and lent dignity to the undignified:

> It had no dignity before.
> But when the band began to play,
> Suddenly the earth was there,
>   And flowers,
>   Trees,
>   And air,
> And like a wave the floor—
> That had no dignity before.[64]

Hughes's attraction to oral performance and music is discussed in "Burden":

> It is not weariness
> That bows me down,
> But sudden nearness
> To song without sound.[65]

Here the "sudden nearness to song without sound" is implicitly compared to weariness, equated with it in seriousness.

Unfortunately, there are no recordings of Hughes's poems with musical accompaniment that were made before 1958, so the available recordings were made in some cases forty years after the original poems were written, with musicians who played in styles different from the styles current when the poems were written and arranged, in some cases in a suite or montage form foreign to the original compositions. In some cases the stanza forms are changed. "Miss Blues'es Child," as printed in *Selected Poems,* uses a twenty-eight-bar vaudeville blues stanza:

> If the blues would let me,
> Lord knows I would smile.
> If the blues would let me,
> I would smile, smile, smile.
> Instead of that I'm cryin'—
> I must be Miss Blues'es child.
>
> You were my moon up in the sky,
> At night my wishing star.

I love you, oh, I love you so—
But you have gone so far!

Now my days are lonely,
And night-time drives me wild.
In my heart I'm crying,
I'm just Miss Blues'es child.[66]

The poem starts with a twelve-bar stanza but then moves on to an eight-bar bridge and ends with an eight-bar stanza which lacks a repeat line. The sentimentality of the middle stanza—the bridge, with its references to the moon and stars—gives the poem an ambience of the stage, and indeed, the credits on the album containing a recording of the song by Big Miller list David Martin, Hughes's collaborator on the popular musical *Simple Takes a Wife,* as collaborator on this song. However, Miller's rendition of the song changes the lyrics to make three twelve-bar stanzas rather than retaining the form of the version in *Selected Poems,* though the music and Miller's manner of singing change at the original version's "bridge," setting that stanza off as different from the others.[67] Hughes apparently had some hand in the recording session itself, though his musical collaborator's arrangers, Budd Johnson and Jimmy Jones, handled the musical end, and Miller chose the songs, all of which are from Hughes's theatrical works. The bulk of the music shows the influence of Count Basie's Kansas City Band or Duke Ellington's "jungle" sound, with a bit of contemporary rhythm and blues mixed in. "Five O'Clock Blues," "Lament," "Mr. Blues' Child," "Red Sun Blues," "Mojo Blues," "Got to Live," and "Wee Small Hours" are all twelve-bar *AAB* stanza blues. However, "Did You Ever Hear the Blues?," which is from the stage play "Simply Heavenly," mixes a number of different types of twelve-bar stanzas:

Did you ever hear the blues
On a battered old guitar?
Did you ever hear the blues
Over yonder, Lord, how far?
Did you ever hear the blues
On a Saturday night?
Did you ever hear the blues
About some chick ain't done you right?

> Baby,
> Did you ever hear the blues?[68]

Each of the first eight lines is sung in one bar, with the final two-line refrain lasting four bars. The second stanza of the song follows the same pattern, but stanzas 3 and 4 follow an *ABC* pattern, and the fifth stanza follows an *AAB* pattern. Hughes states in his liner notes that he "attempted to write blues lyrics influenced by the folk stream and modeled in most cases directly after folk patterns,"[69] and, as I have shown, a stanzaic mixture such as Hughes employs in "Did You Ever Hear the Blues?" has precedent in that folk stream. The *AB*-refrain pattern is also on the album in Miller's rendering of "Tired As I Can Be," emphasizing the singer's weariness through the repeated repetition of the word "tired":

> Gonna wake up some morning with the sun in my hand
> Gonna throw the sun way across this land.
> 'Cause I'm tired,
> So tired!
> I'm tired,
> Tired as I can be.[70]

The two remaining songs, "Good Old Guy" and "Cool Saturday Night," mix sixteen- and eight-bar stanzas with bridges. The recordings done by Miller indicate Hughes's awareness of various stanzaic patterns and, to some extent, confirm previous observations about the influence of various blues stanzaic structures on Hughes's blues poems.

Hughes himself made some recordings of his poems with a collection of respected jazz and rhythm and blues musicians like Red Allen, Vic Dickenson, Sam "The Man" Taylor, Horace Parlan, and Charles Mingus, with music arranged and conducted by white jazz critic Leonard Feather and black jazz bassist Charles Mingus. Hughes had learned early in his career not to sing:

> The blues poems I would often make up in my head and sing on the way to work. (Except that I could never carry a tune. But when I sing to myself, I think I am singing.) One evening I was crossing Rock Creek Bridge, singing a blues I was trying to get right before I put it down on paper. A man passing on the opposite side of the bridge stopped, looked at me, then turned around and cut across the roadway.

He said, "Son, what's the matter? Are you ill?"

"No," I said, "Just singing."

"I thought you were groaning," he commented. "Sorry!" And went his way.

So after that I never sang my verses aloud in the street anymore.[71]

Thus, on one recording, *The Weary Blues and Other Poems*, Hughes recites his poems while jazz groups play various arrangements and soloists occasionally "improve" a stanza or two. Hughes was doing readings with groups in clubs at this time partly as a result of the interest generated by Beat precursors and Beat poets like Kenneth Rexroth and Lawrence Ferlinghetti. Although his recording session was probably far more "arranged" than a club reading, his comments about those performances are illuminating. Apparently Hughes, when collaborating with musicians, liked to see as much interaction between music and text as possible, giving the musicians a free rein to express themselves in relation to his theme. His beliefs were quoted in an article by Nat Hentoff:

> ... The music should not only be background to the poetry but should comment on it. I tell the musicians—and I've worked with several different modern and traditional groups—to improve as much as they care to around what I read. Whatever they bring of themselves to the poetry is welcome to me. I merely suggest the mood of each piece as a general orientation. Then I listen to what they say in their playing, and that affects my own rhythms when I read. We listen to each other.[72]

Thus in performance Hughes might have improvised rhythmically and lyrically as he encouraged the accompanists to do—a regular jam session between poet and musician.

But, of course, the recording session was much more arranged, though Hughes did leave blowing space for soloists. "Blues Montage" is a pastiche of Hughes's blues poems that are read primarily to twelve-bar blues accompaniment, again often in a Basie style. Hughes reads the poems in different ways in relation to the music. The section starts with a twelve-bar musical passage that stops for Hughes's recital of "Hey!," which ends, "Wonder what the blues'll bring," and cues the band to start up another twelve-bar blues for "Too Blue":

I got those sad old weary blues.
I don't know where to turn.
I don't know where to go.
Nobody cares about you
When you sunk so low.

What shall I do?
What shall I say?
Shall I take a gun
And put myself away?

I wonder if
One bullet would do?
As hard as my head is,
It would probably take two.

But I ain't got
Neither bullet nor gun—
And I'm too blue
To look for one.[73]

Since the first stanza does not fit a twelve-bar pattern, Hughes enters around bar 8 and arrives at stanza 2 of his poem at the beginning of the second twelve-bar passage. There the band plays a stop-time passage for the first three lines of his second stanza, which he reads as a singer might sing them, one bar to a line. The last three stanzas form a twelve-bar pattern, and Hughes reads them approximately in the rhythm a singer would sing them, though he ends early to allow the band to swell at the end. This poem makes particularly good use of the music, as does "Six-Bits Blues":

Gimme six-bits' worth o' ticket
On a train that runs somewhere.
I say six bits' worth o' ticket
On a train that runs somewhere.
I don't care where it's goin'
Just so it goes away from here.

Baby, gimme a little lovin',
But don't make it too long.
A little lovin', babe, but
Don't make it too long.

Make it short and sweet, your lovin',
So I can roll along.

I got to roll along![74]

In the recording, pianist Al Williams sets up a locomotive rhythm
with an octave walking bass that suggests both the train and travel,
and Hughes recites right along with the music up to the exclamatory tag, *"I got to roll along,"* whereupon the band rolls on out for
the rest of the twelve-bar stanza. It is difficult not to think of Joe
Turner and Pete Johnson's recording of "Roll 'Em Pete," particularly at that point where Johnson launches into a driving,
boogie-woogie piano solo after Turner sings:

Roll it, boy!
Let 'em jump for joy!
Yeah man!
Happy as a baby boy.
My baby brought me,
A brand new choo choo toy.[75]

In a musical sense, "rolling" refers to bass notes played on the
piano, often in a boogie-woogie number, as this one is, in part as an
attempt to imitate the sound of a train, so the choice of the music to
accompany Hughes's "Six-Bits Blues" is especially appropriate. It
is just another way that Hughes indicates his familiarity with the
blues tradition.

There is a sexual pun at work here as well, since "rolling" also
means having sexual intercourse, to which the singer refers in his
second stanza. By associating his traveling energy with his sexual
energy through the use of this play on the same word, Hughes
suggested that the speaker's exuberant traveling is an act of rest-
lessness and enjoyment and an act of potential fulfillment. The
psychological need for getting away, the sexual need for intercourse, and, perhaps, even the musical need for a rolling bass are
all embedded in the word "roll" here. This double pun once again
underscores how important Hughes thought music was, as in "Burden," since the musical imperative is associated with psychological
and sexual imperatives as well. It is, like rambling and sex, another
way of fulfillment, a way of coping with the problems of the

speaker. Interestingly, the speaker does not mention those problems in the poem, probably because he is trying to escape them. Therefore he concentrates on the *methods* of escape. "Six-Bits Blues" is a particularly powerful performance, one that shows how close Hughes often wanted his poetry and music to be, and one that uses musical techniques to reinforce the theme. Along with "Bad Man," on which Hughes really gets into the spirit of the performance by actually growling when he says "bad," it is the most successful cut on the album.

On the other hand, Hughes does not read other poems in the rhythm of a singer, preferring, perhaps, to simply have the blues backdrop as a suggestion of the constant presence of the blues, no matter what is being said or how it is being said. "Note on Commercial Theatre," which does not employ a blues stanza in its poetic form, is read freely over a twelve-bar blues, and "Hey! Hey!," which does employ a twelve-bar blues stanza in its poetic form, is not read to fit in with the twelve-bar blues backing. "Blues at Dawn," which is a five-line, vaudeville-influenced stanza, is read over a bluesy jazz trumpet played by itself, creating a moody atmosphere. Two eight-bar poems, "Could Be" and "Life Is Fine," are read to eight-bar blues backing, the latter with stops for the interjections in the poem and an exuberant Dixieland chorus after the final "Life is fine!," which gets into the spirit of the lyrics. Overall, this composition, which combines Hughes's various blues lyrics, reveals the poet's varied approaches to the use of blues stanzas, rhythms, and music. Sometimes the music is for mood only, at other times it sets down an appropriate rhythm for the theme of the song; sometimes the rhythms of the poetic stanza and the musical stanza coincide, and at other times they do not. Hughes simply did not have one way of using these aspects of the blues tradition. In a very real sense, his audience, like the musicians who sometimes accompany him, brings their knowledge of the blues to his poems. After all, in a "folk" setting the audience is an extremely important part of the performance and, given Hughes's reliance on the folk-blues tradition for his poetry, the audience is extremely important to his performance as well. A knowledge of the various structures and rhythms does not guarantee that *all* stanzas can be definitely identified as one type of blues stanza or another, but it does help the reader to at least begin to understand what Hughes was trying to do. What he did, stanzaically, rhythmically, and typographically, he often did very well.

Just as Hughes employed a variety of blues stanzas in bringing the oral and written word closer together, so he also drew on the variety of subject matter dealt with in folk and professional blues. Far from being a limited genre, the blues takes its subjects where it finds them. Although the relationships between men and women are by far the most frequent subject, those relationships are described in surprisingly varied ways. Many other subjects, such as poverty, politics, and pie-in-the-sky pipe dreams, also find their way into blues from the back alleys to Broadway. They may be harshly realistic, unabashedly lascivious, euphemistically suggestive, unadorned or highly decorated, naive and sweet, sentimental, and sometimes fantastical, depending on who wrote and performed them. So, with his exposure to blues in a number of different settings, we would expect Hughes to be aware of the diverse subject matter employed in the blues and to draw upon that subject matter for his blues poems.

2

Hughes recognized that the blues are diverse in terms of subject matter. In his discussion in *Phylon* in 1941, Hughes outlined some of the possibilities:

> There are many kinds of Blues. There are the family Blues, when a man and woman have quarreled, and the quarrel can't be patched up. There's the loveless Blues, when you haven't even got anybody to quarrel with. And there's the left-lonesome Blues, when the one you care for's gone away. Then there's also the broke-and-hungry Blues, a stranger in a strange town. And the desperate going-to-the-river-Blues that say:
>
> > I'm going down to de river
> > And take me a rockin' chair—
> > If the blues overcome me,
> > I'm gonna rock on away from here!
>
> But it's not always as bad as that, because there's another verse that declares:

Goin' down to de railroad,
Lay ma head on de track.
I'm goin' to de railroad,
Lay ma head on de track—
But if I see de train a-comin'
I'm gonna jerk it back!

For sad as the Blues may be, there's almost always something humorous about them—even if it's the kind of humor that laughs to keep from crying.[76]

Hughes attempted to present a variety of the subjects dealt with in the blues, and in order to do that it was necessary to speak in voices other than his own. Hughes told Nat Hentoff that much of his poetry "is in the form of a kind of dramatic monologue,"[77] indicating that there are speakers other than Hughes who are expressing themselves *and* characterizing themselves as they speak, not only through their language but by their choice of the blues as the vehicle of expression. This dramatic dialogue technique is obvious, for example, in the poems that have female speakers. Of Hughes's blues poems which have speakers whose sex is identifiable from external evidence (i.e., pronouns, references to the opposite sex, presumed heterosexuality, and placement in sections of books with sexual indicators like "Blues For Men" or "Mammy Songs" in *Shakespeare in Harlem*), about one-quarter have women speakers; just a slightly greater fraction use men as speakers. Of course, there are many poems that do not have any such indicators, but the ones that do are written to support, in some ways, Hughes's assertions about "feminine" and "masculine" blues. The bulk of Hughes's poems with women speakers are concerned with love—lost love, mistreatment, revenge for mistreatment, and separation by death. Roughly one-third of Hughes's blues poems with identifiable male speakers are about lack of jobs and food and being far from home with no way to get back, but there are also "lost love" blues in the poems with male speakers. However, none of the blues poems with female speakers discuss work, and "Blue Monday" is the only poem with a speaker whose sex cannot be identified that deals with that subject. The categories outlined in his *Phylon* piece, even in Hughes's own poems, do not divide up as neatly as he might have implied.

Hughes's blues poems were written, as may be expected, as thematic blues. That is, they "maintain a single coherent theme throughout the song,"[78] or tell a story in the manner of many recorded professional blues singers, as opposed to the often loosely associative, disconnected, or even contradictory texts sometimes collected from many folk-blues artists. While Hughes may have used some lyrics that drew on the folk-blues tradition, he constructed his poems in the manner of the professional blues singer who finds thematic development important, probably so that as many people as possible could follow the logic of stanzaic progression (and thus buy his records or support other commercial endeavors). Since Hughes had commercial concerns, since he was influenced by the vaudeville blues composers who valued a thematically coherent composition as well, and since he was a storyteller to whom narrative coherence mattered, it is natural to expect that his blues would be thematic. Even his poems most influenced by folk blues, like "Bound No'th Blues," are written thematically.

Of course, some of the character of Hughes's blues poems derives from his use of objects, subjects, and themes that are employed in the blues tradition as well. Hughes attempted to explore, for example, the aching combination of hope and despair which characterizes the blues by using symbols like the sun; he investigated economic and interpersonal sources of the blues and the ways of dealing with them that sometimes compounded the problems; he examined daily problems experienced by blacks in relation to folk beliefs and the difficulties fostered by their striving for upward mobility in a white-dominated society; he dealt with subjects related to violence and death, and with the longing for some kind of relief from the harsh city life that brings thoughts of a (nonexistent) rural pastoral past; and he even dealt with the nature of the blues and the blues singer. As with Hughes's use of blues stanzas, sometimes his treatment of these issues was traditional; at other times his approach was novel, or was a literary extension of the oral tradition.

For instance, the sun as a harbinger of a new beginning or an ending is common in blues, and in one of the most famous of all traditional blues lyrics, the sun symbolizes the hope for better times:

> The sun gonna shine in my back door some day
> Sun gonna shine in my back door some day,
> Oh the wind gonna rise and blow my blues away.[79]

"Red River Blues," another well-known folk blues, contains a startling image:

> Which-a-way
> Which-a-way
> Do that blood Red River run?
> Run from my window
> To the rising sun.[80]

Many slaves were brought to Texas by boat on the Red River, and the boats moved first northwest and then north from the entrance to the river on the Mississippi below Natchez. The river can symbolize the possibility of both slavery and freedom (*rising* sun): a reminder of how the slaves were brought to their enslavement as well as a symbol of possible escape and the hope for freedom. The ambivalent symbol of the river gains impact from the combination of the upward transcendence of escape toward the rising sun and the nearness of the means of escape set off against the extreme length—geographically, sociologically, and psychologically—of the journey to be undertaken. These are just two examples of references to the sun in blues lyrics, both from the folk tradition and commonly recorded. Hughes himself opened the blues action of *Fine Clothes to the Jew* with a reference to the setting sun in "Hey!":

> Sun's a settin',
> This is what I'm gonna sing.
> Sun's a settin',
> This is what I'm gonna sing:
> I feels de blues a comin',
> Wonder what de blues'll bring?[81]

Here, Hughes associates the blues with endings, darkness, and the unknown (and it should be remembered that in the blues tradition the blues were often called "devil" music and had "evil" associations). We might normally expect a section to begin with the sun rising, but Hughes opens with a sun setting to capture the speaker's mood of apprehension about his impending troubles and to set up the apprehensions felt by the other speakers of the section. However, "Hey! Hey!," which ends the volume, echoes the lines of "Hey" but presents a different mood:

> Sun's a risin',
> This is gonna be ma song.
> Sun's a risin',
> This is gonna be ma song.
> I could be blue but
> I been blue all night long.[82]

The new mood of hope, which Hughes says is finally characteristic of the blues, takes its rightful place at the end of the volume with a sun rising and the singer expressing hope and rejecting a blue mood. However, the hope *is* still being expressed in a blues stanza which will be ready for the next symbolic troubled night that comes along.

Hughes used a reference to the sun in "Black Maria" to illuminate the singer's simultaneous feelings of apprehension and hope concerning the approach of a "Black Maria," a police vehicle that delivers arrested or convicted people to the "proper authorities":[83]

> Must be the Black Maria
> That I see,
> The Black Maria that I see—
> But I hope it
> Ain't comin' for me.
>
> Hear that music playin' upstairs?
> Aw, my heart is
> Full of cares—
> But that music playin' upstairs
> Is for me.
>
> Babe, did you ever
> See de sun
> Rise at dawnin' full of fun?
> Says did you ever see de sun rise
> Full of fun, full of fun?
> Then you know a new day's
> Done begun.
>
> Black Maria passin' by
> Leaves de sunrise in de sky—

And a new day,
Yes, a new day's
Done begun![84]

This poem is notable for the tension that it builds. In the first stanza the speaker expresses his worries about the coming of the Black Maria, though he never specifies why it would be coming for him. Perhaps, as is often the case, the law needed no reason to pick up a black man; perhaps there really was some crime involved. Hughes, however, concentrates on the way the singer expresses his despair and hope. Through the speaker's feeling that the music upstairs is "playing for him," or directed toward him, we get a sense of the speaker's paranoia, since the people upstairs do not necessarily even know that he is downstairs. The speaker expresses his hope with the dawning-sun image, but Hughes qualifies that hope by having the speaker say that a new day has "done begun." The phrase is perfectly appropriate in terms of capturing colloquial speech patterns, but it is also brilliantly evocative of the speaker's conflicting emotions as the vehicle approaches. When the Maria passes it "leaves de sunrise in de sky," brightening the speaker's outlook, but lingers even in the speaker's greeting of a new day at the end. With the words side by side, we can see that when done is done, something else has begun immediately. There are other Black Maria's, other apprehensions that will continually come along. Finally, the title itself may be an equivoque; it refers to both the police vehicle and the Virgin Mary, who by giving birth to the new possibility brought new hope, through a miracle of divine intervention. Perhaps the speaker believes in his momentary optimism that hope is possible, but the possibility of the return of the vehicle is one with which he'll always have to contend as well. In this sense "black" has a double meaning, since he might expect something good but in fact receives the same penalty he has always gotten because of his color. This type of careful, plotted, intricate, even ingenious wordplay is not typical of the folk blues or even blues written by vaudeville composers. It is a part of Hughes's literary addition to the genre. However, Hughes rarely, if ever, wrote lines as startling or breathtaking as those sung by some blues artists, such as the line from "Red River Blues" (see footnote 80). He approached the blues more as an imaginative craftsman than a creatively arresting lyricist, as a comparison of his lines with many of the other blues lyrics included here will demonstrate. Not all blues lyrics are creatively arresting, of course, but they *can* be very much so.

Lack of money caused by joblessness or insufficient pay is one of the major sources of the difficulties described by the blues singer; Ramblin' Thomas sang about being arrested as a vagrant:

> I picken up the newspaper
> And I looked in the ads,
> Says I picken up the newspaper
> And I looken in the ads,
> And the policeman come along
> And he arrested me for vag.[85]

For Blind Lemon Jefferson, low-paying work meant lack of food:

> I stood on the corner
> And almost bust my head.
> I stood on the corner
> And almost bust my head.
> I couldn't earn enough money
> To buy me a loaf of bread.[86]

Hughes included in *Shakespeare in Harlem* three poems that referred to joblessness or hunger, printed one after the other in the text: "Evenin' Air Blues," "Out of Work," and "Brief Encounter." "Out of Work" deals with the subject most extensively:

> I walked de streets till
> De shoes wore off my feet.
> I done walked de streets till
> De shoes wore off my feet.
> Been lookin' for a job
> So's that I could eat.
>
> I couldn't find no job
> So I went to de WPA.
> Couldn't find no job
> So I went to de WPA.
> WPA man told me:
> You got to live here a year and a day.

A year and a day, Lawd,
In this great big lonesome town!
A year and a day in this
Great big lonesome town!
I might starve for a year but
That extra day would get me down.

Did you ever try livin'
On two-bits minus two?
I say did you ever try livin'
On two-bits minus two?
Why don't you try it folks,
And see what it would do to you?[87]

Hughes's poem starts off with a fairly common example of hyperbole in the blues—wearing out the bottom of one's shoes[88]—this time in the service of finding a job. Finding no job, the speaker appeals to a relief agency, the Works Progress Administration, which FDR set up in the years following the stock market crash to provide jobs for the jobless. The WPA, however, provides no relief, telling the speaker that he has to have lived in the town for a year and a day in order to qualify for a job.[89] This sets up one of Hughes's best ironic stanzas, which deals with the unreasonable demand of the WPA. Hughes's use of the expletive "Lawd" at the end of the first line of stanza 3 emphasizes the speaker's feelings of helplessness and frustration and adds to the orality of the poem. It also refers, implicitly, to the inability of religion to ameliorate his situation: It can do little about overwhelming social and governmental forces except emphasize the supremacy of the next life. When Hughes drops the exclamation in the repeat line, he switches "in this," which would normally be repeated in the fourth line, up to line 3 in order to rhythmically fill in the space vacated by the exclamation. This shifts the emphasis in line 4 very appropriately to the cause of his exasperation, the town. This line gains immeasurably from its new setting as an emphatic exclamation cut loose from the words that connect it to the meaning of the rest of the sentence. Since in the oral tradition the words "in this" would likely be sung as unstressed syllables, Hughes maintains an appropriate rhythm in the line in terms of that oral tradition, but he also emphasizes his meaning by the visual placement of the line. The heightened exasperation paves the way for the biting sarcasm of the final two lines of the stanza. Having built up to this pitch, the speaker directly addresses his audience in the final stanza, inviting them to put themselves in his place in order to see how they would respond to his situation. The stanza implies that having no money would do the same thing to them that it has done to him—make them broke, hungry, frustrated, ignored, and bitter, appealing for sympathy. That sentiment, in turn, extends the criticism of the WPA programs and excessive bureaucracy beyond the personal level to a blanket indictment, implicitly making this blues a broad general protest rather than a specific one—a very subtle touch. It is one common in African oral performance, if not in form, at least in meaning. Artist, performer, and audience are united.

Hughes dealt not only with a number of kinds of economic difficulties in his poems, like trouble with landlords in "Stranger in Town," "Red Clay Blues," and "Ballad of the Landlord," but also with various aspects of interpersonal relationships as well. There are, for example, many blues poems about being mistreated by a spouse or lover. In "Cora," the mistreated woman takes matters into her own hands:

> I broke ma heart this mornin'.
> Ain't got no heart no mo'.
> Next time a man comes near me
> Gonna shut and lock ma door
> Cause they treats me mean,—
> The ones I loves.
> They always treats me mean.[90]

What is most interesting here is that despite the fact that the men she loves treat her badly, Cora says she broke her own heart. The implication is that Cora knows that the broken heart is inevitable, so she assertively breaks her own heart in order to control her own emotions and destiny. This poem is clearly one that was intended as a dramatic monologue. The title, simply the woman's name, seems more related to titles in Edgar Lee Masters's *Spoon River Anthology* than to the blues tradition. Very rarely does a blues song have a name as its title unless it is followed by the word "blues."[91] The fact that the word "blues" doesn't appear in the title is significant, suggesting that this poem is not just presenting the blues side of Cora. This poem *is* Cora; this is what defines her now, this is her existence. It is either a peculiar kind of "assertive resignation," a courageous and perceptive heroism, or a refusal to recognize that she in fact did not break her own heart.

There are, of course, other ways of dealing with mistreatment, and Hughes dealt with the subject with a novel and appropriate twelve-bar stanza in "Only Woman Blues":

> I want to tell you 'bout that woman,
> My used-to-be—
> She was de meanest woman
> I ever did see.
> But she's de only
> Woman that could mistreat me!
>
> She could make me holler like a sissie,
> Bark like a dog.
> She could chase me up a tree
> And then cut down de log—
> Cause she's de only
> Woman that could mistreat me.
>
> She had long black hair,
> Big black eyes,
> Glory! Hallelujah!
> Forgive them lies!
> She's de only
> Woman's gonna mistreat me.
>
> I got her in Mississippi.
> Took her to Alabam'.
> When she left
> I said, Go, hot damn!
> You de last and only
> Woman's gonna mistreat me.[92]

In this poem Hughes employed an *ABC* twelve-bar stanza, however, the last four bars of each stanza present a line that doesn't rhyme but acts as a modulated refrain. That refrain charts the resolve of the speaker to never be mistreated by any other woman, emphasizing in the first two stanzas the woman's power over him. By eliminating the coordinating conjunction and the adverb that had preceded the thought expressed in the refrains of stanzas 1 and 2, the celebration of the woman's beauty is juxtaposed with the speaker's increasingly assertive refrain statement. The final stanza, which in its brevity and terseness brilliantly captures the speaker's bitter attitude about the importance and worth of their relationship, again bypasses a coordinating conjunction or an adverb and becomes even more emphatic in the speaker's direct address to the woman. The poem thus demonstrates two different functions: it is a performance for an audience not involved in the situation being described, perhaps to alleviate in some way the speaker's sorrow, and in the last two lines the speaker works through to a new outlook, which is expressed in the direct statement to the woman who was previously being discussed. The blues song, then, becomes a kind of therapy, a way of working out difficulties and a way of *facing*, not evading, the problem at hand; the singer is not a pitiful whiner but, in the end, a proud and resolute man. Nonetheless, the rendering of "Woman's gonna mistreat me" as a separate line retains the speaker's realistic expectation that mistreatment can and will occur. Hughes integrated these two functions at least partially by using one type of humor that is found in the blues tradition, the humor of overstatement or hyperbole that he emphasized in stanza 2. This type of humor is set off against what might be called the humor of painful recognition in stanzas 3 and 4. Here the audience's recognition of an experience that may be similar to its own either now or sometime in the past might evoke either laughter or brotherhood in misery. The speaker's spirited resolution of his problem in a way that many lovers stuck in a relationship of unequal power would like to resolve might evoke an affirmative laugh as well. The blues tradition contains broad, slapstick humor as well as wry humor, sardonic humor, touching humor, and understated humor, and Hughes used various types of humor in such poems as "Morning After," "Evenin' Air Blues," "Early Evening Quarrel," "As Befits a Man," "Life Is Fine," "Bound No'th Blues," and "Lady's Boogie," among others.

The speaker of "Hard Daddy" goes the speaker of "Only Woman Blues" one further in her reaction to a lover who offers her no aid or sympathy:

> I wish I had wings to
> Fly like de eagle flies.
> Wish I had wings to
> Fly like de eagle flies.

I'd fly on ma man an'
I'd scratch out both his eyes.[93]

In this poem Hughes demonstrated another way of relying on the blues tradition: He borrowed established blues lines and filled in words that were more appropriate to his meaning. Hughes did this, for example, in "The Weary Blues," which I have already discussed, as well as in "Sylvester's Dyin' Bed" (where he used the standard introduction "I woke up this mornin'"), "Morning After" ("Had a dream last night"), "Reverie on Harlem River" ("Did you ever"), and "Life Is Fine" ("I went down to the river"), among other places. The final stanza in "Hard Daddy" opens with a variant of a traditional religious and secular lyric, like the version used by Peg Leg Howell in "Turtle Dove Blues":

If I had wings like
Noah's turtle dove,
If I had wings like
Noah's turtle dove,
If I had wings like
Noah's turtle dove,
I would rise and fly and
light on the one I love.[94]

Hughes substituted for the dove of Howell's lyric the eagle, which is more appropriate for carrying out the woman's retribution. In addition, the implied religious association, because of the use of words that often precede flying away to heaven or to Jesus, makes the speaker's retributive secular purpose even more forceful.

In Hughes's blues poems, as in many blues songs, the very nature of the genre prevents both sides of a dispute from being presented adequately. However, in "Early Evening Quarrel" Hughes followed a tradition of comedy blues dialogues practiced by such male-female recording teams as Butterbeans and Susie, Grant and Wilson, and Billy and Mary Mack, and by such couples brought together in the studio as John Byrd and Mae Glover, and Lonnie Johnson and Victoria Spivey or Clara Smith. In "You Had Too Much" Johnson and Smith alternate suggestive twelve-bar stanzas concerning sexual activity, but halfway through they both get in on the lyrics of the same stanza:

Smith: I used to take em'
               In a row.

Johnson: But you lost yourself, mama,
               Ten years ago.

Refrain: 'Cause you've had too much.
               Aw, you've had too much.
               But you'll never be the same
               'Cause you've had too much.[95]

Hughes's poem opens with one twelve-bar stanza each from Hattie and Hammond, who are arguing over the fact that Hammond has not brought sugar back for Hattie's coffee. The next three stanzas of four lines each present, as Edward Waldron has pointed out, "the staccato pace of his arguing couple and still make use of the blues format."[96] It is likely that the pacing that Hughes heard for these stanzas was similar to that of "Did You Ever Hear the Blues?": twelve bars at one line per bar, which would end the lyric at the same time the music would end and would also move along the banter at an appropriate clip.

Of course, Hattie and Hammond's argument over sugar is a symbolic one. When Bessie Smith sang "I Need a Little Sugar in My Bowl," she was doing more than raising cain about coffee drinking. Bessie was singing about out-and-out sex, though in the Hughes poem the reference may simply be to sweetness. Still, the question arises about the presence of sexual material in Hughes's poems. Certainly it is not lacking in the blues. Euphemistically, genitalia may be referred to as "pigmeat," "stew-meat," "hot dog," "tuna," "barbecue," "jelly roll," "gravy," "biscuits," "yams," "apples," "peaches," "plums," "bananas," "potatoes," "tomatoes," "lemons," "coffee," "sugar," "pudding," "candy," and "dry goods"; a "snake," "bull cow," "Jersey Belle," "bee," "spider," "train," or a "crosscut saw". One might "crochet," "press someone's button," "fish in somebody's sea," become a "deep sea diver" or a "dough" or "biscuit roller," a "jockey" or a "rider"; "whip it to a jelly" or "rock and roll." Perhaps the reference may simply be to "my stuff" or "that thing," or the "yas, yas." You could even just "jazz" somebody. Beyond that, there are the unexpurgated blues recordings like Lucille Bogan's "Shave 'Em Dry," Walter Roland's "I'm Gonna Shave You Dry," or Jelly Roll Morton's "Winin' Boy," none of which was commercially issued at the time of recording, but all of which reflected a very real if "underground" strain of blues lyrics that would have appalled the middle-class sensibility. The following are selections from Bogan's "Shave 'Em Dry":

> I got nipples on my titties
> Big as the end of my thumb
> I got something between my legs
> 'll make a dead man come.
>
> *Refrain:*
> Aw
> Daddy won't you shave 'em dry.
> I want you to grind me daddy,
> Grind me 'til I cry.
>
> Say I fucked all night
> And all the night before, baby,
> And I feel just like I wanna
> Fuck some more.
>
> *Refrain:*
> Aw great God daddy grind me
> Honey, shave me dry
> And if you hear me holler, baby,
> Want you to shave 'em dry.
>
> Now your nuts hang down like a damn bell clapper,
> And your dick stands up like a steeple.
> Your goddam asshole stands open like a church door,
> And the crabs walks in like people.
>
> *Refrain:*
> Ow, daddy!
> Whoo!
> Baby, won't you shave 'em dry.[97]

Of course, the same censorship that kept this song off the market would have suppressed anything similar that Hughes might have written. If Hughes was branded the "poet low-rate" of Harlem for his poems in *Fine Clothes to the Jew,* it is hard to tell what might have happened had he written his own unexpurgated version of "Shave 'Em Dry." It is very unlikely that Hughes would have written a poem like that anyway. The closest he ever got to this type of lyric was in the songs of Jimboy in *Not Without Laughter.* Hughes made only very occasional and euphemistic references to sex in his poems. In "Midwinter Blues" a woman describes a situation where her man has left her in the middle of the winter "when de coal was low."[98] If this is a sexual reference, it would probably come out in the vocal performance or physical gyrations of a singer who would perform the song. Victoria Spivey discussed a Ma Rainey performance of "Bo Weevil Blues":

> Ain't nobody in the world been able to holler "Hey Boweevil" like her. Not like Ma. Nobody. I've heard them try to, but they can't do it. "Hey Bo Weevil." All right. 'Cos Bo Weevil he was eating up everything down South. That worm could eat up all the food and everything. And she holler "Hey Bo Weevil you been gone a long time." Now there was two *meanings* to that. I was such a smart little hip chicken, I knew just which bo weevil she was talking about.[99]

The performance might have a great deal to do with how a lyric is understood, especially if the reference is to a type of dance that could be a euphemism for having sex. The other possible sexual reference in *Fine Clothes to the Jew* is in "Ma Man":

> Eagle-rockin',
> Daddy, eagle-rock with me.
> Eagle rockin',
> Come an' eagle-rock with me.
> Honey baby,
> Eagle-rockish as I kin be![100]

This was certainly used as a sexual euphemism in blues lyrics. Sara Martin recorded an "Eagle Rock Me Papa" in 1924, and the Bessemer Blues Singers recorded a reference to it as part of "My Mama's Baby Child":

> She just could "Sally Long" with me mama,
> 'Eagle Rock' me too.
> Can't nobody rock me
> Like my sweet little mama do.[101]

The independent, unrepentant woman is one of the personae put forth by the vaudeville blues singers, as in Ida Cox's "Wild Women Don't Have the Blues":

> I hear these women ravin'
> 'Bout their money men,

About their triflin' husbands
And their no good friends.
These poor women sit around
All day and moan,
Wondering why their wandering papas
Don't come home,
But wild women don't worry,
Wild women don't have no blues . . .

I've got a disposition,
And a way of my own.
When my man starts kicking
I let him find another home.
I get full of good liquor,
Walk the streets all night,
Go home and put my man out
If he don't act right.
Wild women don't worry.
Wild women don't have them blues.[102]

Cox's later assertion that the only women who get by are wild women is certainly a statement far beyond one that Hughes would have made in his blues poems, but one that the "hot mama" vaudeville queens could make with ease, both as part of a stage persona and in real life. What is out of the ordinary in Hughes's "Ma Man," compared to the rest of his blues poems, is the implication that the woman wishes to have sex and is not repentant about it. In "Listen Here Blues" the singer bemoans the loss of her virginity, and in "Midnight Chippie's Lament" the prostitute even pleads with her loneliness to come and keep her company. Later, in "Easy Boogie" and "Lady's Boogie," the references to boogie and boogie-woogie take a sexual connotation as one part of their total meaning.[103] However, by and large, Hughes did not make many overt references to sex, and he made none to homosexuality. Ma Rainey and Bessie Smith both recorded blues songs dealing with that subject, and, although not very common, there were a number of other blues songs like "Sissy Man Blues," "Freakish Man Blues," "B. D. Woman's Blues," and "Boy in the Boat" (which Georgia White recorded but which was never issued) that broached the subject.[104] It seems likely that a combination of the external censorship of Hughes's audience and of book publishing companies and an internal desire to clean up and "legitimize" the blues and eradicate the so-called "pornographic" element influenced him to use few references to any kind of sexuality in his blues poems.

Hughes did make a number of references to alcohol in his poems. In "Ma Man" liquor makes the man play the banjo better. In "Listen Here Blues" it proves to be the downfall of the woman. In "Morning After," one of Hughes's best humorous blues poems, it precipitates a joke:

> I was so sick last night I
> Didn't hardly know my mind.
> So sick last night I
> Didn't know my mind.
> I drunk some bad licker that
> Almost made me blind.
>
> Had a dream last night I
> Thought I was in hell.
> I drempt last night I
> Thought I was in hell.
> Woke up and looked around me—
> Babe, your mouth was open like a well.
>
> I said, Baby! Baby!
> Please don't snore so loud.
> Baby! Please!
> Please don't snore so loud.
> You jest a little bit o' woman but you
> Sound like a great big crowd.[105]

There are, of course, many references to alcohol in blues lyrics, such as Willie McTell's "I drink so much whiskey I stagger when I'm sleep" and Bill Broonzy's "I went to the doctor with my head in my hands," and Ma Rainey sang a "Sleep Talking Blues" that dealt with a man getting into trouble by calling out another woman's name in his sleep. But Hughes's lyric strains harder for a punch line than these songs.[106] Hughes's attitude toward alcohol in his blues poems seems to have been that it can be the bearer of either good or bad times, and this attitude was perhaps a source of the criticism of middle-class-minded downgraders of Hughes's poetry. Hughes did not make any references to drugs in his blues poems, probably because they would have been considered even more taboo than alcohol, so he did not tap any of the resources of the blues tradition dealing with that subject.[107]

Hughes dealt with another common blues subject, superstition, in "Bad Luck Card," which discusses a visit to a gypsy; "Blues on a Box," where playing music is seen as a way to drive away hard luck; and "Gal's Cry for a Dying Lover," which refers more extensively to common rural African-American superstitions. Like "Bound No'th Blues," the latter is a blues that takes place in the country, where such superstitions were still alive because, after all, there were still owls present. However, such traditions would be remembered by recently transplanted city-dwellers as well:

> Heard de owl a hootin',
> Knowed somebody's 'bout to die.
> Heard de owl a hootin',
> Knowed somebody's 'bout to die.
> Put ma head un'neath de kiver,
> Started in to moan an' cry.
>
> Hound dawg's barkin'
> Means he's gonna leave this world.
> Hound dawg's barkin'
> Means he's gonna leave this world.
> O, Lawd have mercy
> On a po' black girl.
>
> Black an' ugly
> But he sho do treat me kind.
> I'm black an' ugly
> But he sho do treat me kind.
> High-in-heaben Jesus,
> Please don't take this man o' mine.[108]

Ma Rainey drew on one of her strengths, her knowledge of the folk and their beliefs, in "Black Cat Hoot Owl Blues":

> Black cat on my doorstep
> Black cat on my window sill,
> Black cat on my doorstep
> Black cat on my window sill,
> If some black cat don't cross me
> Some other black cat will.

Last night a hoot owl
Come and sit right over my door.
Last night a hoot owl
Come and sit right over my door.
A feelin' seemed to tell me
I'd never see my man no more.

I feel my left side a-jumpin'!
My heart a-bumpin'
I'm mindin' my P's and Q's.
I feel my brain a-thumpin'
And I've got no time to lose.
Now I'm just superstitious,
Tryin' to overcome these blues.[109]

Rainey's version is notable for the pun on "black cat," referring both to an animal and to a man, and for her remarkable explanation of why she is superstitious—she is trying to overcome the blues, to explain or rationalize her experience. Hughes's poem is notable for the way it reflects the self-conscious paranoia of the black-skinned woman. The superstitions, of course, have no basis in fact. However, the woman in the poem not only believes in them, but, because of the way she had been treated and abused because of her skin color, the omens cause her to worry about losing her man. She is used to "bad luck" because of the way she has been looked down upon because of her skin color. By association, the social attitude of black and ugly is compared to the superstitions, not in the woman's mind but in the minds of those reading the poem. Thus, once again, Hughes used a dramatic monologue in a blues poem, in this case to reflect not only an individual's point of view but to make an implicit condemnation of irrational attitudes about skin color as related to a person's intrinsic worth.

Thus, Hughes's poem introduces another subject common to blues poems that appears elsewhere in "Misery," "Gypsy Man," "Argument," "The New Girl," and "Black Gal": social stratification by skin color. Such stratification was based on the middle-class conception of lighter skin being the most desirable color, since it was closer to white. The African-American magazines and newspapers ran ads for "skin lighteners and beautifiers" and for powders that would make the skin more pale:

> Now if you want your woman
> To look like the race,
> You buy high brown powder,
> Palmer's skin success.
> Buy her high brown powder,
> Palmer's skin success.[110]

However, references abound in blues lyrics to the superiority of the "high yellow," "yellow," "bright," "high brown," "brown," "chocolate," and "black" woman, often based on either the individual color or the preference of the singer of the song. In blues songs, sometimes the references can be humorous, as in "Black Gal Swing," which brags about the wildness of the black woman:

> Now a yellow gal rides in an automobile,
> A brownskin gal does the same,
> But a black gal carries in an old haywagon,
> She's gettin' there just the same.
>
> A yellow gal drinks good old whiskey,
> A brownskin gal does the same,
> But a black gal drinks shoe polish,
> She's gettin' drunk just the same.
>
> A yellow gal will bite you,
> She will pop you with a stick,
> A brown skin gal does the same,
> But a black gal get a rusty razor and run you all over town,
> You know that woman's raisin' hell just the same.[111]

But they could also be horrifying as well:

> My woman's so black she stays apart of this town.
> Can't nothin' go on when the poor girl is around.[112]

Hughes's poems do not comment on the situation in as lively or incisive a manner as many blues songs, but they do raise the issue as one of real concern to the speakers. "Black Gal" treats the subject most extensively, but "Gal's Cry For a Dying Lover" is interesting in the way that the omission of a pronoun challenges the phrase "black an' ugly," a phrase which itself can be found in blues songs. In this example it is a defensive response in an aphoristic boast:

> Now my hair is nappy
> And I don't wear no clothes of silk.
> Now my hair is nappy
> And I don't wear no clothes of silk.
> But the cow that's black and ugly
> Has often got the sweetest milk.[113]

Hughes writes in "Gal's Cry":

> Black an' ugly
> But he sho do treat me kind.

This leaves the reader/listener in momentary darkness as to *who* is "black an' ugly." It is clear in line 3 that the phrase refers to the woman, but the lapsed moments give the reader time to question the logic of why a man who is "black an' ugly" would not treat someone kind, and to carry over that questioning when the reference is made clear. Again, leaving out the pronoun would be perfectly acceptable in the oral tradition, but here Hughes used the absence to emphasize the artificiality of the prejudice and the stereotype.

Another convention in blues songs is to raise the spectre of suicide, though suicide is never carried out in the blues song. The river is often mentioned as the location of a suicide, as in Peg Leg Howell's "Rock and Gravel Blues":

> Honey, let's go to the
> River and sit down.
> Honey, let's go to the
> River and sit down.
> If the blues overtakes us
> Jump overboard and drown.[114]

When Hughes's speakers refer to suicide, drowning in a river is most often mentioned. In "Suicide," the river is the final choice:

> Ma sweet good man has
> Packed his trunk and left.
> Ma sweet good man has
> Packed his trunk and left.
> Nobody to love me:
> I'm gonna kill ma self.

I'm gonna buy me a knife with
A blade ten inches long.
Gonna buy a knife with
A blade ten inches long.
Shall I carve ma self or
That man that done me wrong?

'Lieve I'll jump in de river
Eighty-nine feet deep.
'Lieve I'll jump in de river
Eighty-nine feet deep.
Cause de river's quiet
An' a po', po' gal can sleep.[115]

In this poem the speaker seems to have some doubt about whether to kill her man or herself in a more violent fashion—with a knife, probably another source of certain middle-class critics' objections to Hughes's volume. However, the speaker finally opts for the river as a source of rest, implying that drowning in the river represents a yearning for the pastoral life free from worries and cares, not for the literal suicide itself. The river is also mentioned as a suicide location in "A Ruined Gal," "Lament Over Love," "Reverie on Harlem River," "Life Is Fine," and "Lonesome Place." "Too Blue" refers to finding a gun to commit suicide, but the speaker rationalizes his fear of dying by saying that he is too blue to look for a gun.

There exist in blues songs more instances of physical violence done to others than to one's self. There is a strong tradition in black folklore of the bad man who beats other men, and women, too, along with shootings, stabbings, even a whipping with pickets from fences![116] An alliance with the devil is often part of the explanation for this behavior:

Me and the Devil
Commenced walkin' side by side.
Me and the Devil
Commenced walkin' side by side.
I'm gonna beat my woman
'Til I get satisfied.[117]

Such a claim seems to be created to explain something the singer does not understand, but to heighten his mysterious and powerful image as well. Hughes's speaker in "Bad Man" similarly does not understand what makes him "bad," though the first stanza suggests that part of his "badness" indeed lies in the image others have created of him. He accepts that image and revels in it:

> I'm a bad, bad man
> Cause everbody tells me so.
> I'm a bad, bad man.
> Everbody tells me so.
> I takes ma meanness and ma licker
> Everwhere I go.
>
> I beats ma wife an'
> I beats ma side gal too.
> Beats ma wife an'
> Beats ma side gal too.
> Don't know why I do it but
> It keeps me from feelin' blue.
>
> I'm so bad I
> Don't even want to be good.
> So bad, bad, bad I
> Don't even want to be good.
> I'm goin' to de devil an'
> I wouldn't go to heaben if I could.[118]

The speaker of this poem suggests that his violence prevents him from becoming blue, but the way he relishes his image as a bad man suggests that communicating his badness to others is his real delight. The poem or song, then, is what keeps him from being blue, just as the "song" of "In a Troubled Key" temporarily prevents violence from surfacing by serving as a warning:

> Do not sell me out, baby,
> Please do not sell me out.
> Do not sell me out, baby,
> Do not sell me out.
> I used to believe in you, baby,
> Now I begins to doubt.
>
> Still I can't help lovin' you,
> Even though you do me wrong.
> Says I can't help lovin' you
> Though you do me wrong—
> But my love might turn into a knife
> Instead of to a song.[119]

Again, Hughes captured the troubled nature of the speaker by altering the repeat lines. The commanding "do not sell me out" of the first line becomes a pleading in the second line with the addition of "please." But in lines 3 and 4, the repeat is again more assertive. In the second stanza, "Still I can't help lovin' you" becomes "Says I can't help lovin' you," equivocating a bit by suggesting that this is what he *says* but may not actually be the case. That sentiment is verified in the closing thought of the poem, which demonstrates the precarious nature of the way the speaker might demonstrate his love and suggests that love can be both creative *and* destructive. The fact that the speaker's song is "in a troubled key" underscores the important relationship between form and meaning in the poem. The form, the "key," is said to be troubled, permeated by the troubled nature expressed in the lyrics, like the "worried man" it takes "to sing the worried song" of the traditional blues lyric. Finally, Hughes recognized that a knife and gun were not necessary to do deadly violence to someone, and perhaps his belief in the power of words and emotions prompted the lack of physical violence in his blues poetry:

> Just a pencil and paper,
> You don't need no gun or knife.
> A pencil and paper,
> Don't need no gun or knife—
> Cause a little old letter
> Can take a person's life.[120]

Violence often leads to the graveyard, in blues songs and in life, but Hughes's "graveyard" poems are not explicitly the result of violence, since the reasons the people have died is not given. "Death Chant," titled "Stony Lonesome" in *Selected Poems,* focuses on the separation between Cordelia and Buddy and uses typography to emphasize both the moaning nature of this blues and the descent of Cordelia into the ground. "Widow Woman" is a philosophical treatise on the nature of freedom based on the speaker's conflicting emotions at the time her lover is buried:

> Oh, that last long ride is a
> Ride everybody must take.
> Yes, that last long ride's a
> Ride everybody must take.

And that final stop is a
Stop everybody must make.

When they put you in de ground and
They throw dirt in your face,
I say put you in de ground and
Throw dirt in your face,
That's one time, pretty papa,
You'll sure stay in your place.

You was a mighty lover and you
Ruled me many years.
A mighty lover, baby, cause you
Ruled me many years—
If I live to be a thousand
I'll never dry these tears.

I don't want nobody else and
Don't nobody else want me.
I say don't want nobody else
And don't nobody else want me—

Yet you never can tell when a
Woman like me is free.[121]

This poem starts with a general statement about death and doesn't seem to become particularized until the response line of stanza 2. However, the modulation of the repeat line is actually where the personal commentary enters. The initial thought merely presents a situation; however, the repeat line starts with a directive—"I say"— and uses an acceptable change in the oral tradition as the springboard for expressing the woman's animosity. However, the final stanza expresses her conflicting emotions about the death—about being free of a man who she had wanted to stay in his place with her while on earth and whose loving was mighty enough to rule her. The final italicized lines, part of the twelve-bar pattern but separated from the stanza, highlight her essential predicament. Another poem about death, "Young Gal's Blues," presents not a lament for a dead lover but for a dead female friend whose passing initiates fears of becoming old and lonely in old age, a touching poem that finally becomes a plea for the speaker's lover to continue loving her.

Another common presence in blues lyrics is that of the train.

Songs that deal with the departure of a lover on a train are numerous in the blues tradition, such as Willie McTell's touching "Dark Night Blues":

> I followed my fair brown
> From the depot to the train.
> I followed my fair brown
> From the depot to the train.
> And the blues came down
> Like dark night showers of rain.[122]

This was the "mean old train" with the "cruel engineer" that carried away the lover, perhaps even on the track that the singer himself had helped lay, as Buddy Boy Hawkins described in "Workin' on the Railroad."[123] However, the railroad could also be a means of bringing a lover back, of escape, of going back home, or of getting away from oppressive conditions and problems:

> I'm goin' down to the station
> Get me a ticket for a one way.
> I'm goin' down to the station
> Get me a ticket for a one way.
> Now I'm goin' keep on ridin'
> I know I'll feel better someday.[124]

On the other hand, a train can present the singer with a conflict of emotions:

> I hate to hear that
> Engine blow boo hoo.
> I hate to hear that
> Engine blow boo hoo.
> Every time it blows
> I feel like ridin' too.[125]

The attitudes toward the train are many and varied in blues songs, so it cannot be tied down to one symbolic meaning. Hughes, in "Blues Fantasy," presented the speaker who sees the train as the means of possibly escaping the blues:

> Weary,
> Weary,
> Trouble, pain.
> Sun's gonna shine

Somewhere
Again.

I got a railroad ticket,
Pack my trunk and ride.

Sing 'em, sister!

Got a railroad ticket,
Pack my trunk and ride.
And when I get on the train
I'll cast my blues aside.

Laughing,
Hey! . . . Hey!
Laugh a loud,
Hey! Hey![126]

However, escape isn't likely. This is, after all, entitled "Blues Fantasy," and Hughes's placement of "Somewhere" and "Again" on different lines emphasizes the wistful, longing tone of artificially inflated hope. The idea of the words as a performance are emphasized by the interjection of "Sing 'em, sister." Rather than being considered a personal expression of the woman's longing, the words become entertainment to be taken somewhat less seriously. The final four lines seem like forced mirth, partially because they break the rhythmic pattern of the other lines, partially because of the awkward repetition of forms of the verb "laugh," partially because of the ellipses that make the two "Hey's" of the second line more stumbling than spirited. That fantasy of escape by train is fully discounted in "Dream Boogie: Variation," where the piano player being described is:

A few minutes late
For the Freedom Train.[127]

So while the train may hold out some hope, it is a severely qualified hope that contradicts the train bound for glory or the Underground Railroad.

Hughes's "Homesick Blues" bears a resemblance to Trixie Smith's "Freight Train Blues" in the traveling-mood sentiment expressed in its opening stanza, and it introduces another common blues subject, the contrast between the North and the South:

De railroad bridge's
A sad song in de air.
De railroad bridge's
A sad song in de air.
Ever time de trains pass
I wants to go somewhere.

I went down to de station.
Ma heart was in ma mouth.
Went down to de station.
Heart was in ma mouth.
Lookin' for a box car
To roll me to de South.

Homesick blues, Lawd,
'S a terrible thing to have.
Homesick blues is
A terrible thing to have.
To keep from cryin'
I opens ma mouth an' laughs.[128]

James Emanuel found that this poem is marred by the rhyming of "have" and "laughs,"[129] but there is certainly nothing wrong with that rhyme in the context of the rhyming methods of the oral blues tradition. Furthermore, the use of a slant rhyme in these lines emphasizes that laughing to keep from crying is a way of trying to manage two different emotions; therefore, the slant rhyme gives each emotion its autonomy while relating them tentatively with assonance. The rhyme is, in fact, a marvelous way of communicating the incongruity of the inactivity. The response line, however, suffers from comparison to the traditional blues line mentioned above:

When you see me laughin'
I'm laughin' to keep from cryin'.[130]

Hughes's response line suffers from the awkward inversion that throws the infinitive phrase to the beginning of the sentence. In addition, it removes the audience, the "you," from the sentence, reduces the number of "laughs" to one, which de-emphasizes the desperate nature of the laughing, and lacks the pithiness of the traditional phrase, which contains laughing and crying in the same line.

The North-South theme is frequent in the blues, and the "Down South Blues" was recorded by Clara Smith, Hannah Sylvester, Lena Wilson, and Sonny Boy Williamson, among others:

> Now, I'm goin' back down South,
> Man, where the weather suits my clothes.
> Now, I done fooled around in Chicago,
> Yank, I done almost froze.
> Now, I done fooled around in Chicago,
> Lawd, I done almost froze.[131]

As Williamson indicates here, a great deal of the homesickness has to do with the harshness of city life, a theme expressed in Hughes's "Evenin' Air Blues":

> Folks, I come up North
> Cause they told me de North was fine.
> I come up North
> Cause they told me de North was fine.
> Been up here six months—
> I'm about to lose my mind.[132]

Again, Emanuel found the rhyme of "fine" and "mind" to be a weakness in the poem.[133] However, the failure of the "promised land" to live up to its "fine" reputation again calls for a slant rhyme in the poem, an indication that the convention of the good life in the North was wrong, but that it was indeed related to the singer's impending loss of sanity. Thus, once again the rhyme serves very well. Despite Emanuel's criticism of a weak rhyme and dialectical inconsistency ("de"-"the") he saw this as a superior blues poem, as did Nancy McGhee.[134] However, the poem does not really seem to live up to that assessment. The second stanza, while presenting an important message, expresses its sentiment in an unlikely and rather silly way:

> This mornin' for breakfast
> I chawed de mornin' air.
> This mornin' for breakfast
> Chawed de mornin' air.
> But this evenin' for supper,
> I got evenin' air to spare.

Hughes certainly thought carefully about what he wished to accomplish in this stanza. The reference to meals indicates that the speaker's problems have to do with his sustenance and survival, and using the first and last meals of the day conveys the emptiness of the speaker's entire day. The stanza also reflects the end of the speaker's tolerance and patience, as in stanza 1: he has had too much of not having enough. This situation renders Hughes's use of "air" as something to eat particularly appropriate; as something intangible yet surrounding the speaker and presumably available in excess, it serves double duty in representing his lack of food and his surfeit of blues. The speaker's decision not to glut himself on his blues leads appropriately to the activity of the third stanza, which discusses a strategy for driving the blues away:

> Believe I'll do a little dancin'
> Just to drive my blues away—
> A little dancin'
> To drive my blues away,
> Cause when I'm dancin'
> De blues forgets to stay.

The problem with the second stanza lies in the affected rural colloquialism "chawed," which is patronizingly cute, and in the farfetched notion of chewing air. While there are outlandish ideas in the blues tradition, neither this colloquialism nor this notion seems appropriate to the folk-blues idiom or the vaudeville blues idiom. Perhaps Hughes wanted the word "chawed" to stand out as this poor Southerner stood apart in the North, but the word strikes a too discordant note. The final stanza draws attention to the necessity of defining blues with situations from real life rather than with just words:

> But if you was to ask me
> How de blues they come to be,
> Says if you was to ask me
> How de blues they come to be—
> You wouldn't need to ask me:
> Just look at me and see.

The stanza neatly reverses the situation of the first stanza. In stanza 1 the speaker was *told* to come North, but here he is *asked* about the blues. Instead of talking about how he "come up North" (an actual place built up to mythical proportions) he talks about "how de blues come to be"—a state of mind. That state of mind is, in fact, the destroyer of the stories about the good life in the North, the exaltation of personal experience over hearsay. The singer finally affirms that the words of the blues must be based on true people and situations like the ones he described in his song, drawing on the restless searching, hunger, and hope in the face of adversity. As Waldron stated, "it is impossible to separate the blues maker from his song, just as it is impossible, finally, to tell the dancer from the dance."[135]

One of the most interesting poems that discusses the topic of North and South is "Red Clay Blues." Shortly after the Third American Writer's Congress in 1939, to which Hughes presented a speech entitled "Democracy and Me," Hughes collaborated on this poem with Richard Wright, whom he had met in Chicago in 1936. The poem appeared in *The New Masses*, the successor to the old *Masses* which followed increasingly strict Communist party ideology under the editorship of Mike Gold. Hughes's work was first published in *The New Masses* in December 1926, and he joined the journal as a contributing editor in September 1930. From that time, the publication provided an outlet for some of Hughes's more vocally protesting political forms, such as "Advertisement for the Waldorf-Astoria," "Merry Christmas," and "Good Morning Revolution." The late 1930s was also a period during which Wright was applying his energies writing for *The Daily Worker* and *The New Masses*, publishing *Uncle Tom's Children* in 1938 and completing *Native Son* as Hughes was attending the Writer's Congress. It was the end of a decade of Leftist activity intensified by the "Black Friday" stock market crash of 1929, and Wright was ready to emerge as a major force, insisting that black writers "must view society as something becoming rather than something fixed and admired" and "must stand shoulder to shoulder with Negro workers in mood and outlook."[136] In 1938, the International Worker's Order published seventeen protest poems by Hughes, with an introduction by Mike Gold, that mirrored a similar sympathy with the plight of workers. "Red Clay Blues" emerged out of similar racial, social, and literary concerns at the brief 1939 reunion of Wright and Hughes:

I miss that red clay, Lawd, I
Need to feel it on my shoes.
Says miss that red clay, Lawd, I
Need to feel it on my shoes.
I want to see Georgia cause I
Got them red clay blues.

Pavement's hard on my feet, I'm
Tired o' this concrete street.
Pavement's hard on my feet, I'm
Tired o' this city street.
Goin' back to Georgia where
That red clay can't be beat.

I want to tramp in the red mud, Lawd, and
Feel the red clay round my toes.
I want to wade in that red mud,
Feel red clay suckin' at my toes.
I want my little farm back and I
Don't care where the landlord goes.

I want to be in Georgia, when the
Big storm starts to blow.
Yes I want to be in Georgia when that
Big storm starts to blow.
I want to see the landlords runnin' cause I
Wonder where they gonna go!
I got them red clay blues.[137]

In this poem the speaker longs to go back where he's been before, for renewal and to recapture what he once had, his farm. The rural, agrarian environment is something that the speaker misses and needs to feel and see. In stanza 1, as the speaker starts the poem, he says he needs to feel the red clay, the earth, on his shoes, which are now walking on concrete. In stanza 2, the pavement is described as being hard on the speaker's feet, and finally, in stanza 3, the speaker imagines himself in the red mud with the clay around his toes. The stanzas present a progressive movement toward freedom and comfort as the prospect of being in Georgia becomes more real in the speaker's mind. In the third stanza, a villain is finally named—the landlord, who has apparently been the cause of the speaker's coming North, since the speaker indicates that he has lost his farm earlier. With this and the final stanza, the additional meaning of the title emerges. Red is associated with blood, with being inflamed, and with Communism. Clay is produced by the chemical decomposition of rocks and is often a symbol of the material of the human body. The associations combined suggest an angry Communist whose life-blood goal is to assist in the decomposition of a system that beats so hard on the working man.

The use of a storm as a vehicle of complaint is not alien to the blues:

> The North wind has begin howling,
> And the skies are pretty and blue.
> The north has begin howling,
> But the skies are pretty and blue.
> And winter is coming
> Wonder what the poor people are gonna do . . .
>
> Poor people are like prisoners
> But they just ain't got on a ball and chain.
> Poor people are like prisoners
> But they just ain't got on a ball and chain.
> But the way they are faring
> I swear it's all the same.[138]

The singer here, though, does not suggest any kind of revolution, saying simply that things may change, but then again may not. In "Red Clay Blues" the speaker wants to see the big storm make the landlords run, upsetting their system and their artificial status as "lords of the land." However, the speaker emphasizes in the final line that his words are not yet realities, simply stating that he has the "red clay blues." The revolution, compared to a *natural* phenomenon, is what will drive away those blues. Significantly, the storm is going to begin in the decayed pastoral world, presumably welling up from the location of the speaker's roots before it gets to the city. Georgia is also one of the thirteen original colonies, making the revolution *there* a strike at the earliest foundations of America as well. It is hard to tell how much Wright and Hughes each contributed to the poem, but they have handled the material well, provided a thoughtful structure, and indicated the strong resolve of the poem by avoiding slant rhymes, oblique rhymes, and other elements which might have indicated an uneasiness about their purposes. "Red Clay Blues" was really the first of the small number of Hughes's published blues poems to use direct social protest, influenced by his Communist activity, but, as I have said, this type of protest was not unknown in the blues tradition either. "Hard Luck" and "Death of Do-Dirty," in *Fine Clothes to the Jew,* deal with protest against authorities, but it is not the general sociopolitical protest of a poem like "Red Clay Blues." "Big Buddy," in *Jim Crow's Last Stand,* is a call for solidarity, for people to fight like men and to split rocks, a symbol of attack on a system that needs to be fractured.

One of Hughes's last protest blues poems appeared in *The Panther and the Lash:*

> Mister Backlash, Mister Backlash,
> Just who do you think I am?
> Tell me, Mister Backlash,
> Who do you think I am?
> You raise my taxes, freeze my wages,
> Send my son to Vietnam.
>
> You give me second-class houses,
> Give me second-class schools,
> Second-class houses
> And second-class schools.
> You must think us colored folks
> Are second-class fools.
>
> When I try to find a job
> To earn a little cash,
> Try to find myself a job
> To earn a little cash,
> All you got to offer
> Is a white backlash.
>
> But the world is big,
> The world is big and round,
> Great big world, Mister Backlash,
> Big and bright and round—
> And it's full of folks like me who are
> Black, Yellow, Beige, and Brown.
>
> Mister Backlash, Mister Backlash,
> What do you think I got to lose?
> Tell me, Mister Backlash,
> What you think I got to lose?

> I'm gonna leave you, Mister Backlash,
> Singing your mean old backlash blues.
>
> You're the one,
> Yes, you're the one
> Will have the blues.[139]

In this poem Hughes raises questions about the identity that white
society has imposed on the black man and the method by which the
system attempts to guarantee the failure of the black man in that
society. A literal white backlash is, of course, something with
which slaves would be very familiar, but that is now to be countered by a backlash of global proportions as people of color unite.
The final stanza is similar in set-up to stanza 1, but the final
response line changes from portraying the passive receiver of action to portraying the speaker's action. The final coda completes
the turnaround: the next "backlash blues" will be the white man's.
The white man's control over identity, economics, education, the
family, and politics would then be at an end. Hughes's poem is a
cousin to Bessie Smith's "Poor Man Blues":

> Mister rich man, rich man,
> Open up your heart and mind.
> Mister rich man, rich man,
> Open up your heart and mind.
> Give the poor man a chance,
> Help stop these hard, hard times.
>
> While you're livin' in your mansion
> You don't know what hard times means.
> While you're livin' in your mansion
> You don't know what hard times means.
> Poor workin' man's wife is starvin',
> Your wife is livin' like a queen.
>
> Please listen to my pleading
> Cause I can't stand these hard times long.
> Oh, listen to my pleading,
> Can't stand these hard times long.
> They'll make an honest man do things
> That you know is wrong.
>
> Poor man fought all the battles,
> Poor man would fight again today.

Poor man fought all the battles,
Poor man would fight again today.
He would do anything you ask him
In the name of the U.S.A.

Now the war is over,
Poor man must live the same as you.
Now the war is over,
Poor man must live the same as you.
If it wasn't for the poor man,
Mister rich man what would you do?[140]

Both Hughes's poem and Smith's song recognize that the system forces unacceptable circumstances on people, but Smith's song does not overtly specify African-Americans as those mistreated. Although there is anger in Smith's song, she still pleads and does not call for solidarity and bucking the system as Hughes does. That is not to say that such calls are unheard of in blues: the numerous references to building a railroad of one's own or finding a heaven of one's own are similar to the idea Hughes expresses in "Backlash Blues."[141] Hughes was more direct in his statements, and he was, after all, publishing the poem nearly forty years after Smith's song was recorded, when such expression was a bit safer, though the number of blues poems like Hughes's "Backlash Blues" did not increase appreciably during the sixties. By then, the "back to Africa roots" movement and the ascendancy of slick soul music created a distinct decrease in the number of young blacks who were singing blues, and many of the older singers had died, had given up music, or had taken to playing for primarily white audiences whose experiences were far different from the blues singers'.

3

In addition to dramatic monologue blues poems written in traditional or variants of traditional blues stanzas, Hughes wrote a number of poems that looked on the blues and the situations that spawned the blues from a viewpoint external to those situations; some were neither blues stanzas nor first-person laments. In "Monroe's Blues," for example, Monroe's troubles are described for seven lines, and Monroe finally speaks in the eighth line, suggesting the poem's relationship with the blues ballad:

Monroe's fell on evil days—
His woman and his friend is dead.
Monroe's fell on evil days,
Can't hardly get his bread.

Monroe sings a little blues.
His little blues is sad.
Monroe sings a little blues—
My woman and my friend is dead.[142]

Here the simplicity of the lines magnifies the intensity of the emotion, and the correspondence between what the speaker says in line 2 and what Monroe says in the final line emphasizes the correspondence between life and the blues. And what is most important about life in the blues is other people. Monroe's blues concerns his inability to get money and food, but focuses on the deaths of the woman and friend. Though the speaker ironically calls this a "little" blues, referring to Monroe's single line, it is obviously not little in its emotional import. Monroe's line is enhanced by its "lonesomeness," its lack of a repeat line or a line to rhyme with it in Monroe's song. The line, in fact, does not even rhyme with the speaker's line unless it is pronounced in a Southern dialect. That locates the line in the roots and heart of the blues tradition and separates it from the third-person approach of the speaker even as it repeats a previous line that did have a true rhyme. The fact that Monroe's line depends on an oral delivery to make it rhyme underscores the importance of orality to the blues; and the first-person outlook, which makes the final line have so much more impact than the way the statement is made in line 2, is emphasized not only by the substitution of "my" for "his," but by Hughes's use of italics. This is, indeed, a "little" eight-line poem, but that all-important eighth line resounds with the feeling of the blues.

In "The Weary Blues" Hughes dealt with the blues singer and his song and their relation to the speaker of the poem. The poem gave its title to Hughes's first volume, published in 1926, and in that volume we see a Langston Hughes enamored of African and Harlem exoticism—in poems like "Jazzonia," "The Cat and the Saxophone," "Nude Young Dancer," and "Danse Africaine." However, that exoticism is tempered by the pride in African roots expressed in "Proem," with its great similarity to Carl Sandburg's "Old

Timers." The exoticism is further tempered by the hidden sorrow of "Cabaret"; the wistful sadness of "Young Prostitute"; the bitterness of "Cross," "The Jester," and "The South"; the disillusionment with urban life in "Disillusion" and "Summer Night"; and the heartfelt longing of "Dream Variation." In fact, the poet seems to undercut his own impressions of exoticism in "Young Singer":

> One who sings "chansons vulgaire"
> In a Harlem cellar
> Where the jazz band plays
> From dark to dawn
> Would not understand
> Should you tell her
> That she is like some nymph
> For some wild faun.[143]

If there is exoticism in this poetry, Hughes recognizes that it resides in the mind of onlookers, not in the minds of the singers, musicians, and prostitutes who might seem at times to be so picturesque. The people in these poems are viewed by someone attempting to see Harlem in all of its aspects, one who can look from the external viewpoint, with its French labels and classical allusions, but who can also feel from the inside that life "ain't been no crystal stair."[144] This volume presents a person attempting to sort out what his life means. He looks at it romantically, idealistically, and realistically in turns because, in a real sense, the world presents itself that way at various times, though it is the varying temperament and mood of the onlooker that make it change.

Donald Dickinson saw the first verse of "The Weary Blues" as "an alliterative innovation in the style of Lindsay's 'The Congo.'"[145] However, the verse, with its references to crooning, its strategic repetition of the "lazy sway" line, and its description of a blues performer and his playing, seems to derive partly from the vaudeville blues tradition as well. For example, Richard M. Jones's "Jazzin' Baby Blues," recorded in 1922 by Alberta Hunter and by Ethel Waters, and in 1923 by King Oliver and by Eva Taylor, discussed the way "that old piano man he sure can jazz 'em some":

> Jazzin' baby blues are drivin' me insane
> There's nothin' to them but that lonesome blue refrain.
> But when that cornet and that flute begin to play,

> Just make me get right up and throw myself away.
> Just play those jazzin' baby
> Blues for me all night and day.[146]

Bessie Smith's recording of Fletcher Henderson's "Jazzbo Brown from Memphis Town" celebrated the clarinet playing of a man with no professional musical training:

> Don't you start no crownin'.
> Lay your money down.
> I've got mine on Jazzbo,
> That Memphis clarinet hound.
> He ain't got no equal
> Nowhere in this land.
> So let me tell you people
> 'Bout this Memphis man.
>
> Jazzbo Brown from Memphis Town,
> He's a clarinet hound!
> He can't dance,
> He can't sing,
> But Lawdy, how he can play that thing!
>
> He ain't seen no music, too.
> He can't read a note.
> But he's the playin'est fool
> On that Memphis boat.[147]

Hughes's poem, too, deals with the singer and his song, but Hughes presents the flip-side of the romantic vaudeville blues image of the wild and celebrated jazz player, good-timing his way through life. It is doubly significant that Hughes gave his volume the title of this poem and that it is the first poem (following "Proem") in the volume. It suggests that the entire volume begins with and is informed by the "weary blues," and the tradition with which one must come to grips.

The poem itself is a third-person description with some interpolated first-person, eight- and twelve-bar blues lyrics, giving it a sophisticated structure not unlike some vaudeville blues songs:

> Droning a drowsy syncopated tune,
> Rocking back and forth to a mellow croon,
>   I heard a Negro play.

Down on Lenox Avenue the other night
By the pale dull pallor of an old gas light
    He did a lazy sway. . . .
    He did a lazy sway. . . .
To the tune o' those Weary Blues.
With his ebony hands on each ivory key
He made that poor piano moan with melody.
    O Blues!
Swaying to and fro on his rickety stool
He played that sad raggy tune like a musical fool.
    Sweet Blues!
Coming from a black man's soul.
    O Blues!
In a deep song voice with a melancholy tone
I heard that Negro sing, that old piano moan—
    "Ain't got nobody in all this world,
    Ain't got nobody but ma self.
    I's gwine to quit ma frownin'
    And put ma troubles on the shelf."
Thump, thump, thump, went his foot on the floor.
He played a few chords then he sang some more—
    "I got the Weary Blues
    And I can't be satisfied.
    Got the Weary Blues
    And can't be satisfied—
    I ain't happy no mo'
    And I wish that I had died."
And far into the night he crooned that tune.
The stars went out and so did the moon.
The singer stopped playing and went to bed
While the Weary Blues echoed through his head.
He slept like a rock or a man that's dead.[148]

Clearly in this poem the blues unite the speaker and the performer in some way. There is an immediate implied relationship
between the two because of the ambiguous syntax. The "droning"
and "rocking" can refer either to the "I" or to the "Negro," immediately suggesting that the music invites, even requires, the participation of the speaker. Further, the words suggest that the
speaker's poem is a "drowsy syncopated tune" as well, connecting
speaker and performer even further by having them working in the
same tradition. The performer remains anonymous, unlike Bessie

Smith's Jazzbo Brown, because he is not a famous, celebrated performer; he is one of the main practitioners living the unglamorous life that is far more common than the kinds of lives the most successful blues stars lived. His "drowsy syncopated tune," which at once implies both rest and activity (a tune with shifting accents), signals the tension between the romantic image and the reality, and very likely influences the speaker to explore the source of the tension between the singer's stoicism and his resignation to his fate as expressed in his blues lyrics. Significantly, the eight-bar blues stanza, the one with no repeat line, is his hopeful stanza. Its presence as an eight-bar stanza works by passing more quickly, reinforcing both his loneliness *and* the fleeting nature of the kind of hope expressed. This is especially true since the singer's next stanza, a twelve-bar blues, uses the repeat line to emphasize his weariness and lack of satisfaction, and his wish to die.

All the singer seems to have is his moaning blues, the revelation of "a black man's soul," and those blues are what helps keep him alive. Part of that ability to sustain is apparently the way the blues help him keep his identity. Even in singing the blues, he is singing about his life, about the way that he and other blacks have to deal with white society. As his black hands touch the white keys, the accepted Western sound of the piano and the form of Western music are changed. The piano itself comes to life as an extension of the singer, and moans, transformed by the black tradition to a mirror of black sorrow that also reflects the transforming power and beauty of the black tradition. Finally, it is that tradition that helps keep the singer alive and gives him his identity, since when he is done and goes to bed he sleeps like an inanimate or de-animated object, with the blues echoing beyond his playing, beyond the daily cycles, and through both conscious and unconscious states.

Another source of the melancholy aura of the poem is the lack of an actual connection between the performer and the speaker. They do not strike up a conversation, share a drink, or anything else. The speaker observes, helpless to do anything about the performer and his weariness save to write the poem and try to understand the performer's experiences and how they relate to his own. Ultimately he finds the man and his songs wistfully compelling; and he hears in his song the collective weary blues of blacks in America and tries to reconcile the sadness with the sweetness of the form and expression.

The poem is a fitting opening not only to this volume, but to all of Hughes's volumes. It combines traditional blues stanzas that emphasize the roots of African-American experience, touches of vaudeville blues as the roots were being "refined," pride in African-American creativity and forms of expression, and a sense of the weariness that ties together generations of African-Americans. With the words "Sweet Blues," Hughes strikes upon the central paradox with which the poem attempts to come to terms. It is one of his central themes.

Onwuchekwa Jemie outlined some of what he saw as the limitations of Hughes's use of traditional blues themes:

> No topical or occasional blues, no prison or chain gang blues, no gambling blues, no blues about someone running his mouth. . . . Elaborate gun bores and weaponry of popular blues are absent. . . . The popular letter motif is rare. . . . There are no talking blues. . . . Social protest is rare in Hughes as in popular blues.[149]

However, there are some inaccuracies in Jemie's assertions, though he is generally right about the scarcity of these subjects. There *are* topical blues ("Out of Work"), occasional blues ("Goodbye Newport Blues" and "Go and Get the Enemy Blues"), chain-gang blues ("Big Buddy"), references to gambling ("Ballad of the Fortune-Teller" and "Midnight Raffle"), references to weapons ("In a Troubled Key," "Suicide," "Too Blue," "Little Old Letter"), and social protest ("Red Clay Blues," "Southern Mammy Sings," and "Backlash Blues"). Of course, social protest is more common in the blues tradition and Hughes's blues poems than Jemie allows, since an expression of pride in separateness and nonconformity constitutes in itself a form of social protest. And although the motif of sending or receiving a letter is rare in Hughes's blues poetry, as Jemie points out, it is because Hughes referred to the written word only sparingly since this is primarily an orally based poetry. True, the letter motif does show up in the blues tradition, which is orally based as well, but it is still understandable that Hughes concentrated on direct oral communication and performances rather than discussing written communication. Ultimately, Hughes used a wide variety of subjects and themes common in blues songs. Sometimes he used them conventionally; other times he extended the meanings in more overt ways. He could not, of course, have covered all of the subjects and themes of the blues, but he made selective omissions, like references to drugs, or de-emphasized certain subjects, like sex and violence, probably as a result of both external pressures and his own desires to help legitimize the blues. The acceptance that Hughes sought was not only for himself, but for the black oral tradition; it was for later black poets to mine some of the more bawdy, violent, or extreme verses.

Still, Hughes performed some interesting experiments with blues structure and theme, employing both the oral and literary devices he had at hand to help him create his poetry. Some of Hughes's most interesting experimentation took place in *Montage of a Dream Deferred*. Hughes described in his introduction what he was trying to do in the volume:

> In terms of current Afro-African popular music and the sources from which it has progressed—jazz, ragtime, swing, blues, boogie-woogie, and be-bop—this poem on contemporary Harlem, like be-bop, is marked by conflicting changes, sudden nuances, sharp and impudent interjections, broken rhythms, and passages sometimes in the manner of the jam session, sometimes the popular song, punctuated by the riffs, runs, breaks and distortions of the music of a community in transition.[150]

Walter C. Farrell, Jr., and Patricia A. Johnson pointed out that be-bop had a central effect on the relationship among poems in the volume:

> In *Montage* Hughes took advantage of the structural characteristics of be-bop by drastically reordering the traditional limitations imposed upon the poem. By breaking down the barrier between the beginning of one poem and the end of another, Hughes created a new technique in poetry. Perhaps one could more accurately describe *Montage* as a series of short poems or phrases that contribute to the making of one long poem.[151]

Of course, this is not necessarily a new technique. Ezra Pound conceived of his *Cantos* as one long poem, and they were written over many years. Other contemporary American poets like Robert Lowell experimented with creating volumes of poetry that represented progressions—disjunctive but nonetheless progressions— among the thematically related poems. It is probably more appropriate to say that Hughes was reacting to the problems presented by the "modernists" like Pound and Eliot as others in the vanguard of poetry at the time were doing. He was searching for new structures, new ways of making poetry fit the modern experience, and he found a fine correlative in his experiments in *Montage,* which explored the advantages of performance and orality as well.

One way to examine Hughes's experimentation in the blues field is to isolate a number of related blues poems and see how they individually and collectively draw on and extend the tradition, thus offering an opportunity to explore his fusion of oral and written traditions and to examine his skills as a literary-jazz improviser. That is not to suggest that Hughes's poems are spontaneous creations. Improvisation is normally thought of as a spontaneous act, but the jazz or blues musician's improvisations are in fact circumscribed by several things: the musician's "vocabulary" (style, patterns, techniques, and riffs), the accepted conventions of the specific genre (which are at work even if they are being deliberately violated), and the boundaries of the individual piece being performed. For example, boogie-woogie pianist Pete Johnson, in his 1947 version of "Swanee River Boogie," performed the melody of the song to a boogie-woogie beat. Thereafter he improvised solos built around the song's chord changes, the boogie-woogie beat, and the variations on the melody of the piece, combined with his arsenal of boogie-woogie riffs and performed in his inimitable style.[152] Hughes, in his 1951 collection *Montage of a Dream Deferred,* generated a set or sequence of six "boogie" poems— "Dream Boogie," "Easy Boogie," "Boogie 1 a.m.," "Lady's Boogie," "Nightmare Boogie," and "Dream Boogie: Variation"—that have in common much more than the "boogie" of the titles. The poems comprise an intricate series of interwoven "improvisations" over a set boogie-woogie rhythm, with Hughes modulating and modifying rhythm, words, imagery, moods, and themes, and constructing a complex interrelationship between music, the musical instrument, the performance, and a set of attitudes exemplified by them.

Structurally, Hughes's six boogie poems share the exciting, rushing rhythms of boogie-woogie: they evoke images of Hughes at work on his poems, pounding out rhythms on his typewriter keyboard. Briefly, boogie-woogie is a form of African-American music, normally performed on the piano, that emerged as a recognizable genre in the 1920s. As blues researcher Karl Gert zur Heide pointed out, "the theme of boogie is the blues, some features derive from ragtime, and the rhythmic interplay of both hands can be traced back to African roots."[153] In boogie-woogie, the improvisations executed by the pianist's right hand on the treble keys are set off against the ostinato or repeated phrases of the left hand on the bass keys. Characteristically boogie-woogie follows the twelve-bar blues chord change pattern—in the key of C, CFC GFC—employing a repeated bass pattern recognizable most often for its eight beats to the bar, and performed at a medium-to-fast tempo that builds an explosive drive and swing appropriate to the dance step with which it shared a name. Besides identifying a dance step and a type of music, however, the term "boogie" functions in other contexts: to boogie is to raise a ruckus or act wildly or uninhibitedly; it also has sexual connotations deriving apparently from the use of "boogie" in the South to refer to a prostitute and "boogie-woogie" to refer to syphilis:

> I'm gonna pull off my pants and keep on my shirt,
> I'm gonna get so low you think I'm in the dirt.
> I'm gonna pitch a boogie-woogie (×3)
> Gonna boogie-woogie all night long.[154]

In this tune singer Big Bill Broonzy has taken a boogie-woogie beat suitable for dancing and provided both the "wild acting" and sexual connotations that go with it. In the tradition, the word carried these connotations, and typically Hughes tried to capture the ambiance of the tradition.

Hughes demonstrated his knowledge of boogie-woogie in *The First Book of Jazz*, in which he and his co-authors identified among the outstanding exponents of boogie-woogie "Pinetop" Smith, Jimmy Yancey, Meade Lux Lewis, Albert Ammons, and Pete Johnson—all important and generally recognized masters.[155] It was the spirited, exuberant, danceable, and often rhythmically complex and intricate music of performers like those men that provided the basis for Hughes's boogie-poem rhythms, just as it was the connotations of the word and the tradition that Hughes tried to capture in his poems.

Hughes obviously wanted us to hear the boogie rhythms in these poems. The first four poems in the boogie sequence ("Dream Boogie," "Easy Boogie," "Boogie 1 a.m.," and "Lady's Boogie") are very "aural"—the words "hear" and "heard" are employed repeatedly, both in a question:

> Ain't you heard
> The boogie-woogie rumble
> Of a dream deferred?

and an assertion:

> I know you've heard
> The boogie-woogie rumble
> Of a dream deferred.[156]

The incessant rhythm and rumbling of boogie-woogie becomes in the poems symbolic of the dream he had delineated in his earlier poem, "Dream Variations":

> To fling my arms wide
> In some place of the sun,
> To whirl and to dance
> Till the white day is done.
> Then rest at cool evening
> Beneath a tall tree
> While night comes on gently,
>   Dark like me—
> That is my dream![157]

By questioning and by asserting the "obvious," Hughes is trying to get black people to recognize that the deferment of that dream is a large part of their lives. If they hadn't heard that boogie-woogie rumble, they could certainly hear it in the rhythms of Hughes's poems. One could treat "Dream Boogie," the first poem of the sequence and a prototype for the other poems in the sequence, as if it were a lyric to be sung to boogie-woogie music, and one could identify the beats and chord changes as they relate to the words. The notation would look as follows:

    C
1 2 34567 8
Good morning, daddy!

1 2 34 5 6 7
Ain't you heard

8 12   3 4   5 6
The boogie-woogie rumble

78   12   3456   7 8
Of a dream deferred?

    F
1234 567
Listen closely:

8   12 34   5 6 7 8
You'll hear their feet

    C
1 2   3   4   5 6   7 8
Beating out and beating out a—

    You think
    It's a happy beat?

G
1   2   3   4 5 6 78
Listen to it closely:

F
1   2 3 4 5 6 78
Ain't you heard.

    C
1   2   3 4 5 6   7   8
Something underneath like a—

    What did I say?

Sure,

I'm happy!

Take it away!

Hey, pop!

Re-bop!

Mop!

Y-e-a-h![158]

What Hughes created was a twelve-line, twelve-bar, boogie-woogie poem, annexing an exclamatory "tag" ending like that occasionally employed in music. Here, though, Hughes has manipulated the form and rhythm: stanzas 2 and 3 are jarred by the dramatic insertion of disturbing questions that achieve their impact by Hughes's rewording the line we would expect in the normal rhythm and progression of thoughts, making it a question. Thus, in stanza 2 "Beating out and beating out a happy beat" becomes:

Beating out and beating out a—

You think

It's a happy beat?

Just as Hughes shifts to the interrogative and separates those questions from their normal stanzaic group, he surely upsets the boogie-woogie rhythm, eventually violating even the rhyming pattern in stanza 3. This violation is significant because stanza 3 draws on the first two stanzas for a repetition of important lines: "Listen closely" of stanza 2 becomes "Listen to it closely" in stanza 3 (Hughes employed a common characteristic of blues lyrics, building slightly modulated lines around loose formulaic patterns), while "Ain't you heard" of stanza 1 is lifted verbatim. Stanza 3, however, becomes deliberately vague—"Something underneath"— in order to force the audience to answer the question that follows, "What did I say?" By upsetting the rhythm and asking the questions, Hughes highlighted the disparity between the rumbling seriousness of the deferred dream and the superficial happiness of the beat or performance. To this masterful maneuvering of the idiom,

230 / Langston Hughes and the Blues

Hughes annexes the "tag" ending—in jazz and blues, a four-bar section appended to the end of a tune that repeats a phrase, offers a final comment, or indicates that the performance is about to end, often for the benefit of those dancing to the music. Hughes's seven-line ending contrasts once again the happiness of the words and music of the performance with the underlying problem. In light of the dramatic irony with which Hughes treated the subject earlier, this return to the facade of carefree happiness adds psychological complexity to the poem. Hughes felt that blacks needed to recognize the reality of deferred dreams, discussed in stanza 3, but in stanza 4 he emphasized the need to retain the spirit of cultural expression and the usefulness of the elaborate role-playing that provided blacks with the opportunity to advance while whites were lulled by the superficial happy roles that blacks played.

The boogie rhythms extend to other poems in the sequence, although the twelve-bar progression is not necessarily present in any of them. "Easy Boogie," "Nightmare Boogie," and "Dream Boogie: Variation" could theoretically fit into the twelve-bar pattern with variations annotated above. One indication that they may not have been intended to fit the pattern is the presence, in "Easy Boogie," of the line "Riffs, smears, breaks" between stanzas 2 and 3 which seems to indicate an instrumental break that would not be characteristic in a standard twelve-bar blues—the breaks would come between the twelve-bar verses. This underscores the importance of "hearing" the boogie-woogie rhythm and spirit of the performance as opposed to following a predetermined structure. "Lady's Boogie" and "Boogie 1 a.m." reemphasize the distinction, each of them eight-line poems (with an additional mock-jive exclamation in the former) in boogie rhythm. These poems, then, are tied together by the rhythm and spirit of boogie-woogie—a rhythm and spirit that Hughes clearly intended for us to hear.

The poems, of course, have other features in common besides boogie-woogie rhythm. The first four poems in the sequence all employ black jive slang: in "Dream Boogie" Hughes used "Daddy!," "Hey pop! Re-bop! Mop! Y-e-a-h!"; in "Easy Boogie" he used "Hey, Lawdy, Mama!"; it's "Daddy!" in "Boogie 1 a.m."; and in "Lady's Boogie" he employed the phrase "Be-Bach!" Coupled with the boogie rhythms this employment of black speech demonstrates the influence of oral culture on Hughes's work, giving to the poems the distinctively black flavor necessary to suggest encoded messages appropriate to a segregated group of people. Music critic John McDonough has pointed out the usefulness of slang code words:

> There is a fraternal link that always seems to bond together those who would challenge or otherwise separate themselves from the mainstream of social custom. Sometimes the trappings and devices of such brotherhood are enjoyed for their own sake—a sort of college game without substance. But more commonly, they have a very specific and necessary function. In a hostile and crowded world, such devices identify each member to the other. It may be a handshake, a secret word or phrase, gesture or symbol. In short, a lexicon of code words that separate the true believers from the indifferent or unfriendly.[159]

Hughes didn't employ code words that whites were unlikely to understand, but the words are readily identifiable with black culture, and by using them he intimated that his message was directed at blacks and, to a great measure, originated with them.

This slang also helps call attention to the similarities and contrasts of the poems. Both "Dream Boogie" and "Boogie 1 a.m.," for example, are narrated by women, as indicated by the address "Daddy." This address, along with "Papa," is common in the blues songs of females and in black culture in general, but the term of address would not be used by a male; "Daddy-O" would be used, but not simply "Daddy." This use of a female speaker, which is also prevalent in Hughes's blues poems, is important in that it indicates that the ideas are not necessarily identifiable with the single viewpoint of the black male, Hughes himself. The suggestion is that concern for the problems of blacks connected with deferred dreams is not simply an intricate artistic stance of the author but the representative stance of sensitive blacks, both male and female, who, especially in terms of the sexual theme of the poems, will be creating future generations.

"Dream Boogie" is a poem of beginnings. It begins the sequence of poems; it is the poem that greets the beginning of the day and poses the nagging and disconcerting questions dealt with repeatedly in the poems. It is appropriate that this is the first poem in the sequence, since awakening from a dream world to reality would accentuate the disparity between those two worlds. In "Dream

Boogie" the speaker asks questions, which contrasts with "Boogie 1 a.m.," a poem of conclusion that addresses the listener at day's end—"Good evening, Daddy"—and asserts that the listener is aware of the rumblings of the dream deferred, presumably after day-long contact with the white-controlled world.

Similarly, "Easy Boogie," the second poem of the sequence, and "Lady's Boogie," the fourth, are related. In contrast to "Dream Boogie," in "Easy Boogie" a man addresses a woman—"Hey, Lawdy, Mama!" The speaker associates the recognition of the steady beat of the dream deferred with the vitality of the sexual act:

> Hey, Lawdy, Mama!
> Do you hear what I said?
> Easy like I rock it
> In my bed![160]

This sexual vitality, implicit in the word "boogie," is also linked with the soul's aspirations through the repetition of sentence construction:

> Down in the bass
> That easy roll,
> Rolling like I like it
> In my soul.

The soul's dreams are seen as vital, lively and life-giving. Thus, through the repetition of phrases and structures, Hughes expanded the importance of his words beyond their initial or superficial meanings.

"Lady's Boogie" exposes the superficial concerns of a posturing "lady" who ". . . ain't got boogie-woogie / On her mind."[161] As in "Easy Boogie," the sexual connotation is at work here, suggesting a sexually ineffectual or inhibited person and connecting that ineffectiveness to the inability to hear the beat of the dream deferred. Hughes suggests that the "Lady" has not listened and could be successful if she did:

> But if she was to listen
> I bet she'd hear,
> Way up in the treble
> The tingle of a tear.

However, the final exclamation, "Be-Bach!," suggests that her pretense makes a mockery of her own people's language in combining the phrase "be-bop" with the name of the classical composer from another culture, mocking the pretension of her position and making it seem ludicrous.

"Easy Boogie" and "Lady's Boogie" also begin to deal with the relationships between the performer/creator, his instrument, and his creation, and the way they relate to the underlying desires and feelings of blacks. Although the "boogie-woogie rumble of a dream deferred" played "underneath," on the bass keys of the piano, had already been introduced in "Dream Boogie," "Easy Boogie" further connects the bass rumble with something "down," something "underneath," something sexual, elemental. It is the walking bass of solidarity:

> Down in the bass
> That steady beat
> Walking walking walking
> Like marching feet

that is connected, through repetition and parallel sentence structure, with the feelings of the soul:

> Down in the bass
> That easy roll,
> Rolling like I like it
> In my soul.[162]

Conversely, "Lady's Boogie" deals with the speaker's attitudes toward a woman who has allowed the pretentions of "society" to interfere with her realizations about the problems of her people. This woman's mind is linked to the notes played in the treble on the piano:

> See that lady
> Dressed so fine?
> She ain't got boogie-woogie
> On her mind—

> But if she was to listen
> I bet she'd hear,
> Way up in the treble
> The tingle of a tear.[163]

Once again the lines relate through their parallel structures: the lady is one whose pretentions prevent her from "hearing," or being aware; who concentrates on appearances rather than sounds or messages; who doesn't listen to the agent that would "enlighten" her, the treble improvisations; whose mind refuses her emotional involvement with the boogie-woogie message. Hughes is, in effect, replicating the amazing dexterity and remarkable rhythmic diversity of the boogie-woogie pianist: he is combining the rumbling, infectious bass beat and rhythm with treble variations and improvisations, relating the former to the "soul" and action, and the latter to the mind and thought of the "movement" in order to foster awareness of the problems of black people and the deferred dream. The staccato alliteration is particularly effective in "Lady's Boogie" ("tingle of a tear"), "Boogie 1 a.m." ("trilling the treble"), and "Dream Boogie: Variation" ("tinkling treble"), particularly when picked out over the momentum of the rolling bass.

These treble and bass patterns are used to introduce and indeed are a part of the compelling unifying image of the poems:

> Trilling the treble
> And twining the bass
> Into midnight ruffles
> Of cat-gut lace.[164]

Here the right-hand treble notes and the left-hand bass notes are united in performance, as the minds and souls or thoughts and feelings of blacks are meant to be united in a common cause: the recognition of the dream deferred, and the organization of a unified front to confront the problems of blacks in America. Hughes did not want to overemphasize the bass/sex/soul of the second poem of the sequence, "Easy Boogie"; neither did he want to concentrate exclusively on the treble/inhibitions/mind of the fourth poem, "Lady's Boogie." It was the poem in between, "Boogie 1 a.m.," that presented the "unified sensibility" for which Hughes aimed, that combined the bass and treble into a single compelling image.

The image itself at once suggests several things: ruffles and lace both suggest the delicate trimming of clothing; however, to be ruffled is to become disturbed, and to ruffle is to cause disturbances, as in water; the lace becomes something to hold things together in light of the "cat-gut" prefix. All these combine to suggest a decorative appearance tied to an underlying anxiety. The "midnight" of "midnight ruffles" identifies the revelation as a black one, and places the revelation at nighttime, the time of dreams, and nightmares.

A variation of the image returns in "Nightmare Boogie" which follows "Lady's Boogie" and, with "Dream Boogie: Variation," helps emphasize the dream theme at the end of the sequence. "Nightmare Boogie" deals with the collective loss of black identity:

> I had a dream
> and I could see
> a million faces
> black as me!
> A nightmare dream:
> *Quicker than light*
> *All them faces*
> *Turned dead white!*[165]

This sentiment is a magnification of the problem recognized in "Lady's Boogie," where the "lady" has lost the ability to hear and understand cultural messages. In "Nightmare," Hughes identified the instantaneous loss of black identity as a phenomenon that occurred more quickly than it could be recognized, more quickly than it could be exposed, thus stressing the urgency of black identity, pride, and unity. What is important here is that the first four lines have a direct parallel relationship to lines 5 through 8: the dream of line 1 is the nightmare of line 5; the seeing of line 2 is the revelation of line 6; the faces of lines 3 and 7 and the colors of lines 4 and 8 define whether the event was a dream or nightmare. At the climax of the metamorphosis from black to white, from dream to nightmare, Hughes eschews a smooth transition, generating a "whirling" midnight incantation, as if awakening to a real solution:

> Boogie-woogie,
> Rolling bass,
> Whirling treble
> Of cat-gut lace.[166]

This variation on the lines of "Boogie 1 a.m." labels the dream deferred as a nightmare that leads to a loss of racial identity, resolvable only by hearing and understanding the "message" of boogie-woogie.

In contrast to the nightmare of the dream deferred, the black pride/identity "movement," the marching, walking feet of "Dream Boogie" and "Easy Boogie," is a whirling awakening to a new dream, which segues very naturally to "Dream Boogie," the first poem of the group. Whereas "Dream Boogie" is an upbeat, urgent poem, "Variation" is much more sad and subdued: it portrays the boogie-woogie pianist, performing his music, his piano screaming for him under his stomping feet, his eyes misting at the prospect of having missed his chance at freedom. Here, however, the "midnight ruffles / of cat-gut lace" of the "Boogie 1 a.m." quatrain and the "Whirling treble / of cat-gut lace" of the "Nightmare Boogie" quatrain becomes "High noon teeth / In a midnight face," identifying the central idea and image of the poems with the actual facial features and identity of the performer, the creator, the one closest to the music itself. Hughes is emphasizing here how easy it is for an individual to fail to recognize the dream deferred, the nightmare as it relates to the individual himself. The final image is not one of the jive-talking, energetic persona of "Dream Boogie"; it is the embodiment of the boogie-woogie tradition, alone and too late, playing the wistful boogie of freedom deferred. By varying and manipulating the words, imagery, moods, and themes of these poems, Hughes has illuminated the issue of the dream deferred from different emotional perspectives. By employing folk culture so well, he, in effect, gave his poems traditional authority, made them unadulteratedly black, and established a continuity that makes them seem to express the ideas *of* the people *for* the people.

4

The pervasive influence of the oral tradition in Hughes's poetry might make an examination of Hughes's revisions of his blues poems seem like a futile, pedantic exercise, particularly given the variable nature of an individual blues lyric as the singer performs it. However, because Hughes was a literary artist, because he was tied to the written as well as the oral tradition, and because he made sometimes drastic revisions of his blues poems, such an examination helps to reveal his attitudes toward his material as they modulated over the years and to illuminate the nature of his use of the oral blues tradition in his written work.

The textual revisions that Hughes made fall into four categories:
1. Changes in spelling and dialect usage
2. Changes in punctuation
3. Alteration and addition of words
4. Structural changes

A number of these alterations can be accounted for by the nature of the difficulty of rendering oral materials in print. However, Hughes's revisions of his various blues poems *can* also be accounted for by his knowledge of the folk-blues tradition, which, though not as far-reaching as Sterling Brown's, was still fairly extensive, and by the fact that he was adept at combining the techniques of the folk-blues artist, the blues composer, and the poet. In addition, some of the textual changes, like the elimination of dialect spelling and punctuation, reflected Hughes's changing aesthetic as related to his social perspective as it developed over the years. Hughes's status as a literary artist, then, necessitates that we examine the nature of his textual changes in order to track the ways in which he exercised the freedom of the oral tradition and combined those interests with the interests of the literary artist who paid close attention to specific words and typographical elements to emphasize them for specific thematic reasons.

One problem here is that without Hughes's comments on the matter, there is no absolute way to tell if textual variants of his poems are the result of artistic revisions, or to know how much supervision Hughes had over the texts of his journal publications. For example, except for a minor point of punctuation, "The Weary Blues" remained the same from its publication in *Opportunity* through its various publications in *The Weary Blues and Other Poems, The Poetry of the Negro,* and *Selected Poems.*[167] That change, the revision of a three-point ellipsis in the two "He did a lazy sway" lines in *Opportunity* to a four-point ellipsis in subsequent versions, serves primarily to make us linger on the words of those two lines slightly longer, since they become two separate sentences. The added pause reinforces the visual picture of the piano player, stressing the identification of the man with his physical activity ("lazy sway") and the relation of that lazy motion to the ambiance of the song ("drowsy syncopated tune"). In effect, the

four-point ellipsis subtly influences us to recognize the close relationship of the singer to the song and of life to the blues; it also
accentuates the speaker's interest in the piano player and his music
and how they both relate to him. This element of punctuation
should not be overemphasized, but neither should it be ignored,
particularly since there is evidence that Hughes paid careful attention to typographical elements in his other poems, as will be discussed later.

The fact that little else changes in the text of "The Weary Blues"
suggests that *Opportunity* was extremely careful with poetic texts
and that therefore we might say with authority that Hughes's
Opportunity publications are reliable in their fidelity to his intentions. Of course, the attention given to "The Weary Blues" at the
time of publication may have influenced Hughes to work the text
over very thoroughly, as Hughes wrote in *The Big Sea* in 1940.[168]
However, whatever the cause of the constancy of the text in this
poem, it does not necessarily follow that later poems published
in *Opportunity* are textually reliable. The poem entitled "Hard
Luck" in the October 1926 issue of *Opportunity* is a case in point:
the poem actually printed under that title is not "Hard Luck" but
"Bad Luck Card," which was, along with "Hard Luck," published
in the following year in *Fine Clothes to the Jew.* We can only
conjecture as to why the mistake was made; perhaps "Hard Luck,"
whose words gave the title for Hughes's impending volume, was
originally scheduled to appear in the journal but was eliminated
because of its anti-Semitic overtones, overtones which Hughes
denied but which still offended some Jews. The poem was then
removed, but the title somehow left intact. Regardless, the problem
of the source of textual problems still remains; for the purpose of
this study I will assume that all changes are the result of Hughes's
revisions unless, as in the case of "Hard Luck," a mistake is obvious.

The poem entitled "Down an' Out," published in *Opportunity*
of October 1926,[169] exemplifies the various types of changes that
Hughes made in his poems as he prepared them for publication. A
comparison of the text as it appeared in *Opportunity* with the text
in the 1942 volume *Shakespeare in Harlem*,[170] where its title was
"Down and Out," demonstrates some of Hughes's textual strate-

gies. The first version below is from *Opportunity;* the second is from *Shakespeare in Harlem.*

Down an' Out

If you loves me
Help me when I'm down an' out.
If you loves me
Help me when I'm down an' out.
Cause I'm a po' gal that
Nobody gives a damn about.

'Stalment man's done took ma clothes
An' rent time's most nigh here.
'Stalment man's done took ma clothes,
Rent time's most nigh here.
I'd like to buy a straightenin' comb
An' I needs a dime for beer.

Talk about yo' friendly friends
Bein' kind to you.
Talk about yo' friendly friends
Bein' kind to you:
Just let yo'self git down an' out
An' then see what they'll do.

Down and Out

Baby, if you love me
Help me when I'm down and out.
If you love me, baby,
Help me when I'm down and out,
Cause I'm a po' gal
Nobody gives a damn about.

De credit man's done took ma clothes
And rent time's most nigh here.
Credit man's done took ma clothes.
Rent time's nearly here.
I'd like to buy a straightenin' comb,
An' I needs a dime fo' beer.

Oh, talking about yo' friendly friends
Bein' kind to you—
Yes, talk about yo' friendly friends

Bein' kind to you—
Just let yo'self git down and out
And then see what they'll do.

The first obvious textual change here is in the title, a sign of Hughes's general attempt to render the oral tradition successfully by African-American Negro dialect verse. Hughes admitted that among the first types of poems he had tried to write were "Negro dialect poems like Paul Laurence Dunbar's,"[171] but the example he gave in *The Big Sea* and his blues poems in dialect are not so heavily weighted with dialect spellings as Dunbar's "An Ante-Bellum Sermon" or "Signs of the Times." Dialect verse is difficult to write, difficult to balance between inconsistency and overdramatization, and in "Down and Out" Hughes uses a restrained dialect that avoided "darkyism" by mixing standard spellings with dialect renderings of more obvious African-American characteristics in speech. The version of the poem in *Shakespeare in Harlem* is different in that some dialect renderings were changed. While Hughes changed "an'" to "and" and "loves" to "love" in stanza 1, he retained the third-person-singular final "s" in stanza 2—"needs"—and in the same line dropped the final "d" on "and" and changes "for" to "fo'," which makes it more consistent with his rendering of "poor" and "po'." He also consistently left out the final "g" of the "ing" ending, as he did in the earlier version.

The additions and changes in words are more substantial. Hughes added the exclamatory tag "Baby" to the beginning of the first line, emphasizing "if," highlighting the conditional nature of the woman's statement, and expressing her own private doubts about the nature of her man's love. Hughes also added "baby" to the end of line 3, and though it is a common term of endearment, it is hard to ignore the fact that the woman is asking to be helped, to be taken care of, to be "babied." In her own plea she calls to the person she has "babied," in language, to reciprocate. The addition of these tags, then, serves to loosen up the lines, to make them more fluid, far less mechanical than the lines in *Opportunity;* the tags also add yet another element of the oral tradition while still exploiting the placement of the words on the page for literary effect; and they contribute thematically to the poem as well.

Other modifications also contribute thematically to the poem. Changing the " 'Stalment man" to the "credit man" in stanza 2 relates to the theme of needing to be helped in stanza 1. But the major theme in stanza 1 is that of belief. "Credit," from the Latin *credo,* "I believe," is certainly appropriate to this context: the woman has believed in the love of her man, but now her conditional statement indicates that her belief is wavering; the credit man, whose belief was based on a contractual agreement in which he would always be clearly at an advantage, is now not only deserting her, but stripping her of the residence and outer garments without which she cannot comfortably exist in society. This effects the transition to the third stanza, in which, having lost her creditable standing with her friends, she finds herself totally deserted. Ultimately, the effect of using "credit man" is to maintain the idea of the life of installment payments, where bankruptcy is staved off from month to month, and to add to this idea the connotations of the various meanings of "credit" to help unify the poem even more. The effect of the private life on the public life and of the relation of the individual to the group are all tied irrevocably to the theme of belief in others and belief in self.

Alterations in punctuation in the *Shakespeare in Harlem* version seem to be working toward heightening the dramatic effects in the poem. For example, the earlier poem rendered the first four lines of stanza 1 as two separate two-line sentences; in the later version, Hughes changed the period at the end of line 4 to a comma. By doing this, he allows the sentiments in 1 and 2 to stand alone as they had in the earlier poem, but then indicates the closeness of the sentiments to lines 5 and 6 by joining lines 3 and 4 to them with a comma. Thus the sentiment gains from two settings: lines 1 and 2 present the woman's own isolation and her plea to one man in a separate sentence, while, when joined with lines 5 and 6, the idea expands to include the general "a po' gal" that not just one person but *nobody* cares about. Thus the punctuation itself helps develop the movement from private to public and individual to general.

In stanza 2 of both versions the first two lines are set off as a separate sentence, as in stanza 1. However, in the later version, Hughes changed the comma that had ended line 3 of the *Opportunity* version to a period, thus making both lines 3 and 4 separate sentences. Psychologically this works perfectly: the woman begins by enumerating specific troubles in the sentence contained in the first two lines. Then, instead of just repeating those lines as they were, Hughes broke the repeat into two separate sentences, making each loom large, independent, each big enough to destroy her on its own. The impression is also one of a piling up of troubles, pushing the woman toward a subdued hysteria and anger. Part of the reason for her being subdued is her perception that her friends have deserted her; part is her realization that she is black and poor in a white society. This is mirrored in the resolution of this stanza: the woman would *like* to buy a straightening comb—a gesture toward being white—which would help her escape some of her problems. But, she realizes that *looking* more white is not *being* white and therefore knows that she will always feel racial prejudice; she feels that, given the loss of her friends, her only escape is alcohol—for which she *needs* a dime.

Changes in the third stanza once again reinforce the oral nature of the words; here Hughes added the exclamations "Oh" and "Yes." The former is a tag used to introduce a subject or express surprise—in this case that the "friendly friends" are in fact not "bein' kind." The change to "Yes" in line 3 reaffirms the woman's expectations that friends will be kind, and also, through the repetition, forces the "Yes" toward an ironic tone that sets up the reader for the final line. This has an even greater urgency since Hughes replaced the end comma and semicolon in lines 2 and 4 with dashes; this builds up a momentum that is released in the final two lines. The reader can almost see the arching of signifying eyebrows. We can also see that the poem is expanding once again toward the general: the final stanza is aphoristic, expressing a general truth drawn from the specifics of the earlier stanza of the song. Thus this second version represents a skillful revision of the poem in *Opportunity;* punctuation, dialect, additional languages, and structure have been adapted to thematic purposes.

A third revision of "Down an' Out," for *Selected Poems,*[172] is substantially different from the earlier two versions:

Down and Out

Baby, if you love me
Help me when I'm down and out.
If you love me, baby,
Help me when I'm down and out,
I'm a po' gal
Nobody gives a damn about.

The credit man's done took ma clothes
And rent time's nearly here.
I'd like to buy a straightenin' comb,
An' I need a dime fo' beer.

I need a dime fo' beer.

This version adopts many of the changes of the *Shakespeare in Harlem* version, and it also replaces "De" with "The" and "needs" with "need," both of which are more consistent with the pattern of rendering dialect in the rest of the poem. Other changes, though, seem in some ways damaging to the poem. By dropping "Cause" in line 5 of stanza 1, Hughes eliminated the implicit question that lines 5 and 6 are answering: "Why should I help you?" The effect is to move the woman further from a direct-address scene as the reader envisions it, isolating her further from a personal relationship and setting stark statements next to each other, in an almost Hemingwayesque manner, which reflects her disorientation and isolation in a hostile world.

The marvelous effect Hughes attained in the second version of stanza 2 by setting off his third and fourth lines into separate sentences vanishes with lines 3 and 4 in this version. If, in fact, Hughes was trying typographic accommodation to achieve lyric compression, he certainly lost dramatic emotion in the poem, since the building toward the last line in the poem is diminished. The precedent for mixing twelve-bar and eight-bar stanzas has already been discussed: David Evans's study of the number of versions of Tommy Johnson's "Big Road Blues" exemplified this most clearly, and Johnson's "Canned Heat Blues," Furry Lewis's "Big Chief Blues," Sunny Boy and His Pals' "France Blues," and King Solomon Hill's "That Gone Dead Train" all are examples of folk-blues songs that mix twelve- and eight-bar blues stanzas.[173] Hughes makes use of the diminution both structurally and thematically. Going from a six-line to a four-line to a one-line stanza reflects typographically the reduction of the woman to her final outlet, alcohol; and the elimination of the final stanza of the *Shakespeare in Harlem* version, chastising the fickleness of friends, removes what could be seen as a destructive and divisive bitterness—a bitterness definitely not needed some four years after the Montgomery, Alabama, bus boycott of 1955. In the context of the poem, the one-line stanza focuses the reader's attention squarely on the woman rather than flaring out to the general and aphoristic; it focuses on the woman's hopeless alternative to being white by repeating the last line of stanza 2, yet it is set off on its own, the plaintive cry of a woman reduced to escapism, a hopeless victim.

What we lose, then, in the final version's portrayal of the woman is the *spirit,* even if that spirit was "misdirected" against those upon whom she should rely in her fight against the pressures of the system and the pressures to attempt to escape her blackness. This desire for escape is replicated in the stanza form. We have been progressively losing the twelve-bar stanza; it is compressed down to the last line that, in fact, expresses the woman's two basic problems at once: her need for money and her desire to escape from herself. This is the essence of her blues, since both are related to blackness. Thus, Hughes made a transition from the standard twelve-bar blues form to the compressed core of the woman's blues as expressed in the single final line. Hughes had experimented with this type of one-line, final stanza in "Six-Bits Blues," published in the same volume in which "Down and Out" appeared, *Shakespeare in Harlem* of 1942.[174] The tone in this poem is similar in the escapist sentiment: "I got to roll along." And in fact the earlier version of "Six-Bits Blues," published in *Opportunity* of February 1939, actually had a third six-line stanza that Hughes reduced to a single line in the later publication (though he did not reduce stanza 2 to four lines as he did in the "Down and Out" of *Selected Poems*).

Hughes's revisions and the changes they effect should be of great interest to the Hughes scholar interested in his poetic technique and stylistic development over the years. In her 1951 study *Poems in Process,* Phyllis Brooks Bartlett devoted three brief paragraphs to the types of revisions Hughes made in five poems (the drafts of which were presented to the Library of Congress), claiming that

> . . . it is possible to make a generalization about Hughes' method of working over his poems. He nearly always hits just the words he wants in the first draft and he gets them in the right order; a deletion is unusual. The only problem that puzzles him is the arrangement of the lines—where to break them so that their appearance on the page will indicate to the reader how they should be read. His revisions are almost exclusively devoted to achieving the right visual effects for his rhythms.[175]

While Bartlett's comments may be generally true for the poems she studied, as we have seen here, Hughes employed revisions to help smooth out dialect, paying close attention to words and punctuation and altering structure for literary purposes, all the while maintaining a close connection with the techniques of the professional blues composers and the oral tradition, creating a masterful mix. However, just because Hughes drew on the oral tradition does not mean we should not study his poems as we would any other great poet in order to gain insight into his craft, as long as we do not let the research and close analysis overwhelm or ignore the vigor of the oral tradition or the message of the poem. The full appreciation of Hughes's work comes only with the consideration of both the oral and literary aspects of his work.

5

It isn't surprising that as the century progressed, both black and white poets were more familiar with and more often employed pop-blues and jazz-blues elements, as opposed to the folk blues employed on occasion by Hughes and Sterling Brown, since popular variations were much more likely to be heard by more people. The amount of "bluesiness" retained in pop songs varies from song to song of course, as does the amount of blues influence on different jazz performers or compositions. So also the influence of jazz on poets who write blues songs inspired by jazz artists becomes another concern when approaching blues poems. From the beginning of jazz performing, it has been obvious that the jazz musician plays the blues differently from the blues musician. The jazz musician has a tendency to be more sophisticated, to improvise in a more complex manner and at greater length, and to deemphasize the words of songs and subordinate them to instrumental expressiveness and variations, though the jazz player often imitates the human voice. The rural blues were less accessible to both white and black poets who lived in an urban environment, so the blues of these jazz players, who performed in the cities, had more of an influence on them. Although the folk blues continued to develop more commercial forms throughout the 1930s and on down to today, most references to blues by both black and white poets seem related more to jazz blues than to folk blues.

The perception of what the jazz musician represented may have something to do with this influence as well. Many saw the jazz musician as a freedom fighter, a challenger of old forms and a transformer of old songs into new, expressive creations. The blues singer often had a reputation as an uneducated alcoholic, a repetitive performer of traditional songs representing a tie to the black slave past rather than a progressive innovator. Under those circumstances, poets looking for new modes of expression might also be expected to draw upon the ways that jazz players played the blues as jazz changed over the decades. We have Langston Hughes performing with a pianist in the 1920s and recording Kansas City jazz blues in the 1950s; the Beats drawing on the jazz blues of bop musicians like Charlie Parker, Dizzy Gillespie, and others in the 1940s and 1950s; and the attempts of many African-American poets from the late 1950s to the present to draw upon the uses of blues in free jazz to enliven their poems. Thus the influence of the blues tradition on poetry must be carefully analyzed to discern exactly what *kind* of blues or what way of using blues is being employed.

Finally, both the etymology and sound of the word "jazz" have associations that poets in the Freud-influenced and fragmented twentieth century might draw upon to aid them in expressing their ideas. Charles Olson referred to the etymological roots of the word in *The Maximus Poems* with the line "jass is gysm," associating jazz with semen.[176] Sylvia Plath called cacophony "the goddess of jazz and quarrels" as her speaker seeks relief from the harsh sounds of the world in "Alicante Lullaby."[177] Therefore, while blues might suggest one particular mood or color, jazz has connotations and associations that presented a significant advantage in terms of what many modernist and postmodernist poets were trying to accomplish, and a brief look at the convergence of those two traditions is useful in establishing the oral and literary bases for such experimentation.

With the 1920s being dubbed the Jazz Age, a time when the "Negro was in vogue" and self-conscious primitism was pervasive, seemingly there would have been great potential for use of the blues idiom being represented so frequently by vaudeville blues singers in the years 1920–26. The modernists were searching for ways to express passionately their alienation and despair, their sense of discontinuity, and their rejection of traditional assumptions and values. However, Ezra Pound sought to "make it new" by plundering the European intellectual past and elements of Eastern culture, and his primary musical interest was in classical music, as his opera and other music reviews attest. T. S. Eliot, too, forsook American soil and early on embraced similar interests; he sought to fill the void left in his life with Anglo-Catholicism.

William Carlos Williams was the modernist who would seem to have been most sympathetic to jazz and blues, searching as he was for a new measure and a new form to challenge the artificial forms of the past, seeking to be colloquial and revolutionary. Biographer Paul Mariani reports that in "April of '45 Williams was . . . trying to become a convert to black jazz."[178] A bit later Williams went to hear Bunk Johnson's New Orleans jazz band, a revival of Johnson's 1920s band at a time when the latest development in jazz was bop; he wrote a respectful if somewhat awkward poem about what he heard and saw. But all of this took place toward the middle of Williams's poetic career, and even if black jazz is an "analogue for the jagged patterns that distinguish Williams' poetic lines,"[179] an attempt to render ethnopoetically the patterns of oral colloquial speech, Williams's early experimentation stemmed from an avant-garde literary tradition, as did the work of Pound and Eliot.

It is interesting, though, that Williams was for a time involved with an avant-garde literary journal edited by Charles Henri Ford entitled *Blues: A Magazine of New Rhythms,* published in Mississippi in 1929 and 1930. The journal was a place where Williams could advance his poetic ideas about the need for a revolution in poetry. Ford's choice of a title suggests a sadness at the current state of poetry, but the offer of a chance for renewal by drawing on an alternate tradition. Williams himself described Ford's poems in 1938: "They form an accompaniment to the radio jazz and other various, half-preaching, half-sacrilegious sounds of a Saturday night in June with the windows open and the mind stretched out attempting to regain some sort of quiet and be cool on a soft couch. . . . The poems form a single, continuous, running accompaniment, well put together as to their words, to a life altogether unreal."[180] Editor Edward B. Germain picked up on Williams's "radio jazz" comment and saw Ford's first book as welding together "radio jazz and iambic pentameter, surrealist imagery and the sonnet form," describing it as "full of kinky jazz blues . . . and witty satires of popular lyrics."[181] What Ford was capitalizing on was jazz-influenced popular music that had been "liberated" somewhat by the rhythms of the blues, for despite his proximity to the rural Southern blues of Mississippi, Ford was not drawing on folk blues but the jazz of commercial enterprise. His one poem on an African-American musical figure is "Chanson Pour Billie," an amalgam of his sympathy for, desire for, and fear of Billie Holiday, whose "grenadine gums are as exciting as a holdup."[182] In the poem there is evidence of the surrealist exaltation of desire for and revolt against authority, and an attempt to reconcile the seemingly contradictory emotions of desire and fear as the speaker desires the "criminal" for his boss.

Williams's manifestoes for the journal *Blues* indicate that although he was not particularly knowledgeable about the blues tradition, he had a sure sense of what blues might represent for the literary artist in an emotional and aesthetic sense:

> Blues is a good name for it, all the extant magazines in America being thoroughly, totally, completely dead as far as anything new in literature among us is concerned. Anything that fractures the stereotyped is definitely taboo, now as always. In the common mind America is just recovering from the post-war hysterias of a few of the more bizarre (*sic*) writers of that unsettled time, returning to the normal paths of good literary practice. In short to dullness, to stupidity, to regimentation, to business. Blues comes as near to stating the implied revolt from this as one could get to entitle a pushing, new venture.[183]

Since Williams has become recognized as a major influence on subsequent American poets, his acceptance of the blues tradition as an expression of similar aims and concerns of the modernists represents a link between him and those who not only employed his modernist techniques but drew upon the blues and jazz tradition as well.

Although Langston Hughes employed aspects of the blues tradition more regularly than any other poet of his time, there were many other poets, black and white, who referred in a number of ways to that tradition. In 1973 Bernard Bell attempted to categorize the various uses of the blues by contemporary African-American poets, but his categories might just as well refer to white poets. Bell's categories—conventional and organic uses of the blues, experiments with the blues motif and form, ritual and intrinsic uses of the blues, and ornamental and thematic uses of the blues[184]— are useful, though they need both expansion and clarification.

"Conventional and organic uses of the blues" should encompass the various traditional structures, forms, motifs, and language as well as the internal logic of the words and the relationship of the creative artist to the community. Since a number of variables determine the nature of the blues lyric and song, it would be useful to relate blues poem to a certain time period, geographical area, or blues style. One problem with this category and the next, "experiments with the blues motif and form," is that a blues poem may be traditional in one way but experimental in another. Dudley Randall's "Jailhouse Blues," A. B. Spellman's "The Joel Blues," Ishmael Reed's "Betty Ball Blues," and Sherley Anne Williams's "Any Woman's Blues" all use a traditional twelve-bar *AAB* stanzaic pattern, and language and themes common to blues. However, Henry DuMas's "Keep the Faith Blues," while it follows the same stanzaic pattern and often employs traditional blues language, refers to philosophical questions not dealt with directly; and Allen Ginsberg's "Sickness Blues," "Pussy Blues," "Stool Pigeon Blues," and "Hardon Blues," all use a twelve-bar musical pattern and some traditional language and motifs, but employ the less common *ABC* stanza and are more blatantly homosexual and sexually explicit than many commercially recorded blues songs. On the other hand, quite a few of Melvin Tolson's poems in *A Gallery of Harlem Portraits,* including "Harlem," "Babe Quest," and "Edna Borland," and "ETA," "XI," and "UPSILON" from *Harlem Gallery,* or Jodi Braxton's "Whatever Happened to Black America? Or: The Setzuan Invisibility Black and Blues" make use of *AAB* blues stanzas within a poem that does not borrow its entire form from that stanza; and William Waring Cuney's "Let Me Tell You Blues Singers Something" presents a religious person using a blues stanza to challenge the blues. Perhaps, like the designation for the bar length of blues stanzas, blues poems need to be discussed as *tending toward* traditional or *tending toward* experimental, with the various aspects being weighed carefully to discern toward which category the poem tends.

Further, the category "experiments with the blues motifs and form" must be applied with a knowledge of the variations on blues created by jazz musicians such as the bop players of the forties and fifties and the free-jazz players of the sixties to the present, since the best of them drew on the blues tradition and influenced many "jazz poets" in their interpretations of the blues. Often in such jazz-influenced blues poems, the poets seem to draw more on the improvisation and beat of the music rather than the structure. If we establish this as a separate category, the label "ritual and intrinsic uses of the blues" might better be listed as "the blues tradition as an emotional, psychic, or spiritual touchstone or center." Such a category might include poems that do not use traditional form, structure, language, or motifs (most important form and structure) but contain the word "blues" in the title, such as Jayne Cortez's "A Blues" or "3 Day New York Blues," Bob Kaufman's "Heavy Water Blues" or "Blues For Hal Waters," Jack Kerouac's *Mexico City Blues,* Michael Harper's "Blues as Prematurity," or Hayden Carruth's "The Cowshed Blues," among many others. Also in this category are poems that mention the blues in a central way or refer briefly to words from blues songs, such as Baraka's "Look For You Yesterday, Here You Come Today," Colleen McElroy's "Caledonia," Sarah Webster Fabio's "Tribute to Duke," and even Robert Lowell's "Skunk Hour" or John Berryman's "Glimmerings." An adjunct to this category would be a list of poems that define the blues or discuss what they represent, including Don L. Lee's "Don't Cry, Scream," James Cliftonne Morris's "The Blues," Al Young's "What is the Blues?" or "The Blues Don't Change," Jayne Cortez's "You Know," The Last Poets' "True Blues," or Alvin Aubert's "Passage."

Finally, the "ornamental and thematic uses" category that Bell listed is the least satisfactory, since "ornamental" sounds as if the blues reference is artificial or extrinsic. Such a label might fail to recognize, as some music critics did with Art Tatum, for example, the central uses of what seemed like ornaments. This category might be better termed "biographical," to include everything from passing references to blues performers to full-scale narrative portrayals of blues singers and performers. The poems might express admiration or pay tribute, as in Robert Hayden's "Homage to the Empress of the Blues," Etheridge Knight's "To Dinah Washington,"

Conrad Kent Rivers's "For All Things Black and Beautiful," or Berryman's *Dream Song 68*. They might discuss the blues singer as a source of artistic inspiration, as in Al Young's "A Dance for Ma Rainey," Jayne Cortez's "Grinding Vibrato," or James Cliftonne Morris's "East River Tugboat." Or they might reveal the exploitation or suffering of the blues performer, as do Stanley Crouch's "Howlin' Wolf: A Blues Lesson Book," Michael Harper's "Last Affair: Bessie's Blues Song" (also a source of artistic inspiration), Cuney's "Bessie Smith," or Carruth's "A Little Old Funky Homeric Blues For Herm." Of course, there are once again poems that cut across or combine a number of these categories; however, these categories seem to cover the uses of the blues in poetry.

The blues, then, have continued to influence in a variety of ways poems by African-American writers and white writers who were attracted to the blues tradition's strength and beauty. But the poetry of Langston Hughes and his use of the blues tradition have drawn other writers to that tradition as well, as witnessed by the number of poems—such as Dudley Randall's "Langston Blues," a tribute which employs the twelve-bar *AAB* blues stanza—that praise Hughes for his use of folklore. For them, as for Hughes, the blues truly does precede the rise of the curtain. And Hughes's description of Jimboy's music in *Not Without Laughter*[185] is a fitting coda to the blues and to the blues poems of Langston Hughes and his disciples:

> The man stopped playing, with a deep vibration of the strings that seemed to echo through the whole world.

NOTES

1. Brown, *Negro Poetry and Drama*, 61.
2. Ezra Pound, *Ezra Pound's Opera: Le Testament de Villon*, Fantasy 12001, n.d. Robert Hughes's liner notes point out that Pound felt that the divorce of music and poetry had been to the advantage of neither. Contrast Pound's opera to any of Hughes's musical collaborations.
3. See Langston Hughes, ed., *I Hear the People Singing, Selected Poems of Walt Whitman* (New York: International Publishers, 1946); "Whitman: Negroes' First Great Poetic Friend" and "Like Whitman, Great Artists Are Not Always Good People," both in the *Chicago Defender;* and "Walt Whitman and the Negro," *Nocturne*. All of these are

discussed in Berry's *Langston Hughes,* 320–21. The Whitman influence is most obvious in Hughes's poems "I Too" and "Old Walt," included in *Selected Poems,* 100, 275.

4. Hughes, *The Big Sea,* 28.

5. In *A Bio-Bibliography of Langston Hughes* (Hamden, Conn.: Archon Books, 1967), 14, Donald Dickinson calls attention to the influence of Sandburg's "Old Timers" on "The Negro Speaks of Rivers." However, the similarity of "Old Timers" to "Proem" in *The Weary Blues* is even more obvious. Hughes discusses the influence of Sandburg on his poetry in his Caedmon recording *Poetry and Reflections.*

6. Hughes, *The Big Sea,* 213.

7. See note 1 in chapter 1 for the Mamie Smith reference, and Bengt Olsson, *Memphis Blues,* 14 and 21, and Guido Van Rijn and Hans Vergeer's liner notes to *Kansas City Blues,* Agram AB 2004, n.d., for information on Jim Jackson and sixteen of his recorded sides. The use of blues and jazz on Broadway by Hughes and Hurston, in classical music by William Grant Still and George Gershwin, and in prose by writers like Van Vechten, E. C. L. Adams, Howard W. Odum, and Claude McKay suggests that the blues could be commercially viable in a number of ways.

8. Tommy Johnson, "Lonesome Blues," Take 1, *Tommy Johnson (1928–30),* Wolf WSE104, n.d. Titon points out in *Early Downhome Blues,* 28–29, that Big Bill Broonzy "believed that blues songs were all derived from 'Joe Turner,'" an early twentieth-century blues song that followed the *AAA* pattern. W. C. Handy also mentions the song on his Mark 56 recording. Titon also gives "Poor Boy Long Ways from Home" as another example of an *AAA* stanza. Sam Butler's 1926 version, included on *Guitar Wizards,* Yazoo 1016, n.d.; Gus Cannon's 1927 version on *Cannon's Jug Stompers,* Herwin 208, n.d.; Barbecue Bob's version on *Brown-Skin Gal,* Agram AB 2001, n.d., and Ramblin' Willard Thomas's 1928 version on *Blind Lemon Jefferson/Ramblin' Willard Thomas,* Collector's Classics CC5 n.d., provide variations. Barbecue Bob's version uses variously *AAA, AAB,* and *AAAB* stanzas, but recordings with such stanzaic mixtures are not common. As a point of interest, Elvie Thomas's "Motherless Child Blues" employs an *AAAA* pattern in its first stanza. See *The Country Girls,* Origin OJL 6, n.d. [1930]. There are, of course, random variations on the basic stanza structures listed in my text. See David Evans, *Big Road Blues,* 22–47, for a more complete discussion. Different methods of line transcription—the ways the oral performance is placed on the page—have already been discussed, but I will discuss them again when I deal with the *AAB* stanza. I have opted to represent the music this way rather than with notes on a staff because it may be more useful to those who do not read music. In all cases it is best to consult the

actual recording itself. For some excellent transcriptions of a variety of downhome blues, consult Titon's *Early Downhome Blues,* 63–137. Hughes discusses his poems in terms of the twelve-bar musical pattern on *Langston Hughes Reads and Talks About His Poetry,* Spoken Arts 7140, 1959.

9. See Titon, *Early Downhome Blues,* 85–86.

10. Leadbelly, "Packin' Trunk Blues," *Leadbelly,* Columbia S30035, n.d. [1935]. Leadbelly came to prominence after his parole from the Louisiana State Penitentiary in 1934, when he traveled with John A. Lomax as a chauffeur/collector/performer and made New York club appearances in the 1930s, and was even more successful as part of the "folk" boom in the 1940s (with Sonny Terry, Brownie McGhee, Josh White, and others). He was a songster who recorded a wide variety of songs for the Library of Congress and a number of record companies. Leadbelly learned most of his blues from Blind Lemon Jefferson, and indeed the "matchbox" line is often associated with Jefferson, though Jefferson used it in an *AAB* stanza, the *B* line of which is not the same as the second stanza line of Leadbelly's version. Actually, Ma Rainey recorded the line earlier than Jefferson, in 1924, in her "Lost Wandering Blues," and Leadbelly's second verse seems to derive from the *B* line of Rainey's "matchbox" stanza. Rainey's version is included on *Queen of the Blues,* Biograph BLP 12032, n.d., and on *Ma Rainey, Complete Recordings in Chronological Order,* VJM VLP 81, n.d. Leadbelly's version of "Good Morning Blues" (a 1935 version is included on *Early Leadbelly,* Biograph BLP 12013, 1969), his introduction to the blues for Northern audiences, was likely the source for the version included by Hughes and Bontemps in *The Book of Negro Folklore,* 357–88.

Here and elsewhere, my references to specific recordings by blues singers mentioned by Hughes are not meant to imply that Hughes was familiar with those particular recordings. Rather, because he knew of these performers in some way, examples from their recordings or repertoire seem to be more sources than music by people Hughes never mentioned in print. On occasion I refer to sources or recordings with which Hughes *may* not have been familiar in order to establish a broader context for Hughes's discussions. These references are made in lieu of examples by the artists Hughes did discuss, and represent more or less commonplaces in blues rather than oddities. Hughes did hear many blues singers that he did not name in his writings, so conventional blues structures and lyrics that were widespread may be assumed to have been known by Hughes.

11. *The Book of Negro Folklore,* 392–94. Another *AAA* stanza is printed among the "traditional blues verses," 395.

12. Gates Thomas, "South Texas Negro Work Songs," 179. Thomas calls the song "C. C. Rider," and states "who C. C. Rider was is to me unknown." It is likely that there was no such person, and that C. C. Rider should be See See.

13. Ma Rainey, "See See Rider," *Ma Rainey*, Milestone M47021, 1974 [1924]. However, perhaps the song began in the form in which Leadbelly sang it and was adapted by Rainey to the *ABB* pattern. It is difficult to tell. Sleepy John Estes also uses the *ABB* pattern in his "My Black Gal Blues," printed in Eric Sackheim's *The Blues Line*, 266.

14. Hughes, "Black Gal," *Fine Clothes to the Jew* (New York: Knopf, 1927), 66.

15. Hughes, "Don't You Want to Be Free?," 364. In this poem, each group of two lines counts as one line in the notation *ABB*. *ABB* refers not to rhyme scheme but to line repetition. Therefore, *ABB* means a line (group of two lines) followed by another line repeated twice (*BB*).

16. Jim Jackson, "Jim Jackson's Kansas City Blues." Claude McKay uses such a stanza in *Banjo* (1929) when he quotes from "Shake That Thing," which derives from Papa Charlie Jackson's largest commercial hit, his 1925 recording of "Shake That Thing." The two full verses that McKay transcribes are slight variations on two of the verses that Charlie Jackson sings. See the excerpts from McKay's *Banjo* in *Voices from the Harlem Renaissance*, 155–63. Jackson's recording, which anticipated the "hokum blues" craze often associated with Tampa Red's and Georgia Tom's recording of "It's Tight Like That," has been reissued on *Fat Mouth 1924–1929*, Yazoo L 1029, n.d. "It's Tight Like That" has been reissued on *Rare Blues of the Twenties*, Historical, n.d. [1928].

17. Memphis Minnie, "Nothing in Rambling," *Blues Classics*, Blues Classics 1, n.d. [1940].

18. Hughes, ed., *The Book of Negro Humor*, 42.

19. Lonnie Johnson, "Jelly Roll Baker," *Blues From New Orleans*, RCA PM 42390, n.d. The King recording is included on *Tomorrow Night*, King KS 1083, 1976. Johnson recorded "I Got the Best Jelly Roll in Town," parts 1 and 2, in 1930 for Okeh Records, which may be a version of the same song. Of course, this euphemism for genitalia had widespread currency, and Guy B. Johnson discusses it in "Double Meaning in the Popular Negro Blues," 13–15. The earliest recorded version of a "Jelly Roll Blues" is by the Excelsior Quartette, and is included on *Hometown Skiffle: Early Folk Blues Vol. 2*, Saydisc-Matchbox SDR 206, n.d. [1922].

20. Titon, *Early Downhome Blues*, 26. Titon uses these words as part of a question concerning whether this was a likely source. It seems so.

21. W. C. Handy, *Father of the Blues* (1941; rpt., New York: Collier Books, 1970), 279.

22. Hughes, *Poetry and Reflections*. From this point on, I will transcribe the examples from blues lyrics the way Hughes wrote down his blues lines. The "*AAB* stanza," for example, will refer to the repetition of the first two lines of the song followed by two more lines (six lines). The reference to a "line" will refer to this two-line grouping.

23. Hughes, *The Weary Blues*, 30.

24. Peg Leg Howell, "Rock and Gravel Blues," *Blues From Georgia*, Roots RL 309, n.d. [1928].

25. Langston Hughes, *Fine Clothes to the Jew* (New York: Knopf, 1927), 86. Edward Brooks, in *The Bessie Smith Companion* (New York: Da Capo, 1982), 4, points out that Bessie Smith made use of a breathing pause in an unconventional place in order to highlight meaning as well.

26. Victoria Spivey, "Blood Hound Blues," *Women of the Blues*, RCA LPV 534, 1966.

27. Hughes, "Suicide," *Fine Clothes*, 20.

28. Blind Lemon Jefferson, "Pneumonia Blues," *Black Snake Moan*, Milestone MLP 2013, 1970 [1929].

29. Hughes, "Homesick Blues," *Fine Clothes*, 24.

30. Bessie Smith, "Black Mountain Blues," *The World's Greatest Blues Singer*, Columbia GP 33, n.d. [1930].

31. Langston Hughes, "Love Again Blues," *Shakespeare in Harlem* (New York: Knopf, 1942), 103.

32. Charley Patton, "Down the Dirt Road Blues," *Charley Patton: Founder of the Delta Blues*, Yazoo 1020, n.d. [1929]. This lyric, substituting some kind of blues for Patton's "overseas blues," is common in blues.

33. Hughes, "Evenin' Air Blues," *Shakespeare in Harlem*, 38.

34. Hughes, "In a Troubled Key," *Shakespeare in Harlem*, 49.

35. Lonnie Johnson, "Trust Your Husband," *Blues From New-Orleans*, RCA PM 42390, n.d. [1939]. Johnson starts with an *ABB* stanza, and follows with an *ABC* and three *AAB* stanzas.

36. Hughes, "Only Woman Blues," *Shakespeare in Harlem*, 50. Because this poem employs a varied structure, a discussion of it will be taken up later.

37. Odum, "Folk Song and Folk Poetry As Found in the Secular Songs of the Southern Negroes," 270. Other *AA* stanzas are printed on pp. 271, 273, 275, 282.

38. Ibid., 282.

39. King Solomon Hill, "That Gone Dead Train," *Tex-Arkana-Louisiana Country*, Yazoo 1004, n.d. [1932]. Other recordings where this type of setting is used in one or more verses are Tommy Johnson's "Canned Heat Blues," *Tommy Johnson, 1928–1930*, Wolf WSE 104, n.d. [1928]; "France Blues" by Sunny Boy and His Pals on *Really! The Coun-*

try Blues, Origin OJL 2, n.d. [1927]; and Furry Lewis's "Big Chief Blues," transcribed in Eric Sackheim's *The Blues Line,* 253.

40. Lonnie Johnson, "There Is No Justice," *Mr. Johnson's Blues,* Mamlish 3807, n.d. [1932]. This chord progression and stanzaic form is often associated with the eight-bar blues "Crow Jane." One of the earliest recorded examples of that song is Bo Weavil Jackson's "Pistol Blues," included on *East Coast Blues 1926–1935,* Yazoo L1013, n.d. [1926]. Titon discusses the "Crow Jane" tune family in *Early Downhome Blues,* 169, providing references to other recordings that use this chord sequence/melody. Richard M. Jones's "Trouble in Mind" was first recorded in 1926 by Chippie Hill and is included on *Trumpet Blues,* Historical HLP 27, n.d. Georgia White recorded the song in 1936, and her version is included on *Georgia White Sings and Plays,* Rosetta RR1307, 1982. The song has, of course, been recorded many times, but these are versions by two artists whom Hughes mentioned at various points in his career, and White's version is said to have given the song new life. See the liner notes to White's LP.

41. Hughes, "Sylvester's Dyin' Bed," *Shakespeare in Harlem,* 67.

42. Blind Willie McTell, "Searchin' the Desert for the Blues," *Blind Willie McTell 1927–1949: The Remaining Titles,* Wolf WSE 102, 1982 [1932].

43. Hughes, "Reverie on Harlem River," *Shakespeare in Harlem,* 123.

44. See Titon, *Early Downhome Blues,* 89–90. Titon's 2/4 transcription, because it has just two beats per bar, makes this a sixteen-bar blues. There are eight beats of musical accompaniment that extend beyond the vocal line.

45. Hughes and Bontemps print "How Long Blues" in *The Book of Negro Folklore,* 396–97. Ida Cox's 1925 version of "How Long Daddy, How Long" has been reissued on *Blues Ain't Nothin' Else But . . . ,* Milestone MLP 2015, 1971. Ma Rainey's "Daddy, Goodbye Blues," recorded in 1928, has been reissued on *Ma Rainey,* Milestone MLP 47021, 1974, with accompaniment by two other artists mentioned by Hughes, Tampa Red and Georgia Tom. Leroy Carr's 1928 recording has been reissued on *Leroy Carr (1928),* Matchbox MSE 210, 1983. Compare with the vocal line transcription on page 148.

46. Hughes, "Southern Mammy Sings," *Shakespeare in Harlem,* 75–76. The next three quoted stanzas are also from this poem.

47. Hughes, "Same In Blues," *Selected Poems,* 270–71.

48. Hill, "The Gone Dead Train," *Tex-Arkana-Louisiana Country,* Yazoo 1004, n.d. [1932].

49. Hughes, "Lover's Return," *Selected Poems of Langston Hughes*

(New York: Vintage, 1974), 112. The earlier version of this poem appeared in *Shakespeare in Harlem,* 119–20.

50. Hughes, "Little Green Tree," *One Way Ticket* (New York: Knopf, 1949), 111. In *Poetry of the Negro,* ed. Langston Hughes (New York: Doubleday, 1949), 99–100. In *Selected Poems,* 137.

51. Handy, *Father of the Blues,* 148–49. Bessie Smith's recording of this song, reissued on *The Empress,* Columbia G30818, n.d., is generally considered to be the best.

52. Ma Rainey, "Lucky Rock Blues," *Queen of the Blues,* Biograph 12032, n.d. [1924].

53. See Dixon and Godrich, *Recording the Blues,* 20–40, for a good discussion of the recordings made during these years. Unfortunately, they refer to the vaudeville blues as the "classic" blues, a confusing term at best. Jemie calls the *AAB,* twelve-bar blues the "classic" form, adding to the confusion. As a side note, Carl Van Vechten's *Nigger Heaven* (1926) uses a number of vaudeville blues songs or songs recorded by vaudeville blues singers; for example, "Nobody Knows the Way I Feel Dis Mornin'," page 52, was recorded by Monette Moore in 1924, Clara Smith in 1924 and 1925, and Clementine Smith in 1925; "My Man Rocks Me," pp. 16, 250, and 252, was recorded by Trixie Smith in 1922. Hughes later wrote some blues lyrics for Van Vechten to replace lyrics for which Van Vechten had not gotten permission. See Faith Berry's *Langston Hughes,* 80.

54. Titon, *Early Downhome Blues,* 203.

55. Hughes, *The First Book of Jazz,* 19. In *Not Without Laughter,* 99–101, the jazz band plays "St. Louis Blues" and the text refers to two other Handy compositions, "Memphis Blues" and "Yellow Dog Blues," which are differentiated from the "plain old familiar blues."

56. Langston Hughes, "Maker of the Blues," *Chicago Defender* (Nov. 28, 1942), 37.

57. Ibid., 38.

58. *Arna Bontemps-Langston Hughes Letters 1925–1967,* selected and edited by Chas. H. Nichols (New York: Dodd and Mead, 1980), 524. The play reached Broadway in 1946, but a planned film was never shot. Hughes also wrote lyrics for a projected revue, *O Blues!,* in 1926, but the revue was not staged.

59. Onwuchekwa Jemie, *Langston Hughes: An Introduction to the Poetry* (New York: Columbia University Press, 1976), 77. See Berry, *Langston Hughes,* 77 and 309, for discussions of Hughes-Handy collaborations.

60. Hughes, "Blue Monday," *Selected Poems,* 130.

61. Margaret Carter, "I Want Plenty Grease in My Frying Pan," *Pot Hound Blues,* Historical HLP 15, n.d. [1926].

62. Robert S. Gold, *Jazz Talk* (New York: Da Capo Press, 1982), 262.

63. Eric Townley, *Tell Your Story* (Chigwell, Essex: Storyville, 1976), 37.

64. Langston Hughes, "Harlem Dance Hall," *Fields of Wonder* (New York: Knopf, 1947), 94.

65. Ibid., 16.

66. Hughes, *Selected Poems,* 113.

67. Big Miller, *Did You Ever Hear the Blues?,* United Artists, 3047, 1959. The liner notes were written by Hughes.

68. Ibid.

69. Hughes, liner notes, *Did You Ever Hear the Blues?*

70. Big Miller, "I'm Tired," *Did You Ever Hear the Blues?*

71. Hughes, *The Big Sea,* 217.

72. Nat Hentoff, "Langston Hughes: He Found Poetry in the Blues," *Mayfair* (August 1958): 27, 43. In his essay "Jazz as Communication," (*The Langston Hughes Reader,* 494), Hughes asserts that the jazz musicians "on the inside" were the best at putting jazz into words.

73. Langston Hughes, *The Weary Blues and Other Poems,* MGM E 3697, 1958. "Too Blue" was published in *One Way Ticket,* 102.

74. Hughes, "Six-Bits Blues," *The Weary Blues and Other Poems,* MGM E 3697, 1958. The poem was published in *Shakespeare in Harlem.* Its earlier publication in *Opportunity* (February 1939, 54) had no "I got to roll along!" tag, but had one more twelve-bar stanza.

75. Big Joe Turner and Pete Johnson, "I Got A Gal," *The Soul of Joe Turner and Jimmy Nelson,* United US 7794, n.d. This is a live recording of "Roll 'Em Pete." I have used this source because I have never been able to determine what Turner sings in the fifth line on the original, which was reissued on *The Story of the Blues,* Columbia G 30008, n.d. All of the other lines in this stanza are the same in both versions.

76. Hughes, "Songs Called the Blues," 144.

77. Hentoff, "Langston Hughes," 43.

78. Evans, *Big Road Blues,* 49–50. See the same text, 131–44, for a more extensive discussion of thematic texts. Hughes claimed on his Spoken Arts recording that he wrote "Bound No'th Blues" in "the exact format of the traditional folk blues."

79. Son House, "Delta Blues," *Son House: The Legendary 1941–1942 Recordings in Chronological Sequence,* Roots RSE1, n.d. [1941]. House's is just one version of this very old and widespread lyric.

80. Virgil Childers, "Red River Blues," *Piedmont Blues Vol. 2,* Flyright 107, n.d. [1938].

81. Hughes, "Hey!," *Fine Clothes to the Jew,* 17.

82. Ibid., 89. Hughes presents a similar kind of hope in the face of

helplessness in "Red Roses," published in *Poetry* 29, no. 2 (1926): 90. There, in three twelve-bar blues verses, the female speaker wishes to be buried in the springtime, the time of rebirth, when tulips and roses will decorate her grave, instead of in the freezing winter. Perhaps the speaker simply hopes to live that long and *that* is why she looks forward to the springtime as well.

83. Townley, *Tell Your Story*, 32.

84. Hughes, "Black Maria," *Shakespeare in Harlem*, 121–22.

85. Ramblin' Thomas, "No Job Blues," in Sackheim, ed., *The Blues Line*, 94.

86. Blind Lemon Jefferson, "Tin Cup Blues," *Black Snake Moan*, Milestone MLP 2013, n.d. [1929].

87. Hughes, "Out of Work," *Shakespeare in Harlem*, 40–41. In her 1926 recording "Going Crazy With the Blues," Mamie Smith sings a common audience identification lament, "If you knew what I've been through / You would feel the same way, too," a line similar to the one Hughes uses here. See the *Women of the Blues* LP for this recording.

88. See Blind Willie McTell, "Mr. McTell's Got the Blues," *Blind Willie McTell: The Remaining Titles*, and Sonny Boy Williamson, "You Got To Step Back," *Sonny Boy Williamson, Vol. 2*, Blues Classics BC 20, n.d. Such hyperbole is common in blues lyrics. For example, Kid Cole sang a traditional blues verse about how bad he had the blues:

> I got the blues so bad
> It hurts my tongue to talk, lordy, lord.
> Got the blues so bad
> It hurts my lovin' tongue to talk.
> I got the blues so bad
> It hurts my lovin' feet to walk.

Kid Cole, "Niagara Fall Blues," *Down South*, Roots RL 313, 1928. Hughes also uses hyperbole in another song that discusses hunger, "Evenin' Air Blues."

89. See Casey Bill Weldon, "WPA Blues," *Red Hot Blues*, Earl 605, 1982 [1936], and Peetie Wheatstraw, "Workin' on the Project," *Kokomo Arnold and Peetie Wheatstraw*, Blues Classics BC4, n.d. [1937], for two examples of blues songs dealing with the WPA.

90. Hughes, "Cora," *Fine Clothes to the Jew*, 58.

91. Blues ballads like "John Henry" and "Stack O' Lee" of course, consist only of the person's name, but John Henry and Stack O'Lee are not the performers. The same is true of songs like Bessie Smith's "Jazzbo Brown From Memphis Town." The only two pre–World War II blues songs I can think of whose titles consist of the singer's name are "Money

260 / Langston Hughes and the Blues

Johnson" by James "Stump" Johnson and "Pete Wheatstraw" by Peetie Wheatstraw. The latter is actually a *nom du disque* rather than the singer's real name, William Bunch.

92. Hughes, "Only Woman Blues," *Shakespeare in Harlem*, 50–51.

93. Hughes, "Hard Daddy," *Fine Clothes to the Jew*, 86.

94. Peg Leg Howell, "Turtle Dove Blues," *Blues From Georgia*, Roots RL 309, n.d. [1928].

95. Lonnie Johnson and Clara Smith, "You Had Too Much," *Mr. Johnson's Blues*, Mamlish 3807, n.d. [1930]. There are blues performances by one blues singer that recreate a dialogue as well: Blind Lemon Jefferson's "Long Lonesome Blues," included on *King of the Country Blues*, Yazoo 1069, n.d. [1926].

96. Edward Waldron, "The Blues Poetry of Langston Hughes," *Negro American Literature Forum*, 5 (1971): 145.

97. Lucille Bogan, "Shave 'Em Dry," *Copulatin' Blues*, Stash ST 101, n.d. [1935]. Jelly Roll Morton's "Winin' Boy" is also included on this LP. Walter Roland's song is on *Copulatin' Blues Vol. 2*, Stash ST 122, 1984 [1935].

98. Hughes, "Midwinter Blues," *Fine Clothes to the Jew*, 84.

99. Quoted in Giles Oakley, *The Devil's Music: A History of the Blues* (New York: Taplinger, 1977), 103.

100. Hughes, "Ma Man," *Fine Clothes to the Jew*, 88. The eagle-rock as a dance is also mentioned in *Not Without Laughter*, 115–16, in a minstrel show. More explicitly sexual blues are also contained in this novel. These are presumably the blues Hughes reported hearing in Baton Rouge and New Orleans (*The Big Sea*, 290). In *Not Without Laughter*, see the lyric reference to "peaches" and "windin' an' grindin'," 51; "easy rider," 53, "a mule to ride," 56; and Harrietta's song, 318. Onwuchekwa Jemie cites the poem as containing Hughes's most explicit sexual image; see *Langston Hughes* (New York: Columbia University Press, 1976), 46.

101. Bessemer Blues Singers, "My Mama's Baby Child," *Birmingham Quartet Anthology*, Clanka Lanka CL 144 001/002, n.d. [1930]. The name of this group hid the identity of the Dunham Jubilee Singers, a fine Alabama gospel singing group.

102. Ida Cox "Wild Women Don't Have the Blues," *Ida Cox Vol. 2*, Fountain FB 304, n.d. [1924].

103. These poems will be discussed later in a section dealing with the boogie poems of *Montage of a Dream Deferred*.

104. See *AC/DC Blues*, Stash ST 106, 1977, for a number of examples.

105. Hughes, "Morning After," *Shakespeare in Harlem*, 44–45.

106. Willie McTell's "Dark Night Blues" is on *Blind Willie McTell:*

1927–1949, The Remaining Titles; Big Bill Broonzy's "Good Liquor Gonna Carry Me Down" is included on *The Young Big Bill Broonzy,* Yazoo L-1011, n.d. [1935]. Ma Rainey's "Sleep Talking Blues" is included on *Ma Rainey* [1928].

107. There are more references to drugs in jazz music than in blues, actually. For examples of recorded blues and jazz songs dealing with drugs, see *Reefer Songs,* Stash 100, n.d.; *Pipe, Spoon, Pot and Jug,* Stash 102, n.d.; *Weed: A Rare Batch,* Stash 107, n.d.; and *Reefer Madness,* Stash 119, n.d.

108. Hughes, "Gal's Cry for a Dyin' Lover," *Fine Clothes to the Jew,* 82.

109. Ma Rainey, "Black Cat Hoot Owl Blues," *Ma Rainey* [1928]. This is only one of many such references to superstition in blues. See Oliver, *The Meaning of the Blues,* 157–60, 165–71, for a number of other references.

110. Ishman Bracey, "Saturday Blues," *Ishman Bracey, 1928–1930,* Wolf WSE 105, n.d. [1928].

111. The Delta Boys, "Black Gal Swing," *Country Blues Classics Vol. 3,* Blues Classics BC 7, n.d. [1941]. This is more of a hokum-style song with a refrain, which is not reprinted here, but "the Delta Boys" were actually two blues singers, Sleepy John Estes and Son Bonds. Wallace Thurman prints a similar lyric in his 1929 novel *The Blacker the Berry* (New York: Collier Books, 1970), 179 and 224, which deals with the problems of a dark-skinned woman in a whiter world. Hurston also prints such a lyric in "Characteristics of Negro Expression," which is included in *The Sanctified Church* (Berkeley: Turtle Island, 1983), 64.

112. Son House, "My Black Mama," *Really! The Country Blues* [1930].

113. Sara Martin, "Mean Tight Mama," *The Immortal King Oliver,* Milestone MLP 2006, n.d. [1928]. Of course the phrases "black and ugly" or "black and evil" can also be found outside of blues songs as well. Hughes makes several pointed references to skin color and the various perceptions and attitudes related to it in *Not Without Laughter* (see especially 7, 30, and 130). Claude McKay discusses the issue briefly in "Mattie and Her Sweetman," in *The Passion of Claude McKay,* 169–73, and Thurman's *The Blacker the Berry,* cited in note 111 above, deals with the subject at length.

114. Peg Leg Howell, "Rock and Gravel Blues," *Blues From Georgia* [1928]. This type of understatement is common in both blues and Hughes's poetry.

115. Hughes, "Suicide," *Fine Clothes to the Jew,* 20.

116. Blind Willie McTell, "Southern Can Is Mine," *Blind Willie McTell: The Early Years,* Yazoo L1005, n.d. [1931], contains the picket fence lyric.

117. Robert Johnson, "Me and the Devil Blues," *King of the Delta Blues Singers,* Columbia CL 1654, n.d. [1937].

118. Hughes, "Bad Man," *Fine Clothes to the Jew,* 21.

119. Hughes, "In a Troubled Key," *Shakespeare in Harlem,* 49.

120. Hughes, "Little Old Letter," *The Old Line* (April 1943), 20.

121. Hughes, "Widow Woman," *Shakespeare in Harlem,* 107–8.

122. Blind Willie McTell, "Dark Night Blues," *Blind Willie McTell: The Remaining Titles* [1928].

123. Buddy Boy Hawkins, "Workin' on the Railroad," *Cream of the Crop,* Roots RL 332, n.d. [1927].

124. Big Bill Broonzy, "Shine On, Shine On," in Oliver, *The Meaning of the Blues,* 308–9.

125. Trixie Smith, "Freight Train Blues," *Trixie Smith,* Collector's Classics CC 29, n.d. [1924].

126. Hughes, "Blues Fantasy," *The Weary Blues,* 37–38.

127. Hughes, "Dream Boogie: Variation," *Selected Poems,* 268.

128. Hughes, "Homesick Blues," *Fine Clothes to the Jew,* 24.

129. James Emanuel, *Langston Hughes* (New York: Twayne, 1967), 138. Onwuchekwa Jemie claims that this type of rhyme is absent in Hughes's blues poems; see *Langston Hughes,* 44.

130. "You Don't Know My Mind Blues" was recorded by vaudeville blues singers Viola McCoy, Josie Miles, and Clara Smith, and by Georgia White as well. The lyric is common in the folk tradition and was recorded by many other blues singers as well. See Rust, *Jazz Records 1897–1942,* 1992.

131. Sonny Boy Williamson, "Down South Blues," *Bluebird Blues* [1938]. Hannah Sylvester's 1923 version of "Down South Blues" has been reissued on *Hard Luck Blues,* VJM 40, n.d. "Yank" of the lyric is Yank Rachell, Williamson's accompanist. See also Ma Rainey, "South Bound Blues," *Queen of the Blues* [1924], and Bessie Smith's "Florida Bound Blues," *Nobody's Blues But Mine,* Columbia CG 31093, 1972 [1925].

132. Hughes, "Evenin' Air Blues," *Shakespeare in Harlem,* 38–39.

133. Emanuel, *Langston Hughes,* 140.

134. Nancy B. McGhee, "Langston Hughes: Poet in the Folk Manner," in *Langston Hughes: Black Genius,* ed. Therman B. O'Daniel (New York: Morrow, 1971), 39–64.

135. Waldron, "Blues Poetry of Langston Hughes," 146.

136. Richard Wright, "Blueprint for Negro Writing," *The New Challenge* 1 (Fall 1937): 55.

137. Langston Hughes and Richard Wright, "Red Clay Blues," *The New Masses* (Aug. 1, 1939): 14.

138. Walter Davis, "Howling Wind Blues," *Think You Need a Shot,* Victor 731015, n.d. [1931].

139. Hughes, "The Backlash Blues," *The Panther and the Lash* (New York: Knopf, 1967), 8–9. Hughes uses a reference to blues for protest purposes in *Ask Your Mama* as well. His reference to "Hesitation Blues," a widespread folk-blues song recorded by Prince's Band in 1915, the Victor Military Band in 1916, and Sara Martin and Eva Taylor in 1923, among many other artists, is mixed with the French Revolutionary chant "Ça ira" in a powerful call to action. See *Ask Your Mama* (New York: Knopf, 1961), 13. Hughes is once again suggesting that the blues people are not politically naive or passive.

140. Bessie Smith, "Poor Man's Blues," *Empty Bed Blues,* Columbia CG 30450, n.d. [1928].

141. See Ida Cox, "Any Woman's Blues," *Ida Cox Vol. 1,* Fountain FB 301, n.d. [1923]; Blind Lemon Jefferson, "Broke and Hungry," *King of the Country Blues* [1926]; and Wright Holmes, "Alley Special," *Country Blues Classics Vol. 3* [1947] for examples of this type of lyric. I read the railroad- and heaven-building in these lyrics as symbolic. Literally the lyrics refer to threats or situations that will offer sexual advantages.

142. Hughes, "Monroe's Blues," *One Way Ticket,* 108. "John Henry," for example, discusses his life and inserts his comment about desiring a cool drink of water.

143. Hughes, "Young Singer," *The Weary Blues,* 28.

144. Hughes, "Mother to Son," *The Weary Blues,* 107.

145. Dickinson, *Bio-Bibliography,* 120.

146. Georgia White, "Jazzin' Babies Blues," *Georgia White Sings and Plays the Blues,* Rosetta RR 1307, 1982 [1940]. The other versions have not, to my knowledge, been reissued, but since this is a composed blues, the lyrics probably remained very similar.

147. Bessie Smith, "Jazzbo Brown from Memphis Town," *Nobody's Blues But Mine* [1926].

148. Hughes, "The Weary Blues," *The Weary Blues,* 23–24.

149. Jemie, *Langston Hughes,* 45.

150. Langston Hughes, Introduction, *Montage of a Dream Deferred* (New York: Henry Holt, 1951), 1.

151. Walter C. Farrell, Jr., and Patricia A. Johnson, "Poetic Interpretations of Urban Black Folk Culture: Langston Hughes and the 'Bebop' Era," *MELUS* 8, no. 3 (1982): 61.

152. Pete Johnson, "Swanee River Boogie," *Boogie Woogie Trio,* Storyville SLP 4006, 1976.

153. Karl Gert zur Heide, *Deep South Piano* (London: Studio Vista, 1970), 11.

154. Big Bill Broonzy, "Let's Reel and Rock," Melotone 706–64, 1936. 78 RPM recording. See Townley, *Tell Your Story*, 44, for a discussion of origins.

155. Langston Hughes, Cliff Roberts, and David Martin, *The First Book of Jazz* (New York: Franklin Watts, 1976).

156. Langston Hughes, "Boogie 1 a.m.," *Selected Poems* (New York: Vintage Books, 1974), 221.

157. Hughes, *Selected Poems*, 14.

158. Hughes, "Dream Boogie," *Selected Poems*, 221.

159. John McDonough, Jacket Notes, *Tea Pad Songs Vol. 2*, Stash ST-104, n.d.

160. Hughes, "Easy Boogie," *Selected Poems*, 229–30.

161. Hughes, "Lady's Boogie," *Selected Poems*, 251.

162. Hughes, "Easy Boogie," *Selected Poems*, 229–30.

163. Hughes, "Lady's Boogie," *Selected Poems*, 251.

164. Hughes, "Boogie 1 a.m.," *Selected Poems*, 250.

165. Hughes, "Nightmare Boogie," *Selected Poems*, 258.

166. Ibid.

167. The version of the poem in *The Langston Hughes Reader* contains the three-point ellipsis in lines 6 and 7 and the misspelling "salf" for "self" in line 20. Hughes's reading of the poem on *The Weary Blues and Other Poems Read by Langston Hughes*, MGM LP E3697, substitutes "one bulb light" for "old gas light" in line 5.

168. Hughes, *The Big Sea*, 215.

169. Hughes, "Down an' Out," *Opportunity* 4, no. 46 (October 1926): 314.

170. Hughes, "Down and Out," *Shakespeare in Harlem*, 101–2.

171. Hughes, *The Big Sea*, 28.

172. Hughes, "Down and Out," *Selected Poems*, 147.

173. See David Evans's discussion in *Big Road Blues* and Steve Tracy, "To the Tune of Those Weary Blues: The Influence of the Blues Tradition on Langston Hughes's Blues Poems," *MELUS* 8, no. 3 (1981): 73–98.

174. Langston Hughes, *Shakespeare in Harlem*, 37.

175. Phyllis Brooks Bartlett, *Poems in Process* (New York: Oxford University Press, 1951), 102.

176. Charles Olson, *The Maximus Poems*, ed. George F. Butterick (Berkeley: University of California Press, 1983), 193. Olson's use of the line is in the context of his seeing the actuarial, the statistical calculator of risks and premiums, as the source of the "Isms" of "Vulgar Socialization." The line puns, then, on the reference to vulgarity and on the "ism" sound

of "gysm," while referring to a close relationship between jazz and sexuality that Olson compares to the relationship between the actuarial and vulgar socialization. The connection between sexuality and jazz and blues is also exploited by Robert Lowell in "Skunk Hour," where he quotes lines from the old blues song "Careless Love" to highlight the sexual sterility and aimlessness of the world he is describing. Since the reference is to a version heard on a car radio, Lowell probably knew the song from a pop recording.

177. Sylvia Plath, "Alicante Lullaby," in *The Collected Poems,* ed. Ted Hughes (New York: Harper and Row, 1981), 43.

178. Paul Mariani, *William Carlos Williams: A New World Naked* (New York: McGraw Hill, 1981), 504.

179. Ibid., 716.

180. William Carlos Williams, Introduction, *The Garden of Disorder and Other Poems,* by Charles Henri Ford (London: Europa Press, 1938), 9.

181. Edward B. Germain, Introduction, *Flag of Ecstasy,* by Charles Henri Ford (Los Angeles: Black Sparrow Press, 1972), 9.

182. Charles Henri Ford, "Chanson Pour Billie," in *Flag of Ecstasy,* ed. Edward B. Germain, 114.

183. William Carlos Williams, "For a New Magazine," *Blues* 1 (1929): 30. Rpt., New York: Johnson Reprint Corporation, 1967. The nine issues of *Blues* contained only two poems that referred explicitly to blues music: Herman Spector's "These Are Those Back-Again, Once-Before, Home-Again Blues," the title a play on the occasionally lengthy and humorous titles of vaudeville blues songs, and William Closson Emory's "Theme for a Blues Song," about an urban prostitute who is mocked by the concrete around her.

184. Bernard Bell, "Contemporary Afro-American Poetry as Folk Art," *Black World* 22, no. 5 (March 1973): 81–83.

185. Hughes, *Not Without Laughter,* 60.

BIBLIOGRAPHY

LANGSTON HUGHES

Volumes of Poetry

Ask Your Mama. New York: Knopf, 1961.
The Dream Keeper and Other Poems. New York: Knopf, 1932.
Fields of Wonder. New York: Knopf, 1947.
Fine Clothes to the Jew. New York: Knopf, 1927.
Jim Crow's Last Stand. Atlanta: Negro Publication Society of America, 1943.
The Langston Hughes Reader. New York: Braziller, 1958.
Montage of a Dream Deferred. New York: Henry Holt, 1951.
One Way Ticket. New York: Knopf, 1949.
The Panther and the Lash. New York: Knopf, 1967.
Selected Poems of Langston Hughes. New York: Vintage, 1974.
Shakespeare in Harlem. New York: Knopf, 1942.
The Weary Blues. New York: Knopf, 1926.

Blues Poems in Journals/Collections

"Barefoot Blues." *Masses and Mainstream* 2, no. 2 (1949): 53.
"Barrel House: Industrial City." In *Seven Poets in Search of an Answer,* edited by T. Yoseloff. New York: B. Ackerman, 1944.
"Bound No'th Blues." *Opportunity* (Oct. 1926): 315.
"Crowing Hen Blues." *Poetry* (Sept. 1943): 313–14.
"Down and Out." *Opportunity* (Oct. 1926): 314.
"Fortune Teller Blues." *Vanity Fair* (May 1926): 70.
"Little Green Tree Blues." *Tomorrow* (July 1945): 15.
"Little Old Letter." *The Old Line* (April 1943): 20.
"Lonesome Place." *Opportunity* (Oct. 1926): 314.

"Red Clay Blues." *New Masses* (Aug. 1, 1939): 14.
"Red Roses." *Poetry* (Nov. 1926): 90.
"Six-Bits Blues." *Opportunity* (Feb. 1939): 54.

Stories

"The Blues." *Simple's Uncle Sam.* New York: Hill and Wang, 1965.
"The Blues I'm Playing." *The Ways of White Folks.* New York: Knopf, 1934.
"Bop," "Shadow of the Blues," "Empty Room." *Simple Takes a Wife.* New York: Simon and Schuster, 1953.
"Jazz, Jive, and Jam." *Simple Stakes a Claim.* New York: Rinehart, 1957.
"Princess of the Blues." *Not Without Laughter.* New York: Knopf, 1968.

Drama

"Don't You Want To Be Free?" *One Act Play Magazine* (Oct. 1938): 359–93.
"Simply Heavenly." In *Five Plays By Langston Hughes,* edited by Webster Smalley. Bloomington: Indiana University Press, 1973, 113–81.

Autobiography

The Big Sea. New York: Knopf, 1940.
I Wonder As I Wander. New York: Hill and Wang, 1964. Reprint. New York: Octagon, 1974.

Essays on Influences/Blues and Jazz

"I Remember the Blues." In *Mississippi Reader,* edited by Frank Luther Mott, 152–55. Columbia: University of Missouri Press, 1964.
"Jazz as Communication." In *The Langston Hughes Reader,* 492–94. New York: Braziller, 1958.
"Maker of the Blues." *Negro Digest* (Jan. 1943): 37–38.
"Music at Year's End." *Chicago Defender,* 9 January 1943. Reprint. *Living Blues* 19 (1975): 7.
"My Adventures as a Social Poet." *Phylon* 6 (1947): 205–13.
"My Early Days in Harlem." In *Harlem: A Community in Transition,* edited by John Henrik Clarke. New York: Citadel Press, 1969.
"The Negro Artist and the Racial Mountain." *Nation* 122 (1926): 692–94. Reprint. In *Voices From the Harlem Renaissance,* edited by Nathan I. Huggins, 305–9. New York: Oxford University Press, 1976.
"Songs Called the Blues." *Phylon* 2, no. 2 (1941): 143–45. Reprint. *The Langston Hughes Reader,* 159–61. New York: Braziller, 1958.

"Tribute." In *Black Titan: W. E. B. DuBois,* edited by John Henrik Clarke et al., 8. Boston: Beacon Press, 1970.
"The Twenties: Harlem and Its Negritude." *African Forum* 1, no. 4 (1966): 11–20.

Letters

Nichols, Charles H., ed. *Arna Bontemps-Langston Hughes Letters, 1925–67.* New York: Dodd, Mead, 1980.

Editor

Black Magic: A Pictorial History of the Negro in American Entertainment. Co-edited with Milton Meltzer. Englewood Cliffs, N.J.: Prentice-Hall, 1967.
Book of Negro Folklore. Co-edited with Arna Bontemps. New York: Dodd, Mead, 1958.
Book of Negro Humor. New York: Dodd, Mead, 1966.
I Hear the People Singing: Selected Poems of Walt Whitman. New York: International, 1946.

Books on Music

Famous Negro Music Makers. New York: Dodd, Mead, 1955.
The First Book of Jazz. (With Cliff Roberts and David Martin.) New York: Franklin Watts, 1976.

SECONDARY MATERIALS
Biography

Berry, Faith. *Langston Hughes: Before and Beyond Harlem.* Westport, Conn.: Lawrence Hill, 1983.
Dickinson, Donald C. *A Bio-Bibliography of Langston Hughes.* Hamden, Conn.: Archon Books, 1967.
Haskins, James S. *Always Movin' On: The Life of Langston Hughes.* New York: Franklin Watts, 1973.
Meltzer, Milton. *Langston Hughes: A Biography.* New York: Crowell, 1968.

Criticism—Books

Barksdale, Richard. *Langston Hughes: The Poet and His Critics.* Chicago: American Library Association, 1977.
Bartlett, Phyllis Brooks. *Poems in Process.* New York: Oxford University Press, 1951.
Emanuel, James A. *Langston Hughes.* New York: Twayne, 1967.

Gibson, Donald B. *Five Black Writers: Essays on Wright, Ellison, Baldwin, Hughes, and Leroi Jones.* New York: New York University Press, 1970.

Jemie, Onwuchekwa. *Langston Hughes: An Introduction to the Poetry.* New York: Columbia University Press, 1976.

Miller, R. Baxter. *Langston Hughes and Gwendolyn Brooks: A Reference Guide.* Boston: G. K. Hall, 1978.

O'Daniel, Therman B., ed. *Langston Hughes: Black Genius.* New York: Morrow, 1971.

Wagner, Jean. *Black Poets of the United States.* Urbana: University of Illinois Press, 1973.

Criticism—Articles

Davis, Arthur P. "The Harlem of Langston Hughes' Poetry." *Phylon* 13 (1982): 276–83.

Farrell, Walter C., Jr., and Patricia A. Johnson. "Poetic Interpretations of Urban Black Folk Culture: Langston Hughes and the 'Bebop' Era." *MELUS* 8, no. 3 (1982): 57–72.

Hentoff, Nat. "Langston Hughes: He Found Poetry in the Blues." *Mayfair* (August 1958): 26, 27, 43, 45–47, 49.

Holmes, Eugene C. "Langston Hughes: Philosopher Poet." *Freedomways* 8, no. 2 (1968): 144–51.

Kramer, Aaron. "Robert Burns and Langston Hughes." *Freedomways* 8, no. 2 (1968): 159–67.

Martin, Dellita. "Langston Hughes's Use of the Blues." *CLA Journal* 22, no. 2 (1978): 151–59.

Presley, James. "The American Dream of Langston Hughes." *Southwest Review* 47, no. 3 (1963): 380–86.

Tracy, Steven C. " 'Midnight Ruffles of Cat-Gut Lace': The Boogie Poems of Langston Hughes." *CLA Journal,* Publication pending.

———. "Simple's Great African American Joke." *CLA Journal* 27, no. 3 (March 1984): 239–53.

———. "To the Tune of Those Weary Blues: The Influence of the Blues Tradition On Langston Hughes's Blues Poems." *MELUS* 8, no. 3 (1981): 73–98.

Waldron, Edward. "The Blues Poetry of Langston Hughes." *Negro American Literature Forum* 5 (1971): 140–49.

FOLKLORE AND THE HARLEM RENAISSANCE

Adelman, Lynn. "A Study of James Weldon Johnson." *Journal of Negro History* 52 (1967): 128–45.

Bell, Bernard. "Folk Art and the Harlem Renaissance." *Phylon* 36 (1975): 155–63.

Brewer, J. Mason. *American Negro Folklore*. Chicago: Quadrangle Books, 1968.

———. "American Negro Folklore." *Phylon* 6 (1945): 345–61.

Broderick, Francis L. *W. E. B. DuBois: Negro Leader in a Time of Crisis*. Stanford: Stanford University Press, 1959.

Brown, Sterling A. "The Blues." *Phylon* 13 (1952): 286–92.

———. "Blues, Ballads, and Social Songs." In *Seventy Five Years of Freedom*, 17–25. Washington: Library of Congress, 1943.

———. "The Blues as Folk Poetry." In *Folk Say I,* edited by B. A. Botkin, 324–39. Norman, Okla.: University of Oklahoma Press, 1930.

———. "The Folk Roots: Excerpt from the Spoken Commentary to the 1939 Concert." *From Spirituals to Swing: The Carnegie Hall Concerts 1938–1939.* Vanguard, LP 47/48, 1973.

———. "Negro Folk Expression: Spirituals, Seculars, Ballads, and Work Songs." *Phylon* 14 (1953): 45–61.

———. *Negro Poetry and Drama and the Negro in American Fiction.* 1937. Reprint. New York: Atheneum, 1972.

———. "Remarks at a Conference on the Character and State of Studies in Folklore." *Journal of American Folklore* 59 (1946): 506–7.

———. "Spirituals, Blues, and Jazz: The Negro in the Lively Arts." *Tricolor* 3 (1945): 62–70.

Collier, Eugenia W. "James Weldon Johnson: Mirror of Change." *Phylon* 4th Quarter (1960): 351–59.

Cooper, Wayne F., ed. *The Passion of Claude McKay.* New York: Schocken, 1973.

Dixon, William. "The Music of Harlem." In *Harlem: A Community in Transition,* edited by John Henrik Clarke, 69–75. New York: Citadel Press, 1969.

DuBois, Shirley Graham. *His Day Is Marching On.* Philadelphia: Lippincott, 1971.

DuBois, W. E. B. *An ABC of Color.* New York: International, 1969.

———. *Dusk of Dawn.* New York: Harcourt Brace, 1940.

———. *The Education of Black People.* New York: Monthly Review Press, 1973.

———. *The Negro.* 1913. Reprint. Millwood, N.Y.: Kraus-Thomson, 1975.

———. *The Negro Problem.* 1903. Reprint. New York: Arno Press, 1969.

———. "Of the Sorrow Songs." In *The Souls of Black Folk*. 1903. Reprint. Greenwich, Conn.: Fawcett, 1961.

———. *The Quest of the Silver Fleece*. 1911. Reprint. Millwood, N.Y.: Kraus-Thomson, 1974.

Dunbar, Paul Laurence. "Representative American Negroes." In W. E. B. DuBois, *The Negro Problem*. 1903. Reprint. New York: Arno Press, 1969.

Dundes, Alan. "The Devolutionary Premise in Folklore Theory." *Journal of the Folklore Institute* 6, no. 1 (1969): 5–19.

Epstein, Dena J. *Sinful Tunes and Spirituals*. Urbana: University of Illinois Press, 1977.

Gabbin, Joanne V. *Sterling Brown: Building the Black Aesthetic Tradition*. Westport, Conn.: Greenwood Press, 1985.

Hayden, Robert. "Preface." In *The New Negro*, edited by Alain Locke, ix–xiv. 1925. Reprint. New York: Atheneum, 1970.

Hemenway, Robert E. *Zora Neale Hurston: A Literary Biography*. Urbana: University of Illinois Press, 1977.

Henderson, Stephen. "A Strong Man Called Sterling Brown." *Black World* 19, no. 11 (1970): 5–12.

———. *Understanding the New Black Poetry*. New York: William Morrow, 1973.

Heyward, Dubose. "Review of *The Weary Blues,* by Langston Hughes." *New York Herald Tribune Books* (1 August 1926): 4.

Hurston, Zora Neale. "Characteristics of Negro Expression." New York, 1935. Reprint. In *The Sanctified Church,* 49–68. Berkeley: Turtle Island, 1983.

———. *Mules and Men*. 1935. Reprint. Bloomington: Indiana University Press, 1978.

———. "Spirituals and Neo-Spirituals." New York, 1935. Reprint. In *The Sanctified Church,* 79–84. Berkeley: Turtle Island, 1983.

Ikonné, Chidi: *From DuBois to Van Vechten: The Early New Negro Literature, 1903–1926*. Westport, Conn.: Greenwood Press, 1981.

Johnson, Charles. "Jazz Poetry and Blues." *Carolina Magazine* 58 (1928): 16–20.

Johnson, James Weldon. *Along This Way*. Reprint. New York: Da Capo, 1973.

———. *Autobiography of An Ex-Coloured Man*. Knopf, 1912. Reprint. New York: Hill and Wang, 1960.

———. "The Dilemma of the Negro Author." *The American Mercury* (Dec. 1928): 477–81.

———. "Preface." *The Book of American Negro Poetry*. New York,

1922. Reprinted in *Voices From the Harlem Renaissance,* edited by Nathan I. Huggins, 281–304. New York: Oxford University Press, 1976.

Kent, George E. "Patterns of the Harlem Renaissance." In *The Harlem Renaissance Remembered,* edited by Arna Bontemps, 27–50. New York: Dodd, Mead, 1972.

Locke, Alain. "Art or Propaganda." New York, 1928. Reprint. In *Voices From the Harlem Renaissance,* edited by Nathan I. Huggins, 312–13. New York: Oxford University Press, 1976.

———. "Foreword." In *The New Negro,* edited by Alain Locke, xv–xvii. 1925. Reprint. New York: Atheneum, 1970.

———. *"The Negro and His Music" and "Negro Art: Past and Present."* 1936. Reprint. New York: Arno Press, 1969.

———. "Negro Youth Speaks." In *The New Negro,* edited by Alain Locke, 47–53. 1925. Reprint. New York: Atheneum, 1970.

———. "Sterling Brown: The New Negro Folk Poet." New York, 1935. Reprint. In *Voices From the Harlem Renaissance,* edited by Nathan I. Huggins, 251–57. New York: Oxford University Press, 1976.

———. "Toward a Critique of Negro Music." *Opportunity* 12, no. 11 (1934): 328–31; no. 12 (1934): 365–67.

Lord, Albert B. *The Singer of Tales.* 1960. Reprint. New York: Atheneum, 1965.

Martin, Tony. *The Pan-African Connection.* Dover, Mass.: The Majority Press, 1984.

Odum, Anna Kranz. "Some Negro Folk-Songs from Tennessee." *Journal of American Folklore* 27 (1914): 255–65.

Odum, Howard W. "Folk-Song and Folk-Poetry as Found in the Secular Songs of the Southern Negroes." *Journal of American Folklore* 24 (1911): 255–94, 351–96.

Odum, Howard W., and Guy B. Johnson. *The Negro and His Songs.* Chapel Hill: University of North Carolina Press, 1925.

———. *Negro Workaday Songs.* 1926. Reprint. New York: Negro Universities Press, 1977.

Oring, Elliott. "The Devolutionary Premise: A Definitional Delusion?" *Western Folklore* 34, no. 1 (1975): 36–44.

Perrow, E. C. "Songs and Rhymes from the South." *Journal of American Folklore* 25 (1912): 137–55; 26 (1913): 123–73; 28 (1915): 129–90.

Redding, Saunders. "The Souls of Black Folk: DuBois' Masterpiece Lives On." In *Black Titan: W. E. B. DuBois,* edited by John Henrik Clarke et al., 47–51. Boston: Beacon Press, 1970.

———. *To Make a Poet Black.* Chapel Hill: University of North Carolina Press, 1939.

"Review of *The Weary Blues* by Langston Hughes." *The Times Literary Supplement* (29 July 1926): 515.

Robeson, Paul. "Tribute." In *Black Titan: W. E. B. DuBois,* edited by John Henrik Clarke et al., 34–38. Boston: Beacon Press, 1970.

Rogers, J. A. "Jazz at Home." In *The New Negro,* edited by Alain Locke, 251–57. 1925. Reprint. New York: Atheneum, 1970.

Scarborough, Dorothy. *On the Trail of Negro Folk-Songs.* Cambridge, Mass., 1925. Reprint. Hatboro, Pa.: Folklore Association, 1963.

Schuyler, George. "The Negro Art Hokum." New York, 1926. Reprint. In *Voices From the Harlem Renaissance,* edited by Nathan I. Huggins, 309–12. New York: Oxford University Press, 1976.

Stuckey, Sterling. "Introduction." In *The Collected Poems of Sterling A. Brown,* selected by Michael S. Harper, 3–15. New York: Harper and Row, 1980.

Sylvander, Carol Wedin. *Jessie Redmon Fauset: Black American Writer.* Troy, N.Y.: Whitson, 1981.

Thurman, Wallace. *The Blacker the Berry.* New York: Collier Books, 1970.

Toelken, Barre. *The Dynamics of Folklore.* Boston: Houghton Mifflin, 1979.

Wagner, Jean. *Black Poets of the United States.* Urbana: University of Illinois Press, 1973.

White, Newman I. *American Negro Folk-Songs.* Cambridge: Harvard University Press, 1928.

Wilson, William A. "The Evolutionary Premise in Folklore Theory and the 'Finnish Method.'" *Western Folklore* 35 (1976): 241–49.

Work, John. *American Negro Songs and Spirituals.* New York: Crown, 1940.

———. *Folk Songs of the American Negro.* New York: Negro Universities Press, 1969.

Wright, Richard. "Blueprint for Negro Writing." *The New Challenge* 2 (Fall 1937). Reprint. In *Voices From the Harlem Renaissance,* edited by Nathan I. Huggins, 394–402. New York: Oxford University Press, 1976.

Young, James O. *Black Writers of the Thirties.* Baton Rouge: Louisiana State University Press, 1973.

BLUES AND JAZZ

Two blues magazines are of special importance to enthusiasts who wish to keep up on the latest research and current performing and LP releases: *Blues Unlimited Publications, Ltd.,* 36 Belmont Park, Lewisham,

London SE 13 5DB, England; and *Living Blues,* Center for the Study of Southern Culture, University of Mississippi, University, Mississippi, 38677.

Abrahams, Roger D. *Positively Black.* Englewood Cliffs, N.J.: Prentice-Hall, 1970.

Albertson, Chris. *Bessie.* 1972. Reprint. New York: Scarborough, 1982.

Barnie, John. "Oral Formulas in the Country Blues." *Southern Folklore Quarterly* 42, no. 1 (1978): 39–52.

Benston, Kimberly. "Tragic Aspects of the Blues." *Phylon* 36, no. 2 (1975): 164–76.

Blesh, Rudi. *Shining Trumpets: A History of Jazz.* New York: Oxford University Press, 1948. Revised edition. New York: Knopf, 1958.

Borneman, Ernest. *An Anthropologist Looks at Jazz.* New York: Jazz Music Books, 1946.

Bynum, David. *The Daemon in the Wood.* Cambridge: Harvard University Press, 1978.

Charters, Samuel. *The Bluesmen.* New York: Oak, 1967.

———. *The Poetry of the Blues.* New York: Avon, 1970.

———. *The Roots of the Blues: An African Search.* New York: Perigree, 1981.

Courlander, Harold. *Negro Folk Music U.S.A.* New York: Columbia University Press, 1963.

Davis, Henry C. "Negro Folk-Lore in South Carolina." *Journal of American Folklore* 27 (1914): 241–54.

Dixon, R. M. W., and John Godrich. *Blues and Gospel Records: 1902–1943.* Chigwell, Essex: Storyville Publications, 1982.

———. *Recording the Blues.* London: Studio Vista, 1970.

Dundes, Alan, ed. *Mother Wit from the Laughing Barrel.* Englewood Cliffs, N.J.: Prentice-Hall, 1973.

Ellison, Ralph. *Shadow and Act.* New York: Random House, 1964.

Evans, David. "Africa and the Blues." *Living Blues* 10 (1972): 27–29.

———. *Big Road Blues.* Berkeley: University of California Press, 1982.

———. "Folk, Commercial, and Folkloric Aesthetics in the Blues." *Jazz Forschung* 5 (1973): 11–32.

———. "Techniques of Composition Among Black Folksingers." *Journal of American Folklore* 87 (1974): 240–49.

Fahey, John. *Charley Patton.* London: Studio Vista, 1970.

Ferris, William. *Blues From the Delta.* Garden City, N.Y.: Doubleday, 1978.

———. "Racial Repertoires Among Blues Performers." *Ethnomusicology* 14 (1970): 439–49.

Garon, Paul. *Blues and the Poetic Spirit*. London: Eddison Press, 1975.
————. *The Devil's Son-In-Law: The Story of Peetie Wheatstraw and His Songs*. London: Studio Vista, 1978.
Gold, Robert. *Jazz Talk*. New York: DaCapo Press, 1982.
Green, Jeffrey P. "Spencer Williams: Composer." In *Storyville* 123 (Feb.-March, 1986): 87–93.
Gruver, Rod. "The Blues as Dramatic Monologues." *John Edwards Memorial Foundation Quarterly* 6 (1970): 28–31.
Guralnik, Peter. *Feel Like Going Home*. New York: Random House, 1981.
Handy, William Christopher. *Father of the Blues*. New York: Collier Books, 1941.
————. *Negro Authors and Composers of the United States*. New York: AMS Press, 1976.
————, ed. *Blues: An Anthology*. New York: A. and C. Boni, 1926. Reprint, edited by Jerry Silverman. New York: Macmillan, 1972.
————, ed. *A Treasury of the Blues*. New York: A. and C. Boni, 1926.
Haralambos, Michael. *From Blues to Soul in Black America*. London: Eddison Press, 1974.
————. "Soul Music and Blues: Their Meaning and Relevance in Northern United States Black Ghettoes." In *Afro-American Anthropology: Contemporary Perspectives*, edited by Norman E. Whitten, Jr., and John F. Szwed, 367–84. New York: Free Press, 1970.
Harper, Michael S. "Don't They Speak Jazz?" *MELUS* 10, no. 1 (1983): 306.
Harris, Sheldon. *Blues Who's Who*. New Rochelle, N.Y.: Arlington House, 1979.
Hayakawa, S. I. "Popular Songs vs. the Facts of Life." In *Mass Culture*, edited by Bernard Rosenberg and David Manning White, 393–403. New York: Free Press, 1964.
Heide, Karl Gert zur. *Deep South Piano*. London: Studio Vista, 1970.
Herskovits, Melville J. *The Myth of the Negro Past*. Boston: Beacon Press, 1958.
————. *The New World Negro*. Bloomington: Indiana University Press, 1966.
Jahn, Janheinz. *A History of Neo-African Literature*. New York: Grove Press, 1968.
————. *Muntu: An Outline of the New African Culture*. London: Faber and Faber, 1961.
Jarrett, Dennis. "The Singer and the Bluesman: Formulations of Personality in the Lyrics of the Blues." *Southern Folklore Quarterly* 42, no. 1 (1978): 31–37.

Johnson, Guy B. "Double Meaning in the Popular Negro Blues." *Journal of Abnormal and Social Psychology* 22, no. 1 (1927): 12–20.

Jones, A. M. "Blue Notes and Hot Rhythm." *African Music Newsletter* 1 (1951).

Jones, Leroi. *Blues People*. New York: William Morrow, 1963.

Krehbiel, H. E. *Afro-American Folksongs*. New York: G. Schirmer, 1914.

Lomax, Alan. "The Homogeneity of African-American Musical Style." In *Afro-American Anthropology*, edited by Norman E. Whitten, Jr., and John F. Szwed, 181–20. New York: Free Press, 1970.

———. "I Got the Blues." *Common Ground* 8, no. 2 (1948): 31–37.

———. "Song Structure and Social Structure." *Ethnology* 1 (October 1962): 452–51.

Lomax, John A. "Self-Pity in Negro Folk-Songs." *The Nation* 105 (July-Dec. 1917): 141–45.

Lomax, John A., and Alan Lomax. *Negro Folk Songs as Sung by Leadbelly*. New York: Macmillan, 1936.

Lord, Tom. *Clarence Williams*. Chigwell, Essex: Storyville, 1976.

Mbiti, John S. *African Religions and Philosophy*. Garden City, N.Y.: Anchor Books, 1970.

Merriam, Alan P. "African Music." In *Continuity and Change in African Cultures*, edited by William R. Bascom and Melville J. Herskovits, 49–86. University of Chicago Press, 1962.

Nicholas, A. X. *Woke Up This Mornin': Poetry of the Blues*. New York: Bantam, 1973.

Oakley, Giles. *The Devil's Music: A History of the Blues*. New York: Taplinger, 1977.

Odum, Howard W. "Folk-Song and Folk-Poetry as Found in the Secular Songs of the Southern Negroes." *Journal of American Folklore* 24 (1911): 255–94.

Odum, Howard W., and Guy B. Johnson. *Negro Workaday Songs*. Chapel Hill, 1926. Reprint. New York: Negro Universities Press, 1977.

Oliver, Paul. *The Blues Tradition*. New York: Oak Publications, 1970.

———. "Can't Even Write: The Blues and Ethnic Literature." *MELUS* 10, no. 1 (1983): 7–14.

———. *Conversation with the Blues*. New York: Horizon, 1965.

———. "Echoes of the Jungle?" *Living Blues* 13 (1973): 29–32.

———. *The Meaning of the Blues*. 1960. Reprint. New York: Collier Books, 1963.

———. *Savannah Syncopators: African Retentions in the Blues*. New York: Stein and Day, 1970.

————. *Screening the Blues*. London: Cassell, 1968.

————. *Songsters and Saints*. Cambridge University Press, 1984.

————. *The Story of the Blues*. Philadelphia: Chilton Books, 1973.

Olsson, Bengt, ed. *Memphis Blues*. London: Studio Vista, 1970.

O'Neal, Jim, and Amy O'Neal. "Living Blues Interview: Georgia Tom Dorsey." *Living Blues* 20 (1975): 16–34.

Oster, Harry. "The Blues as Genre." *Genre* 2 (1969): 259–74.

————. *Living Country Blues*. Detroit: Folklore Associates, 1969.

Owens, William A. *Tell Me A Story, Sing Me A Song* . . . . Austin: University of Texas Press, 1983.

Palmer, Robert. *Deep Blues*. New York: Viking Press, 1981.

Parry, Adam, ed. *The Making of Homeric Verse: The Collected Papers of Milman Parry*. Oxford: Clarendon Press, 1971.

Peabody, Charles. "Notes on Negro Music." *Journal of American Folklore* 16 (1903): 148–52.

Pearson, Barry Lee. *Sounds So Good to Me*. Philadelphia: University of Pennsylvania Press, 1984.

Reed, Ishmael. *Shrovetide in Old New Orleans*. Garden City, N.Y.: Doubleday, 1978.

Rosemont, Franklin. "Preface." In *Blues and the Poetic Spirit*, by Paul Garon. London: Eddison Press, 1975.

————. "A Revolutionary Poetic Tradition." *Living Blues* 25 (1976): 20–23.

Russell, Tony. *Blacks Whites and Blues*. London: Studio Vista, 1970.

Rust, Brian. *Jazz Records 1897–1942*. New Rochelle, N.Y.: Arlington House, 1978.

Sackheim, Eric, ed. *The Blues Line: A Collection of Blues Lyrics*. New York: Schirmer Books, 1975.

Sargeant, Winthrop. *Jazz: Hot and Hybrid*. New York: E. P. Dutton, 1946.

Schuller, Gunther. *Early Jazz*. New York: Oxford University Press, 1968.

Stearns, Marshall. *The Story of Jazz*. New York: Oxford University Press, 1958.

Stewart-Baxter, Derrick. *Ma Rainey and the Classic Blues Singers*. New York: Stein and Day, 1970.

Thomas, Gates. "South Texas Negro Work Songs." In *Rainbow in the Morning*, edited by J. Frank Dobie, 154–60. Hatboro, Pa.: Folklore Association, 1965.

Thomas, Will H. *Some Current Folk-Songs of the Negro*. Austin: Folk-Lore Society of Texas, 1912.

Thompson, Robert Farris. *Flash of the Spirit: African and Afro-American Art and Philosophy.* New York: Random House, 1983.

Titon, Jeff Todd. "Autobiography and Blues Texts: A Reply to 'The Blues as Dramatic Monologues.'" *John Edwards Memorial Foundation Quarterly* 6 (1970): 79–82.

———. *Early Downhome Blues.* Urbana: University of Illinois Press, 1978.

———, ed. *Downhome Blues Lyrics.* Boston: Twayne, 1981.

Townley, Eric. *Tell Your Story.* Chigwell, Essex: Storyville, 1976.

Tracy, Steven C. "The Blues in Future American Literary Histories and Anthologies." *MELUS* 10, no. 1 (1983): 15–28.

———. "A *MELUS* Interview: Big Joe Duskin." *MELUS* 10, no. 1 (1983): 65–86.

———. "A *MELUS* Interview: Etheridge Knight." *MELUS* 12, no. 2 (1985): 7–23.

Turner, Lorenzo Dow. *Africanisms in the Gullah Dialect.* University of Chicago Press, 1949.

Van Vechten, Carl. "The Black Blues." *Vanity Fair* 24, no. 6 (1925): 57, 86, 92.

———. "Negro 'Blues' Singers." *Vanity Fair* 26, no. 1 (1926): 67, 106, 108.

———. *Nigger Heaven.* New York: Knopf, 1926.

Vreede, Max E. *Paramount 12000/13000 Series.* London: Storyville, 1971.

Waterman, Richard Alan. "African Influence on the Music of the Americas." In *Acculturation in the Americas,* edited by Sol Tax, 207–18. Chicago: University of Chicago Press, 1952.

———. " 'Hot' Rhythm in Negro Music." *Journal of the American Musicological Society* 1 (1948): 4.

Webb, W. Prescott. "Notes on Folk-Lore of Texas." *Journal of American Folklore* 28 (1915): 291–96.

Whiting, Bartlett Jere. *Early American Proverbs and Proverbial Phrases.* Cambridge, Mass.: Belknap Press, 1977.

Williams, Martin. *The Jazz Tradition.* Revised edition. Oxford: Oxford University Press, 1983.

Williams, Sherley A. "The Blues Roots of Contemporary Afro-American Poetry." In *Chant of Saints: A Gathering of Afro-American Literature, Art, and Scholarship,* edited by Michael S. Harper and Robert B. Stepto, 123–35. University of Chicago Press, 1979.

Wright, Richard. Foreword. *Blues Fell This Morning,* by Paul Oliver. London: Cassell, 1960. Reprint. New York: Collier, 1972.

Selected Discography of LP Recordings

The following is a discography of material consulted in the preparation of this text supplemented by listings of recordings that best represent the material under discussion. The discography includes recordings of Hughes's poems by himself and others and his commentary on jazz; related recordings by Sterling Brown, W. C. Handy and others; reissued recordings that exemplify various blues traditions, primarily those of blues during the pre–World War II period, when many of Hughes's blues poems were written; and recordings of blues performers named frequently by Hughes in his prose writings, including post–World War II recordings. The bulk of these recordings are still commercially available from Down Home Music, 10341 San Pablo Ave., El Cerrito, CA 94530. If any of these LP's have gone or go out of print, the proprietors will be able to tell you whether the material is currently available on other issues.

LANGSTON HUGHES

Hughes Reading His Poems

Anthology of Negro Poets. Folkways FL9791, 1966 [with Brown, McKay, Cullen, Walker, Brooks].

Langston Hughes Reads and Talks About His Poetry. Spoken Arts 7140, 1959.

Poems by Langston Hughes. Asch A454, 1945.

Poetry and Reflections. Caedmon 1640, n.d.

The Weary Blues and Other Poems Read by Langston Hughes. MGM E3697, 1958.

Writers of the Revolution. Black Forum, BF 453, 1970 [with Margaret Danner].

Commentary by Hughes

Spann, Otis. *Rarest Recordings.* JSP 1070, n.d.

Narration by Hughes

The Glory of Negro History. Folkways FC 7752, 1955.
Rhythms of the World. Folkways FP 740, 1955.
The Story of Jazz. Folkways FJ 7312, n.d.

Hughes Poems/Songs Recorded by Others

Dee, Ruby, and Ossie Davis. *The Poetry of Langston Hughes.* Caedmon 1272, 1969.
Miller, Clarence "Big." *Did You Ever Hear the Blues?* United Artists 3047, 1959.
Spann, Otis. "Goodbye Newport Blues." In *Muddy Waters at Newport.* Chess 1949, 1960. Co-written with Muddy Waters. See also the section below dealing with 1950s Chicago blues.

RELATED RECORDINGS

African Music

African Journey: A Search for the Roots of the Blues. Vanguard SRV73014/5, n.d.
African Music: Rhythm in the Jungle. Victor, n.d.
Savannah Syncopators: African Retentions in the Blues. CBS 52799, n.d.

Brown, Sterling

Sixteen Poems of Sterling A. Brown. Folkways FL 9494, 1973.
Sterling Brown and Langston Hughes. Folkways FL 9790, 1967.

Handy, W. C.

W. C. Handy Narrates and Sings His Immortal Songs. Mark 56, 684, n.d.

Johnson, James Weldon

God's Trombones and Selected Twentieth Century Negro Poetry (Read by J. W. Johnson, Alice Childress, and P. Jay Sidney). Lexington LE 7716, 1967.

Pound, Ezra

Ezra Pound's Opera: Le Testament de Villon. Fantasy 12001, n.d.

Zora Neale Hurston Field Recordings
Boot That Thing. Flyright-Matchbox SDM 257, 1974.
Out in the Cold Again. Flyright-Matchbox, SDM 257, 1974.
Red River Runs. Flyright-Matchbox SDM 259, 1979.

PRE–WORLD WAR II BLUES
Anthologies
Bluebird Blues. RCA 518, 1965.
Blues in the Mississippi Night. United Artists UAL 4027, 1959.
Chicago Blues 1935–42. RCA RC 350, n.d.
Country Blues Classics Vol. 3. Blues Classics 7, n.d.
The Great Harmonica Players Vol. 2. Roots RL321, n.d.
Hard Times. Rounder 4007, n.d.
Hometown Skiffle: Early Folk Blues Vol. 1. Saydisc-Matchbox SDR 206, n.d.
Kings of the Twelve String. Gryphon GLP 13159, n.d.
Rare Blues of the Twenties Vol. 1. Historical HLP1, n.d.
Really! The Country Blues. Origin OJL 2, n.d.
The Story of the Blues. Columbia 30008, n.d.
Travelling This Lonesome Road. RCA International 1175, 1970.
Trumpet Blues. Historical, HLP 27, n.d.

PRE–WORLD WAR II VAUDEVILLE BLUES
AND WOMEN'S BLUES
Anthologies
The Country Girls. Origin OJL 6, n.d.
Easin' In. Muskadine 105, n.d.
Mean Mothers: Independent Women's Blues. Rosetta 1300, 1980.
Piano Singer's Blues: Women Accompany Themselves. Rosetta 1303, 1982.
Streetwalking Blues. Stash 117, n.d.
When Women Sang the Blues. Blues Classics 26, 1976.
Women of the Blues. RCA LPV 534, 1966.
Women's Railroad Blues: Sorry But I Can't Take You. Rosetta 1301, 1980.

Recordings by Individual Artists
Austin, Lovie. *Lovie Austin and Her Blues Serenaders.* Fountain FJ105, n.d.

Cox, Ida. *Ida Cox*. BYG 529073, n.d.
————. *Ida Cox. Blues Ain't Nothin Else But* . . . . Milestone 2015, n.d.
————. *Ida Cox Vol. 1*. Fountain FB 301, n.d.
————. *Ida Cox Vol. 2*. Fountain FB 304, n.d.
Glinn, Lillian. *Lillian Glinn*. VJM VLP 31, n.d.
Hegamin, Lucille. *Blue Flame*. VJM VLP 50, n.d.
Henderson, Fletcher. *Fletcher Henderson, Vol. 1*. Neovox 306, n.d.
Wilson, Edith. *Edith Wilson, 1921–22*. Fountain FB 302, n.d.

See artist list of blues performers named by Hughes for more recordings by female blues singers.

PRE–WORLD WAR II MISSISSIPPI BLUES
Anthologies

Jackson Blues. Yazoo 1007, n.d.
Mississippi Blues 1927–1936. Yazoo 1001, n.d.
Mississippi Blues 1927–1940. Origin OJL 5, n.d.
Mississippi Blues No. 2: The Delta 1929–1932. Origin OJL 11, n.d.
Walking Blues. Flyright 545, n.d.

Individual Recording Artists

Bracey, Ishman. *Ishman Bracey (1928–30)*. Wolf WSE 105, n.d.
House, Son. *Son House: The Legendary 1941–42 Recordings in Chronological Sequence*. Roots RSE 1, n.d.
Hurt, Mississippi John. *Mississippi John Hurt, 1928 Sessions*. Yazoo 1065, n.d.
James, Skip. *Skip James, 1931*. Yazoo 1072, n.d.
Johnson, Robert. *Robert Johnson: King of the Delta Blues Singers*. Columbia CL 1654, n.d.
Johnson, Tommy. *Tommy Johnson (1928–30)*. Wolf WSE 104, n.d.
Patton, *Charley Patton: Founder of the Delta Blues*. Yazoo 1020, n.d.

PRE–WORLD WAR II TEXAS BLUES
Anthologies

Blues from the Western States. Yazoo 1032, n.d.
Tex-Arkana Louisiana Country. Yazoo 1004, n.d.
Texas Blues: Dallas 1928. Fountain FB 305, n.d.

Recordings by Individual Artists

Hopkins, Lightnin'. *Early Recordings Vol. 2*. Arhoolie 2010, n.d.

Pullum, Joe. *Black Gal.* Agram 2012, n.d.

Thomas, Henry. *Ragtime Texas.* Herwin 209, n.d.

See artist list of blues performers named by Hughes for recordings by Blind Lemon Jefferson and Leadbelly.

PRE–WORLD WAR II MEMPHIS BLUES

Anthologies

Frank Stokes' Dream: The Memphis Blues. Yazoo 1008, n.d.

Memphis Blues 1928–1930. RCA NL89276, n.d.

Missouri and Tennessee. Roots RL 310, n.d.

Recordings by Individual Artists

Cannon, Gus. *Cannon's Jug Stompers.* Herwin 208, n.d.

Jackson, Jim. *Kansas City Blues.* Agram AB2004, n.d.

See artist list of blues performers named by Hughes for recordings by Memphis Minnie.

PRE–WORLD WAR II ALABAMA BLUES

Anthologies

Alabama Country 1927/31. Origin OJL 14, n.d.

Barefoot Bill's Hard Luck Blues. Mamlish 3812, n.d.

The Blues of Alabama 1927–31. Yazoo 1006, n.d.

PRE–WORLD WAR II ST. LOUIS BLUES

Anthologies

The Blues in St. Louis. Origin OJL 20, n.d.

Hard Time Blues. Mamlish 3806, n.d.

St. Louis Town 1929–1933. Yazoo 1003, n.d.

Recordings by Individual Artists

Arnold, Kokomo, and Peetie Wheatstraw. *Kokomo Arnold and Peetie Wheatstraw.* Blues Classics BC4, n.d.

Davis, Walter. *The Bullet Sides.* Krazy Kat 7441, n.d.

———. *Think You Need a Shot.* Victor 731015, n.d.

———. *Walter Davis 1937–1941.* Best of Blues BOB 5, 1987.

See artist list of blues performers named by Hughes for recordings by Lonnie Johnson.

PRE–WORLD WAR II EAST COAST/PIEDMONT BLUES
Anthologies
Blues From Georgia. Roots RL 309, n.d.
Bull City Blues. Magpie 1812, n.d.
East Coast Blues 1926–1935. Yazoo 1013, n.d.
Nobody Knows My Name. Heritage 304, 1984.
Western Piedmont Blues. BRI 003, n.d.

Recordings by Individual Artists
Barbecue Bob. *Masters of the Blues Vol. 10.* Collector's Classics 36, n.d.
———. *Brown-Skin Gal.* Agram AB2001, n.d.
Blind Blake. *Ragtime Guitar's Foremost Exponent.* Yazoo 1068, n.d.
Fuller, Blind Boy. *Blind Boy Fuller 1936–1940.* Old Tramp 1202, 1987.
———. *Truckin' My Blues Away.* Yazoo 1060, n.d.
McTell, Blind Willie. *Blind Willie McTell 1927–1933.* Yazoo L1005, n.d.
———. *Blind Willie McTell: 1927–1949, The Remaining Titles.* Wolf
WSE 102, 1982.
———. *Blind Willie McTell: 1940.* Melodeon 7323, n.d.

See artist list of blues performers named by Hughes for recordings by
Brownie McGhee, Sonny Terry, and Josh White.

CHICAGO BLUES:
THE 1930s AND 1940s
Anthologies
Blues Roots, Chicago: the 30's. RBF 16, n.d.
Lake Michigan Blues 1934–1941. Nighthawk 105, n.d.
Windy City Blues 1935–1953. Nighthawk 101, n.d.

Recordings by Individual Artists
Broonzy, Big Bill. *The Young Big Bill Broonzy.* Yazoo 1011, n.d.
Carr, Leroy. *Leroy Carr (1928).* Matchbox MSE 210, 1983. (Actually,
Carr was based in Indianapolis.)
Clayton, Doctor. *Pearl Harbor Blues.* RCA International 731045, n.d.
Dorsey, Georgia Tom. *Come On Mama Do That Dance.* Yazoo L1041,
n.d.
Tampa Red. *It's Tight Like That.* Blues Documents 2001, n.d.
Weldon, Casey Bill. *Red Hot Blues.* Earl 605, 1982.
Williamson, Sonny Boy. *Sonny Boy Williamson Vol. 2.* Blues Classics
20, n.d.
———. *Sonny Boy Williamson Vol. 3.* Blues Classics 24, n.d.

CHICAGO BLUES:
THE 1950s AND 1960s

Much of the best Chicago blues of the 1950s and 1960s was recorded for Chess Records, which has reissued recordings by its major artists, such as Muddy Waters, Howlin' Wolf, Sonny Boy Williamson, Little Walter, and Elmore James. The company was sold to Sugar Hill, who in turn sold the recordings to MCA in 1985. A new series of reissues by these Chess recording artists is probably forthcoming. See *Blues Unlimited* and *Living Blues* magazines for current information. The following list is limited because of the current status of Chess Records and the fact that the blues of Chicago are only peripherally related to our concerns. For more in-depth listings of postwar Chicago, Memphis, and Detroit blues, see Palmer's *Deep Blues*, 284–89.

Anthologies

The Blues World of Little Walter. Delmark 648, 1985.
Chicago Slickers, 1948–1953. Nighthawk 102, n.d.
On the Road Again. Muskadine 100, n.d.

Recordings by Individual Artists

James, Elmore. *Elmore James: Something Inside Me.* Fire (Japan) PLP 005/6/7.
Lenoir, J. B. *J. B. Lenoir.* Chess ACMB 208, 1976.
———. *J. B. Lenoir.* Crusade 1, n.d.
Waters, Muddy. *Muddy Waters: The Chess Box.* Chess (Japan) PLP 6040–6050. A remarkable eleven-LP set of 162 sides recorded between 1947 and 1967—all of his recordings for Aristocrat and Chess save for some untraced sides and LP sessions.

KANSAS CITY BLUES

Anthologies

Kansas City Piano. Decca 79226, n.d.

Recordings by Individual Artists

Kimbrough, Lottie, and Winston Holmes. *Lottie Kimbrough and Winston Holmes.* Wolf 114, n.d.
Turner, Big Joe. *Have No Fear, Big Joe Turner is Here.* Savoy 2223, 1977.
Turner, Big Joe, and Jimmy Nelson. *The Soul of Joe Turner and Jimmy Nelson.* United US7794, n.d.

PRE–WORLD WAR II PIANO BLUES
Anthologies
Boogie Woogie Rarities 1927–1932. Milestone 2009, n.d.
Pitchin' Boogie. Milestone 2018, 1971.
Rugged Piano Classics. Origin OJL 5, n.d.
Territory Blues: Piano Blues Vol. 10. Magpie 4410, n.d.

Recordings by Individual Artists
Blythe, Jimmy. *Moods of Jimmy Blythe.* Whoopee 105, n.d.
Ezell, Will. *Pitchin' Boogie.* Oldie Blues 2830, n.d.
Montgomery, Little Brother. *Crescent City Blues.* Bluebird AXM2-5522, 1977.

See artist list of blues performers named by Hughes for recordings by Albert Ammons, Pete Johnson, Meade Lux Lewis, and the Boogie Woogie Trio.

JAZZ AND JAZZ-BLUES
Anthologies
AC-DC Blues Vol. 1. Stash ST 106, 1977.
Copulatin' Blues. Stash ST 101, n.d.
Copulatin' Blues Vol. 2. Stash ST 122, n.d.
Pot, Spoon, Pipe, and Jug. Stash ST 102, n.d
Reefer Songs. Stash ST 100, n.d.
Tea Pad Songs Vol. 1. Stash ST 103, n.d.
Tea Pad Songs Vol. 2. Stash ST 104, n.d.
Them Dirty Blues. Jass Box 1, n.d.

Recordings by Individual Artists
Armstrong, Louis. *Jazz Classics in Digital Stereo.* BBC REB 597, n.d.
———. *The Louis Armstrong Story Vol. 1.* Columbia CL851, n.d.
———. *Mister Armstrong Plays the Blues.* Biograph BLP-C6, n.d.
Basie, Count. *The Indispensable.* RCA 43688, n.d.
Blake, Eubie. *Blues and Ragtime Vol. 1.* Biograph 1011, n.d.
———. *Ragtime 1900–1930.* RCA 45687, n.d.
———. *Shuffle Along.* New World 260, n.d.
Dodds, Johnny. *Jazz Classics in Digital Stereo.* BBC REB 603, n.d.
Ellington, Duke. *The Beginning: Vol. 1.* MCA 1358, n.d.
———. *The Works of Duke: Vol. 1–5.* RCA Duke 1, n.d.
Johnson, James P. *Father of the Stride Piano.* Columbia CL 1780, 1962.

Joplin, Scott. *Ragtime: Vol. 1–5.* Biograph BLP 1006, 1008, 1010, 1013, 1014, n.d.
Morton, Jelly Roll. *Jazz Classics in Digital Stereo.* BBC REB 604, n.d.
Moten, Bennie. *Bennie Moten's Kansas City Orchestra 1923–25.* Swaggie 820, n.d.
Oliver, King. *The Immortal King Oliver.* Milestone MLP 2006, n.d.
———. *West End Blues.* CBS 63610, 1973.
Reinhardt, Django. *Django Reinhardt and the American Jazz Giants.* Prestige 7633, 1969.
Rushing, Jimmy. *Good Mornin' Blues.* Affinity AFS 1002, n.d.
Smith, Willie "The Lion." *The Original 14 Plus Two.* Columbia Special Products 15775, n.d.
Waller, Fats. *Integrale, Vol. 1–10.* RCA Fats 1, n.d.
Williams, Clarence. *Clarence Williams' Blue Five.* Rhapsody RHA 6031, n.d.
———. *Clarence Williams' Jazz Kings.* VJM VLP37, n.d.

Readings of Jazz Poetry

Baraka, Amiri. *New Music—New Poetry.* India Navigation 1048, 1981.
Ferlinghetti, Lawrence, et al. *Jazz Canto.* World Pacific 1244, 1958.
Ginsberg, Allen. *First Blues.* John Hammond Records W26 37673, 1982.
Harper, Michael. *Hear Where Coltrane Is.* Signature Series 1984.
Joans, Ted. *Jazz Poems.* S Press 451, n.d.
Kerouac, Jack. *Blues and Haikus.* Hanover 5006, n.d.
The Last Poets. *This Is Madness.* Celluloid 6105, 1984.
Lee, Don L. *Rappin' and Readin'.* Broadside Voices LP BR 1, n.d.
Patchen, Kenneth. *Reads With Jazz in Canada.* Folkways FL 9718, 1959.
———. *Reads His Poetry With the Chamber Jazz Sextet.* Cadence CLP 3004, n.d.
Reed, Ishmael. *Conjure.* American Clave 1006, 1984.
Reed, Ishmael, et al. *New Jazz Poets.* Broadside 461, n.d.
Rexroth, Kenneth. *Poetry and Jazz at the Blackhawk.* Fantasy 7008, n.d.
Rexroth, Kenneth, and Lawrence Ferlinghetti. *Poetry Readings in the Cellar.* Fantasy 7002, 1957.
Sanchez, Sonia. *Black Box No. 3,* n.d.

RELIGIOUS

Birmingham Quartet Anthology. Clanka Lanka CL 144, 001/002, n.d.

RECORDINGS BY BLUES PERFORMERS
NAMED BY HUGHES

Ammons, Albert. *Boogie Woogie.* Boogie Woogie 1001, n.d.
——. *Boogie Woogie and the Blues.* Commodore 15357, 1970.
——. *King of Blues and Boogie Woogie.* Oldie Blues 2807, n.d.
Bentley, Gladys. "How Much Can I Stand." In *Mean Mothers: Independent Women's Blues.* Rosetta 1300, 1980.
——. *The Complete Blues Sessions of Gladys Bentley and Mary Dixon.* Collector's Classics CC52, n.d.
Boogie Woogie Trio. *Boogie Woogie Kings.* Euphonic 1209, n.d.
——. *Boogie Woogie Trio.* Storyville 670184, n.d.
——. *Boogie Woogie Trio.* Storyville 4006, 1976.
——. *The Complete Library of Congress Recordings.* Jazz Piano 5003, n.d.
Boogie Woogie Trio, et al. *From Spirituals to Swing.* Vanguard 47148, 1973.
Carr, Leroy. *Blues Before Sunrise.* Columbia 1799, 1962.
——. *Blues That Make Me Cry.* Agram 2008, n.d.
——. *Leroy Carr Vol. 2.* Collectors' Classics 50, n.d.
——. *Naptown Blues.* Yazoo 1036, n.d.
——. *Scrapper Blackwell.* Yazoo 1019, n.d.
Hill, [Bertha] Chippie. *Bertha "Chippie" Hill.* Hot Society 1005, n.d.
——. "Christmas Man Blues" and "Weary Money Blues." In *When Women Sang the Blues.* Blues Classics 26, 1976.
——. "Hangman Blues" and "Trouble in Mind." *Trumpet Blues, 1925–1929.* Historical 27, n.d.
——. "Panama Limited Blues." In *Women's Railroad Blues: Sorry But I Can't Take You.* Rosetta 1301, 1980.
——. "Some Cold Rainy Day." In *Come On Mama Do That Dance.* Yazoo 1041, n.d.
Jefferson, Blind Lemon. *Black Snake Moan.* Milestone MLP 2013, n.d.
——. *The Immortal Blind Lemon Jefferson.* Milestone MLP 2004, n.d.
——. *King of the Country Blues.* Yazoo 1069, n.d.
Johnson, Lonnie. *Blues by Lonnie Johnson.* Prestige-Bluesville 1007, n.d.
——. *The Blues of Lonnie Johnson.* Swaggie 1225, 1969.
——. *It Feels So Good.* (With J. C. Johnson, James P. Johnson, and Clarence Williams.) Queen Disc 043, n.d.
——. *The Jazz Makers.* (With Eddie Lang.) Swaggie 1229, 1967.
——. *Lonnie Johnson: Blues From New Orleans.* RCA PM42390, n.d.

————. *Lonnie Johnson: Masters of the Blues, Vol. 6*. Collectors Classics 30, n.d.

————. *Lonnie Johnson Sings Twelve-Bar Blues*. King 958, n.d.

————. *Losing Game*. Prestige 7724, n.d.

————. *Mr. Johnson's Blues*. Mamlish 3807, n.d.

————. *The Originator of the Modern Blues*. Blues Boy 300, n.d.

————. *Stringing the Blues*. (With Eddie Lang.) CBS JC2L24, 1975.

————. *Tomorrow Night*. King 1083, 1976.

————. *Woke Up This Morning . . . Blues in My Fingers*. Origin 23, 1980.

Johnson, Pete. *All Star Swing Groups*. Savoy 2218, 1977.

————. *Boogie Woogie Mood*. MCA 1333, 1980.

————. *Kansas City Piano*. (Includes Count Basie.) Decca 79226, n.d.

————. *Master of Blues and Boogie Woogie*. Oldie Blues 2806, n.d.

Jordan, Louis. *The Best of Louis Jordan*. MCA 24079, 1975.

————. *G.I. Joe*. Jukebox Lil JB602, n.d.

Leadbelly. *Good Mornin' Blues: Early Leadbelly*. Biograph 12013, 1969.

————. *Leadbelly*. Columbia 30035, n.d.

————. *Leadbelly*. Playboy 34735 1973.

————. *The Midnight Special*. RCA Victor 505, 1964.

Lewis, Meade Lux. *Boogie Woogie Kings Vol. 8*. (With Cripple Clarence Lofton.) Euphonic 1208, 1974.

Lofton, Cripple Clarence. *Cripple Clarence Lofton and Walter Davis*. Yazoo 1026, n.d.

McGhee, Brownie, and Sonny Terry. *Back to New Orleans*. Fantasy 24708, n.d.

————. *Carolina Blues*. Flyright 105, n.d.

————. "Harmonica Blues." In *Piedmont Blues Vol. 2*. Flyright 107, n.d.

————. *Hometown Blues*. Mainstream 308, n.d.

————. *Let's Have a Ball*. Mapgie 1805, 1978.

————. "Mountain Blues" and "The New John Henry Blues." *From Spirituals to Swing*. Vanguard 47/48, 1973.

Memphis Minnie. *Blues Classics by Memphis Minnie*. Blues Classics 1, n.d.

————. *Early Recordings with Kansas Joe McCoy*. Blues Classics 13, n.d.

————. *Gonna Take the Dirt Road Home*. Origin OJL 24, n.d.

————. *Hot Stuff*. Magpie 1806, 1977.

————. *In My Girlish Days*. Travelin' Man 803, n.d.

————. *Love Changin' Blues*. Biograph 12035, n.d.

————. *Memphis Minnie 1934–1941*. Flyright 108, 1973.

————. *Memphis Minnie and the McCoy Brothers.* MCA 3529, 1976.
Rainey, Ma. *Complete Recordings in Chronological Order.* VJM 81, n.d.
————. *Complete Recordings in Chronological Order.* VJM 82, n.d.
————. *Ma Rainey.* Milestone M47021, 1974.
————. *Ma Rainey's Black Bottom.* Yazoo 1071, n.d.
————. *Oh My Babe Blues.* Biograph 12011, n.d.
————. *Queen of the Blues.* Biograph 12032, n.d.
Smith, Bessie. *Any Woman's Blues.* Columbia 30126, n.d.
————. *The Empress.* Columbia 30818, n.d.
————. *Empty Bed Blues.* Columbia 30450, n.d.
————. *Great Original Performances.* BBC REB 602, n.d.
————. *Nobody's Blues But Mine.* Columbia CG31093, 1972.
————. *Soundtrack.* Jazz Live 8025, n.d.
————. *The World's Greatest Blues Singer.* Columbia 33, n.d.
Smith, Clara. "Freight Train Blues." In *Women's Railroad Blues: Sorry But I Can't Take You.* Rosetta 1301, 1980.
————. "Let's Get Loose." In *Let's Get Loose.* New World 290, 1978.
————. Five songs included on *Rare Recordings of the Twenties.* CBS 64218, 1973.
Smith, Pinetop. *The Piano Jazz: Boogie Woogie Pianists.* Swaggie S1326, n.d.
Smith, Trixie. "Choo Choo Blues" and "Freight Train Blues." *Women's Railroad Blues: Sorry But I Can't Take You.* Rosetta 1301, 1980.
————. "My Daddy Rocks Me." In *The Blues and All That Jazz.* MCA 1353, n.d.
————. *Trixie Smith.* Collector's Classics CC29, n.d.
Spivey, Victoria. *Recorded Legacy of the Blues.* Spivey 2001, n.d.
White, Georgia. "The Blues Ain't Nothin' But???" In *Piano Singer's Blues: Women Accompany Themselves.* Rosetta 1303, 1982.
————. "Daddy Let Me Lay It on You" and "Dead Man's Blues." In *Blues Box I,* MCA Coral 7526/1-4, 1975.
————. *Georgia White Sings and Plays.* Rosetta 1307, 1982.
————. "I'll Keep Sittin' on It." In *Copulatin' Blues.* Stash 101, n.d.
————. "Jazzin' Babies Blues." In *The Blues and All That Jazz.* MCA 1353, n.d.
————. "Rock Me Daddy." In *Tea Pad Songs Vol. 2.* Stash 104, n.d.
————. "Your Worries Ain't Like Mine." In *When Women Sang the Blues.* Blues Classics 26, 1976.
White, Josh. *Josh at Midnight.* Elektra 102, n.d.
————. *Joshua White Vol. 1.* Earl 606, 1982.
————. "Silicosis Is Killin' Me." In *Hard Times.* Rounder 4007, n.d.

Wilson, Edith. *Edith Wilson 1921–2*. Fountain FB302, n.d.
———. *He May Be Your Man*. Delmark 637, 1976.
Yancey, Jimmy. *Boogie Woogie Man*. (With Albert Ammons and Pete Johnson.) RCA 730.561, 1972.
———. *Chicago Piano Vol. 1*. Atlantic 7229, n.d.
———. *Piano Blues of Jimmy Yancey*. Swaggie 824, n.d.

GENERAL INDEX

Pound, Ezra, 7, 90, 141, 224–25, 247, 251
Prince's Band, 263
Professor Longhair, 120

Rainey, Ma, 21, 74, 93, 106, 108, 113, 119, 122, 123, 136, 139, 150, 163, 171, 196, 197, 198, 199–200, 253, 254, 262
Rampersad, Arnold, 20
Randall, Dudley, 249, 251
Razaf, Andy, 94
Reed, Ishmael, 249
Reinhardt, Django, 88
Rexroth, Kenneth, 178
Rivers, Conrad Kent, 251
Robeson, Paul, 18–19, 39, 44, 48, 109, 132
Robinson, Edwin Arlington, 31
Roethke, Theodore, 7
Roland, Walter, 194
Rosemont, Franklin, 103
Rubin, Louis D., 58

Sackheim, Eric, 78, 127
Sandburg, Carl, 8, 15, 31, 142–43, 218–29
Sargeant, Winthrop, 61
Scarborough, Dorothy, 78, 85–86, 87, 89, 92, 95, 102
Schuller, Gunther, 60
Schuyler, George, 28, 45
Shines, Johnny, 98–99
Slavery, 3, 19, 59, 61, 67, 68, 69, 70–74
Smith, Bessie, 39, 44, 94, 95, 98–99, 101, 109, 113, 118, 119, 129, 136, 137, 138, 139, 157, 172, 194, 197, 216–17, 220, 221, 222, 255, 259, 262
Smith, Clara, 119, 120, 136, 193–94, 210, 257, 262
Smith, Clementine, 257
Smith, Cricket, 11
Smith, Joe, 171
Smith, Mamie, 11, 91, 93, 119, 136, 143, 259

Smith, Pinetop, 120, 139, 226
Smith, Trixie, 119, 208, 257
Smith, Willie "The Lion," 109, 136
"Sorrow Songs," 19
Spann, Otis, 10, 145
Spector, Herman, 265
Spellman, A. B., 249
Spivey, Victoria, 119, 120, 156, 193, 196
S. S. Malone, 109–10
"Stack O' Lee," 259
Stearns, Marshall, 60
Still, William Grant, 32, 252
Stokowski, Leopold, 32
Stovepipe, Daddy, 94
Stravinsky, Igor, 32
Sunny Boy and His Pals, 243
Surrealism, 103
Survey Graphic, 40
Sylvester, Hannah, 210, 262
Synge, John Millington, 23

Taft, Michael, 79
Talley, Thomas, 34
Tampa Red, 120, 137, 254
Tanner, Henry Ossawa, 20
Tatum, Art, 250
Taylor, Eva, 219, 263
Taylor, Sam "The Man," 177
Terry, Sonny, 120, 253
Third American Writer's Congress, 212
Thomas, Elvie, 252
Thomas, Gates, 53, 149, 254
Thomas, Henry, 77, 88, 106
Thomas, Willard "Ramblin'," 70, 88, 188, 252
Thompson, Robert Farris, 67
Thurman, Wallace, 261
Titon, Jeff, 70, 79, 80, 100, 103, 127, 147, 252–53, 254
Toelken, Barre, 12
Tolson, Melvin, 249
Toomer, Jean, 48
Turner, Big Joe, 106, 107, 180, 258
Turner, Lorenzo Dow, 125

INDEX OF POEMS

Index of Songs

NOTE ON THE AUTHOR

Steven C. Tracy has a doctorate in English. His numerous writings about American literature, blues lyrics and performers, and the work of Langston Hughes have appeared in such publications as *Phylon,* the *College Language Association Journal, Callaloo,* and *MELUS.* He has also published many reviews of blues recordings in music journals in this country and in Europe, and has delivered papers at meetings of the Popular Culture Association and the American Studies Association. Tracy is a contributing editor for the Heath Anthology of American Literature for the section dealing with the blues. Tracy is also a long-time blues performer.